OAKWOOD LIBRARY OF RAILWAY HISTORY

Isle of Portland Railways

Volume Three
Railway, Associated and
Other Bus Services

B.L. Jackson

THE OAKWOOD PRESS

© Oakwood Press & B.L. Jackson 2000

British Library Cataloguing in Publication Data
A Record for this book is available from the British Library
ISBN 0 85361 566 7

Typeset by Oakwood Graphics.
Repro by Ford Graphics, Ringwood, Hants.
Printed by Cambrian Printers, Aberystwyth, Ceredigion.

Abbreviations

Various abbreviations are used in both the text and fleet lists of this publication, most are standard references used by both the PSV Circle, the Omnibus Society, and generally in most omnibus publications. Others are to save the unnecessary use of words.

NOTC	National Omnibus & Transport Company (also referred to as 'National').
ENOC	Eastern National Omnibus Company.
SNOC	Southern National Omnibus Company.
WNOC	Western National Omnibus Company.
ECW	Eastern Coachworks.
LL	Last licensed date given in taxation records.
LO	Last registered owner given in taxation records.
b	In service with operator by this date.

Prefix

B	Single-Deck bus.	H	Highbridge Double Deck.
CH	Char-a-banc.	OT	Open Top Double Deck.
C	Coach.	DP	Dual Purpose, usually, bus body, coach seats.
L	Lowbridge Double Deck.		
LD	Lodekka (low height highbridge-type seating).	MB	Mini Bus.

Suffix

C	Centre Entrance.	RO	Rear Entrance, Open Staircase.
F	Front Entrance.	D	Dual entrance-exit.
R	Rear Entrance.	T	Toastrack type body.
RD	Rear Door.		

Front cover: A specially commissioned painting by Mike Jeffries of GWR Maudslay ML3 No. 1209, YR 6217, with a Buckingham B32R body, proceeding along Weymouth Esplanade during 1933.
Rear cover: A selection of bell punch type tickets issued in the Weymouth area.
Title page: Portland Express Brush-bodied AEC Regal MV 2675 stands at Portland Bill with the lighthouse in the background. What a different scene over 65 years ago, no car park and ticket machines to reduce your spending power even before you reach the cafe.
Dennis Fancy

Published by The Oakwood Press (Usk), P.O. Box 13, Usk, Mon., NP15 1YS.
E-mail: oakwood-press@dial.pipex.com
Website: www.oakwood-press.dial.pipex.com

Contents

Portland Bill viewed from the top of the lighthouse. Below, the cause of the dissension between National and the Portland private operators. The National Dennis has arrived on a timetabled service. To the right two char-a-bancs have drawn up outside the cafe, no doubt on a pick-up-and-go operation. To the right of the huts the earthworks of a quarry tramway can be seen (described in *Isle of Portland Railways Vol. I*). Beyond is the old Lower Lighthouse and the cliffs stretching back towards Grove Point.   *Author's Collection*

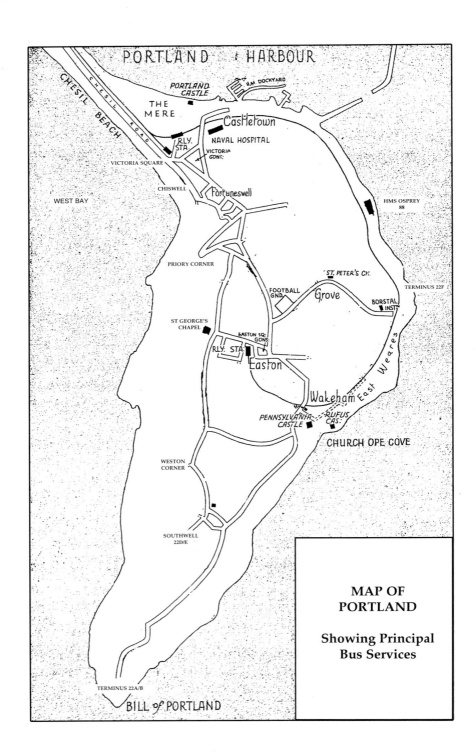

MAP OF
PORTLAND

Showing Principal
Bus Services

Acknowledgements

Many people have assisted in the writing of this book, often unwittingly by supplying a snippet of information that has helped to complete the complex history of local bus services. The main inspiration for this work has been *Railway Motor Buses and Bus Services in the British Isles* by John Cummings, and the three volumes of *The Years Between* by Messrs Crawley, MacGregor, and Simpson.

Many books, newspapers, periodicals, and other sources have been referred to as have various minute books and other documents held at various record offices, and the three principal local papers, *Southern Times*, *Weymouth Telegram*, and *Dorset Evening Echo*. The assistance of the following organisations is gratefully acknowedged: The Dorset County Archives Department, Dorset County Library Service, Weymouth & Portland Museum Services. The Public Record Office (Kew), The Great Western Museum (Swindon), The National Motor Museum Library Beaulieu, the Omnibus Society, the PSV Circle, Bristol Vintage Bus Group and Dorset Transport Circle.

The local Studies Department of Weymouth library has been of great assistance, in particular Mrs Maureen Attwooll, whose vast knowledge of local history is invaluable. The staff of Southern National, many of whom have now taken their final journey, who over the years recalled the past days with pride. The Hoare family of Bluebird Coaches, Mike Jeffries for the excellent cover painting. Thanks are also due to Bob Crawley, John Cummings and Roger Grimley for their expert advice and the latter two for checking draft copies, and to George Pryer for overseeing the complete proof reading of the work. I am also grateful to the following for their assistance, N. Aish, R. Atkinson, Cliff Austin, Mrs S. Barter, N. Biles, V.C. Biles, John Brown, G. Bruce, C.L. Caddy, A.B. Cross, H. Cailes, M.S. Curtis, D.Fancy, A.G.H. Jeanes, Phillip Kelley, D.M. Habgood, A. Hutchings, P. Lacey, A.M. Lambert, W. Macey, M. Marshall, G.R.Mills, S. Morris, C. Owen, D.J.N. Pennels, G. Pritchard, R.C. Riley, L. Ronan, R.H.G. Simpson, D.Smith, Mrs B. Tallack, M.J. Tattershall, B. Thompson, Mrs V. Tilley, C. Tolman, B. Thompson, Alan Townsin, J. Way, J. Woodsford.

Finally I should like to thank my wife, herself a Portlander, for her encouragement and help whilst this work was being written.

An enamel sign 'to the National Buses' these were to be found at many railway stations where Western and Southern National services ran, the Portland stations being no exception. *Author*

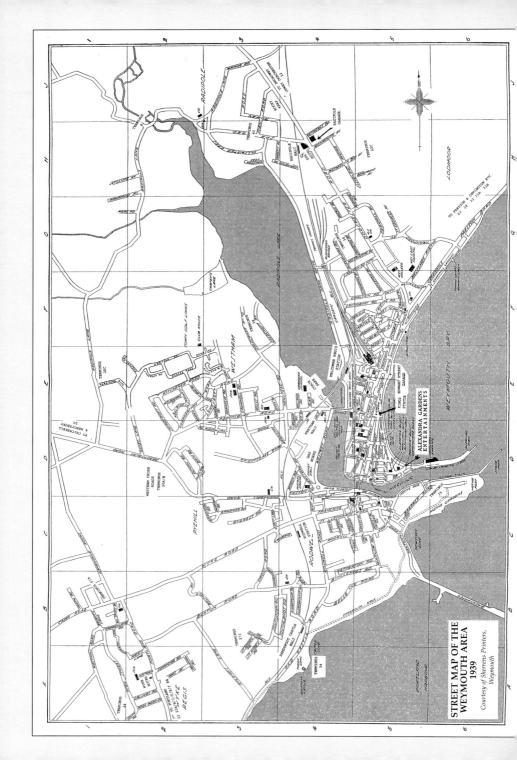

STREET MAP OF THE WEYMOUTH AREA
1939

Courtesy of Sherrens Printers,
Weymouth

Introduction

At first glance the title of this work might sound a little strange! However the reader will soon become aware of the railway connection, in particular with the Portland branch and surrounding area. With the proposed tramway schemes, the Great Western Railway buses were part of their defence strategy. This led to the National combine, added to this there were the independents, many become involved with the railway story either by ownership or opposition to it.

This is the story of natural progression, as railways replaced the stage coach, so with the fullness of time the bus and coach were to usurp the railways, and in the case of Portland were able to provide a service the railway could never match. Indeed the motor car can now provide a personal service superior to the bus, such has been the progress of the past hundred years!

Being a seaside resort the story of the local tour operator is also involved, a trip taken on a char-a-banc was a lost passenger to the railway, or local paddle steamers, both suffering as a result of the internal combustion engine.

The differences of opinion between Weymouth Town Council and the operators in the early days now makes interesting reading, the problems of operation and the competition for the seasonal trade, although local to this book, could well be in many other seaside resorts, change the name of both the play and the actors, the story would be very similar under any other name!

The words optimism, hope, and failure, must have been applied many times in the early days, for vehicles, drivers, and passengers alike. Something of a novelty pre-1914, World War I was to produce a reliable motor vehicle and men with the knowledge to perfect and operate the machine. Returning from the war, many men tried their hand, some failed others succeeded.

The work of the Traffic Commissioners following the 1930 Act is demonstrated in the history of several operators within this work. For the historian the amount of information given in the remaining records is varied ranging from just a name and vehicle registration number, to a full description of the vehicle. The Dorset County Council registration records pre-1920 give a full description of the vehicle, the registration number, make and type of vehicle, including alterations to the vehicle and changes of owner. After 1920 the registration number, make and type and first owner only are given, it relied for example on the clerk making the entry to state whether it was a Ford Hackney, or Ford 14 seat bus, a problem with manufacturers who offered a wide range of vehicles. The difference for the historian is either following up an unwanted taxi, or missing a very interesting bus! Likewise vehicles obtained from outside the county are difficult to trace accurately. Information obtained from Council records although invaluable is not always complete, as not all vehicles are quoted in Minutes. Therefore the fleet lists of the various operators is only as complete as remaining records have allowed.

It would be impossible to list the Southern National vehicles employed at Weymouth, for the sake of completeness vehicles acquired by Southern National from local fleets have their histories fully documented in the accounts of their original owners. It is not possible to give full details of all the various chassis and bodies mentioned in this work, however earlier models in particular are described, to give an idea of the problems faced. Readers who require full details of many of the later vehicles can refer to the many excellent books covering the subject.

In this volume the author has attempted to cover the 70 years since the first horse-drawn omnibus opened a stage carriage service in Weymouth, a convenient cut off date being 1969 with the formation of the National Bus Company. The years after will be the responsibility of the next generation of historians.

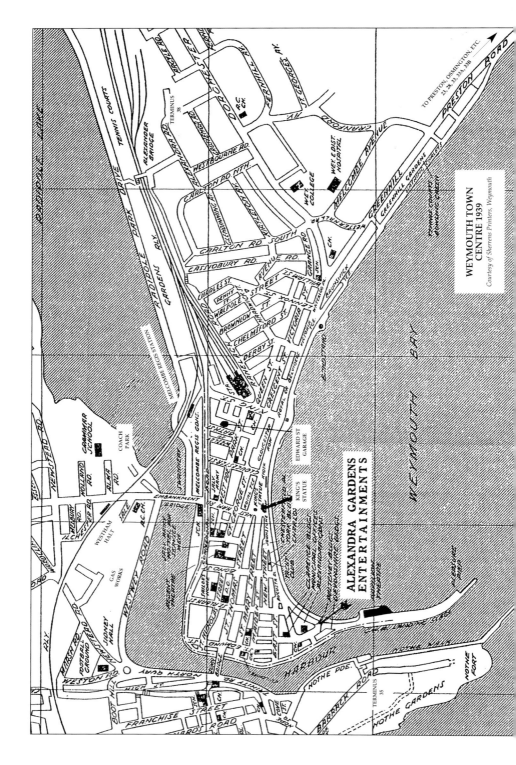

WEYMOUTH TOWN
CENTRE 1939
Courtesy of Sherrens Printers, Weymouth

Chapter One

Setting the Scene

Apart from the stagecoach, the only other means of road transport for the common man was the carrier's cart that travelled between villages and towns, usually on market days, conveying both goods and any persons who were willing to suffer the journey in the back of such a vehicle. The first vehicles of note to provide excursions were the Wagonettes, which were large horse-drawn carts with a bench seat down each side. This idea was developed into the char-a-banc, in which bench-type seats were placed in rows across the wagon, usually being arranged in tiers, thus allowing the passengers at the rear to see over those in front.

These conveyances were administered by the local council Hackney Inspector, who was also responsible for the horse-drawn cabs of the period. With the arrival of the motor taxi, the motor char-a-banc, and omnibus these also became the responsibility of the said official, whose administration was controlled by The Town Police Clauses Acts of 1847 and 1889 and the Stage Carriage Act of 1832, which in effect had little impact on the prevailing situation, having been drawn up to control horse-drawn traffic! Early char-a-banc and bus operators were a new breed of men and difficult to control. Where the railways had been brought up on tradition, the pioneer bus men were brought up on expediency, and considered the occasional fine for running an unlicensed service or any other minor misdemeanour as part of the running costs!

Councils had different committees looking after their Hackney affairs. In Weymouth it was the Watch Committee, no doubt a wise choice, whilst the Highways Committee looked after these matters on Portland. In Dorchester, a search of the Sanitary Committee minutes has revealed the affairs of bus operators! This state of affairs continued until the 1930 Road Traffic Act, when buses and coaches became the responsibility of the newly formed Traffic Commissioners, much to the annoyance of some councillors and officials!

The control of vehicles by the councils pre-1930 was, by modern standards, somewhat haphazard. Apart from Greater London, where the Metropolitan Police controlled the situation with stringent licensing and construction and use regulations, in the provinces it was up to each individual council how to determine the Hackney regulations, whilst in rural areas there appeared to be no governing body. Even more surprising was the fact that there was no universal test for drivers or examination of vehicles until the 1930 Act, whereas Railways had been under strict control for safety matters since the 1870s.

Despite the fact that nationally there had been some very serious accidents involving coaches and buses, and locally the Ridgeway Hill accident of 1922, implementation of any Regulations was slow to come about. In May 1923 Weymouth Council decided that all Hackney carriages had to be insured to cover passenger liability. At the June Watch Committee meeting it was reported that during the past 12 months wheels had come off motor buses on three occasions, the Town Clerk being instructed to write to the owners drawing their attention to the matter!

The Council could not have been well pleased with an article in *Motor Transport* during September 1923, entitled 'Passenger Travel Facilities In Weymouth and District'. In a scathing attack on some vehicles it stated:

We are confident that the local authority would improve the reputation of the town if they were more strict in regard to ply-for-hire vehicles. There are a few Fords fitted with bodies that are an absolute disgrace. The condition of the chassis may be satisfactory, but the appearance and condition of the bodies, which looked as if they have been made out of soap boxes, are terrible. We would rather ride on a manufacturer's test body than one of the vehicles in question. When running they rattle and squeak from every quarter.

At the next meeting the Hackney Inspector was instructed to interview the owners of the vehicles referred to in *Motor Transport*.

It was not until July 1925 that the question of testing brakes on hackney carriages was considered, the Hackney Carriage Inspector making arrangements with the motor coach and omnibus proprietors for periodical testing of their vehicles. It was only in the previous year that the Council insisted that a rear emergency door be fitted to all enclosed vehicles with a front entrance. In 1925 it was also decided that no person under the age of 20 would be granted a licence to drive a hackney carriage, and no person under 18 years of age be employed as a conductor.

An area of regulation the Watch Committee strictly enforced was the licensing of vehicles as hackney carriages. There was also the difficult task of looking after local interests, without appearing to be openly hostile to outside organisations. During February 1914 the Council received a letter via solicitors asking whether they would be prepared to grant a licence to a syndicate or company to be formed for plying for hire or running a motor omnibus service in the Borough. The Council was of the opinion that the motor service to be provided during the coming season by local enterprise would meet the requirements of the public. A deputation of local motor proprietors asked that no licences be granted to outside firms, both Mr A'Court and Mr Bugler stating that they intended putting on motor char-a-bancs, and Mr Puffett already had one. In December 1917 an application by Mr A.J. Harding for a licence to ply for hire in the Borough with a char-a-banc was granted, although having a licence and being able to operate with the war situation and petrol restrictions were two different things! Likewise on 3rd January, 1918 Mr Standley Kings-Mill was granted a licence to operate a char-a-banc between Montevideo Camp (Chickerell), and Weymouth, subject to police approval of the vehicle and route to be taken.

Whereas before the war there had been a lack of enthusiasm for running various services, there were now many people interested in joining a rapidly expanding industry. A study of the Council Minute books reveals some interesting entries, and there is doubt whether some who received licences ever actually operated, or if they did it was so short lived as to escape the historian.

In May 1919 the application by T.R. Brooke of Bournemouth to ply for hire with two 30-seat Dennis char-a-bancs was granted for one year, subject to police approval, this being one event that failed to materialise! On 22nd September, 1920 an application was made to the Watch Committee, that if proceeded with could well have changed the future of omnibus services in the area. The fledgling Bournemouth-based Hants & Dorset Motor Services Ltd applied for licences to operate a regular service between Bournemouth-Dorchester-Weymouth. The committee deferred the matter pending receiving particulars of fares, etc. These were duly submitted, and the company asked that a vehicle be allowed to stand at the pier end of the Alexandra Gardens, to which the Council agreed, and issued the necessary licences. However the service never commenced, Hants & Dorset having more pressing commitments in Bournemouth. It is known that the company wished to expand westwards to Dorchester and Weymouth, but unfortunately their lack of action at that time cost them dear. The National Omnibus

& Transport Company headed for Weymouth, and a boundary war between them and both Hants & Dorset and Wilts & Dorset ensued across the Dorset countryside!

Bolt Bros of Dorchester were granted a licence to operate between Weymouth and Dorchester in September 1921, being allowed to pick up at the Alexandra Gardens. This service would seem to have been short-lived with the arrival of Road Motors Ltd.

Mr J. Rand applied to run a motor bus from the Spa Hotel at Radipole to Portesham via Abbotsbury Road and Charlestown, but the committee would only grant a licence if the service operated via Broadwey and Nottington - clearly a case of keeping him out of Weymouth from where others were operating towards Chickerell. That December (1921) an application from the Western Road Transport Company to operate a motor bus service in the district was refused, the Council being of the opinion that existing services were adequate.

In March 1922 W.F. Waters was granted a licence to ply for hire between Langton Herring and Weymouth, and Messrs Ford & Son to run between Weymouth and Came Down Golf Links. F.C. Ashford of Preston was allowed a service from Sutton Poyntz and Preston to Weymouth, whilst two years later J. Spiller, a local carrier, was refused permission to ply for hire with an omnibus from Osmington. In January 1923 G.E. Foote was refused a licence to run an service between Weymouth and Abbotsbury via Nottington. There was a hostile reaction to the National Omnibus & Transport Company in 1923 when they applied to run services within the Borough, although at the January 1924 Weymouth Town Council meeting the Watch Committee agreed that 'no objections be offered to the Town Clerk accepting a free pass from the National Omnibus & Transport Company', a matter that was to cause contemptuous remarks at a later date!

W.E. Blanchard applied to operate a bus service between Weymouth and Portland in September 1927, this also being refused.

The Council were now becoming very concerned about the number of vehicles plying for hire and regulated their number and also attempted to control the activities of the touts. A strict check was kept on outsiders' activities within the town, and they were almost paranoid about Portland operators picking up within the Borough, and several other in-comers were prosecuted. There was also, in those unregulated days, the problem of services for special events. An unsolicited advert in the *Dorset Daily Echo* on 30th July, 1925 stated: 'Weymouth Races, A Bus Service, will run to and from the King's Statue every half hour, from 12 o'clock. Fare 1s. per head'.

By the late 1920s the vehicles were becoming sophisticated, and as for the char-a-banc, the term died out within the trade during the 1930s with the introduction of covered coaches. First came the variety with fixed side windows and a roll-back roof, known as the 'All Weather' coach, which was quickly superseded by the sliding roof of the late 1930s luxury coach, although to the public the term 'char-a-banc outing' was still used 20 years later. The bus and coach business also became an established industry and needed integrated nationwide control, rather than the local *ad hoc* arrangements then in force.

The 1930 Act took responsibility for 'Public Service Vehicles' away from local councils, leaving them only with restricted powers over the positioning of bus stops, etc. They had no control over fares, timetables, or other licensing matters, and could only make objections at a Traffic Commissioners' hearing, like any other objector. The railway companies also had a right to object, but did not come under the jurisdiction of the Act themselves.

To administer the Act the country was divided into 'Traffic Areas', each presided over by a chairman and a panel of representatives who sat at public inquiries known as 'Traffic Courts'. Originally Weymouth and the whole of Dorset came under the control of the 'Southern Area', this was disbanded on 31st December, 1933, and Dorset except for the East became part of the 'Western Traffic Area'.

Char-a-bancs lined up at the King's Statue during the 1920s give an idea of the potential trade available, and the problems of control for the Town Council Watch Committee.

Author's Collection

A view of the King's Statue between 1925 and 1928. Bottom left a small Crossley, in the centre PR 2645 the Greyhound, Daimler CK, with the Greyhound Ford 'T' alongside. Behind another small Crossley and a horse-drawn wagonette. In front of the Statue two vehicles of Jeanes, 'White Star' fleet, whilst a National 'Dennis' loads behind the statue. *Author's Collection*

High Summer at the King's Statue in the late 1920s. The tour boards are out, and the touts tell of unheard of sights to be seen! A motley collection of char-a-banc and horse-drawn wagonettes, alongside the Statue a National 'Dennis' bus. Today all these people could easily be accommodated in three modern coaches. *Author's Collection*

The Act was all embracing. Drivers had to hold a Public Service Vehicle driving licence which involved a strict test, while conductors also had to be licensed, the vehicles had to be up to the high standards required and were subject to annual inspection by Ministry examiners. The operator had to hold an operator's licence, and each route had to be individually licensed. In the case of stage services, a timetable and fare table had to be strictly adhered to, and the operation of extra vehicles in the form of duplicates was also restricted. Express services, excursions, and tours were also licensed, and where two or more operators made the same journey, the fares had to be the same and all agreed by the Commissioners, thus avoiding undercutting and the worst excesses of a free for all. There was also the added complication, in particular with express services, where a service crossed into or passed through a neighbouring 'Traffic Area' it required a 'Backing Licence', a procedure that at times caused friction.

There were many trials and tribulations during the first few years - especially as the old brigade of the 'Get a load and Go' attitude were forced into line! Several examples of the problems faced by both the operators and Commissioners are described within this work. It was often said the Act was the friend of the the large company as opposed to the small man, it being true the larger companies were better at presenting their case with expert staff and advocates, whilst the small operator had always muddled through and now had to face the complex world of the Traffic Courts. But there were many cases where the Commissioners upheld the small operator, and once given his licence he was protected by the power of those courts from any predators.

An example of their powers was demonstrated in September 1933, when 11 operators were summoned at Weymouth for committing 36 offences when operating excursions to the town. In February 1934 Webb of East Chaldon, was prosecuted for running to Weymouth on an unlicensed day and for overloading.

Whatever one's opinion of the 1930 Act, it served well through the great years of the motor bus. The deregulation of services seen in recent years has been a two-edged sword. The operator now has freedom to operate services in competition, but unlike the days before the Act, he is weighed down with rules and regulations and the bureaucracy that goes with them. Only future historians will be able to fully judge the results.

Before the Motor Bus. Wagonettes line up at the King's Statue as passengers board for the various destinations on offer. The first wagonette is *Badminton* the third is *Vivid*. Despite being referred to as the age before pollution, the ladies still had to make sure they avoided the 'horse exhaust'.   *Author's Collection*

One of the few photographs of the Weymouth Omnibus Company horse buses to survive. Taken pre-May 1905 passengers board at the bottom of St Mary Street outside the Golden Lion Hotel, the gentleman in uniform just stepping aboard is John Gill a railway inspector at Weymouth with special responsibility for the Harbour Tramway. The detail of the horse bus and the one approaching down St Mary Street are clearly shown.   *Author's Collection*

Chapter Two

Before the Motor Bus, Horse-Drawn Days and the Tramway Question

Carriages and Waggonettes

From the time Weymouth became a fashionable holiday resort, various types of horse-drawn carriages became available. These were usually provided by job masters who supplied carriages to the top-class hotels. Most of their work could best be described as being of a 'private hire' nature to meet the requirements of their clientele. A group of interested parties decided that coach rides to various places of interest could become a lucrative business, resulting in the formation of the Weymouth Coaching Club (Limited). This was not a financial success as rival coaches and the opening of the Abbotsbury branch railway soon affected their most popular trip, and in March 1888 it was decided that the Club be voluntarily wound up.

There was strong competition for the Summer trade. Generally the wagonettes operated from the King's Statue to the various beauty spots, these attractions lasting well into the motor char-a-banc era! The most popular destination was Upwey Wishing Well, *en route* to which the wagonette left the main road just past the Swan Inn at Broadwey, turning into Littlemead to travel along the shallow bed of the River Wey, before rejoining the road in Watery Lane and proceeding via Church Street to the Wishing Well. A slogan used by one of the drivers was 'By the Wey, Over the Wey, and Thro' the Wey'.

Incredibly, two wagonettes kept going until World War II, *The Royal* and *Royal Pearl* and in the dark days of August 1940 (during the Battle of Britain) the *Daily Mail* reported from Weymouth that 'The man with the double-decker horse carriage is shouting for customers'. One operator 'Suger-em' Shorey, a well-known local character who continued into World War II, was granted a Hackney Licence for 1945/6, although it is doubtful if he operated. In the following years he used the wagonette to deliver firewood around the town from his home, the old Toll House situated halfway across Preston Beach Road.

Likewise on Portland carriages and wagonettes provided transport and excursions around the Island, mostly meeting trains at Portland station or paddle steamers at Castletown Pier and conveying visitors to the prison or sightseers to Portland Bill. Another 'attraction' was to watch convicts at work in the quarries, a number of houses in Grove Road having 'Tea Rooms' upstairs, which offered a good view of proceedings!

The *Southern Times* of 6th May, 1893 mentioned a regular omnibus service on the island: 'Mr E. Collins of Easton Square has commenced running a small Brake on the omnibus principle. The route is from Easton Square to the railway station, in Victoria Square, and as the fares are very moderate and the journey very frequent, we imagine the bus will be very popular both with residents and visitors'.

The Weymouth Omnibus Company

In 1895 a group of local businessmen and traders formed the Weymouth Omnibus Company, which was registered on 19th April, 1895 with offices in Lower St Alban Street. The object of the company was to purchase various cab businesses and negotiate with local authorities to run services and operate tramways. The capital was £3,000 divided into 600 shares of £5 each. Little is known about the formation of

WEYMOUTH OMNIBUS COMPANY, LIMITED.

EXTENSION AND ALTERATION OF SERVICE.

ON and after MONDAY, APRIL 29th, 1895, the OMNIBUSES will RUN to and from RADIPOLE at the undermentioned times until further notice :—

To RADIPOLE, *via* ST. MARY-STREET, leaving GUILDHALL :—

From RADIPOLE, *via* ST. THOMAS-STREET for the BRIDGE and GUILDHALL, leaving

GUILDHALL :—	SPA-ROAD :—	LODMOOR-HOUSE :—
8.45 A.M.		9.0 A.M.
9.30S ,,	9.55 A.M.	10.0 ,,
10.30 ,,		11.0 ,,
11.30S ,,	11.55 ,,	12.0 NOON.
12.30 P.M.		1.0 P.M.
1.30 ,,		2.0 ,,
2.30S ,,	2.55 P.M.	3.0 ,,
3.30 ,,		4.0 ,,
4 30S ,,	4.55 ,,	5.0 ,,
5.30 ,,		6.0 ,,
6.30 ,,		7.0 ,,
7.30S ,,	7.55 ,,	8.0 ,,

S denotes journey to Spa-road.

FARES.—Guildhall to Lennox-street ... ... 1d. ⎫
Lennox-street to Lodmoor House ... ... 1d. ⎬ And *vice versa*
Lodmoor House to Spa-road ... ... 1d. ⎭

TEMPORARY OMNIBUS SERVICE TO WESTHAM.

To FRANKLIN-ROAD, WESTHAM, *via* ST. MARY-STREET, leaving GUILDHALL :—

From WESTHAM, *via* ST. THOMAS-STREET for the BRIDGE and GUILDHALL, leaving FRANKLIN-ROAD :—

GUILDHALL :—	FRANKLIN-ROAD :—
11.0 A.M.	11.30 A.M.
12.0 NOON	12.30 P.M.
1.0 P.M.	1.30 ,,
3.0 ,,	3.30 ,,
4.0 ,,	4.30 ,,
5.0 ,,	5.30 ,,

FARE.—Guildhall to Franklin-road 1d., and *vice versa*.

The Westham Service is temporary, and the Company hope shortly to extend it.

CHARLES J. SAMWAYS,
Secretary.

The first advert for the Weymouth Omnibus Company Ltd, published in the *Southern Times* for 27th April, 1895.

this company, there being no press reports of its formation or any subsequent meetings. In the event the company provided a service of horse-drawn buses between Lodmoor Hill and the Guildhall. This commenced very quickly, and the success of the venture can be judged by the fact that from 29th April, 1895 five journeys a day were extended to Radipole.

The exact terminal point at Radipole cannot be determined as the Spa Hotel was not built at that time, a building on the corner of Spa Road (at present a Chinese takeaway) then being a public house called 'The Bridge Inn'. However, it appears that the omnibus travelled at least part way along Spa Road, as an advert in December 1898 for a house to let in that road stated, 'Omnibus passes the door several times daily'.

From the same date as the Radipole extension a service was commenced from the Guildhall to the Waverley Arms in Westham, a novel feature of both services being that the inward journeys to the Guildhall travelled down St Thomas Street whilst the outward journeys were made via St Mary Street.

On 6th May adjustments were made to the Dorchester Road service, whilst the Westham service was doubled from six to 12 journeys.

A report in the *Southern Times* at the time stated:

We understand that the company are very pleased with the success of the service up to the present time, the returns having more than reached their expectations. The company hope with the extended service now offered a much larger revenue may be obtained.

Whereas only seven persons had subscribed to seven shares by 18th April, 152 shares had been taken up by the end of August, most subscribers taking five shares. At that time Charles F. Samways of St Thomas Street was the company Secretary, and by early 1897 the company was operating from a coach house and stables in Holly Road, Westham.

Despite a search of the local papers very little is recorded of the company. The rate books for the first part of 1898 stated that the coach house was occupied by Charles Samways and owned by the omnibus company, although by December the owners were the same but H.J. Young was the occupant. A year later Young had also become the owner, at which time the frontage of the site was developed. A terrace of five cottages, 'Overdale Terrace' (now 14-22 Holly Road) was built, and by November 1900 'Overdale House' had been constructed with Young as the owner.

By February 1900 the few remaining company documents reveal that 165 shares had been taken up. By then Robert Henry Young had become Managing Director, holding 151 shares, the remaining 14 being held by other family members. The fact that the shares, which had been held mostly by traders and businessmen of the town, had all been acquired by the Young family is interesting, but again no details of these transactions appeared in the local press! In the 1902 company returns R.H. Young was also listed as company Secretary and Chairman - clearly it had become a family business.

Robert Young came from a farming community at Sherborne, moving to Weymouth in his early twenties. By 1893 he occupied Lynch Farm, to the west of Weymouth, trading as a farmer and horse dealer and branching out into the haulage business which tendered for work with Weymouth Town Council.

The commencement of the GWR motor omnibus service from Radipole Spa Hotel in June 1905 obviously affected the horse bus trade although the Westham route remained untouched. In fact Westham was a fast growing community. Almost nonexistent in 1860, it had a population of 2,500 in 1891. Originally part of the parish of Wyke Regis, it was incorporated into the Borough of Weymouth in 1895 and became an ecclesiastical parish in its own right in 1901. Its western boundary was then at what later became the Adelaide Hotel. By the turn of the century it was a much sought-after area in which to live, and a large amount of building was taking place. In general it would appear that Young ran a very successful and well respected Jobmasters business. Again the newspapers reported little on the horse buses, until an accident on 8th January, 1906 when a bus collided with the fencing on Westham bridge, smashing a 12 ft length, the bus company paying £3 19s. 8d. for the damage! Later that year in May, Young's char-a-banc named *Queen* ran into a hedge when a horse bolted.

By February 1907 Young was in failing health, which resulted in the business being sold by auction on 21st October, 1907. The three horse buses were London-built two-horse vehicles with garden type seats on the upper deck. Two had a seating capacity of 26, the other 24 passengers. These were purchased for £41 by Henry Carter of Rockey Knap, Radipole, Weymouth, a well known local carter. He also purchased five additional bus horses for £56 14s., thus (with other associated equipment) the omnibus business passed to Henry Carter.

According to the auctioneer's records three old horse buses were sold for £6 4s., one at £2 14s., and two at £1 15s., whilst the other conveyances and equipment went to various buyers, the entire sale raising £783 11s. 6d.

Robert Young passed away on 6th January, 1908 aged 48 years. His widow, Mrs Annie Young then become the company Chairman. That June, at an extraordinary general meeting of the company, it was decided that by reason of its liabilities the business would be voluntarily wound up. On 31st August another general meeting was held for the purpose of having an account laid before them showing the manner in which the winding up had been conducted, and the property of the company disposed of.

Whilst the final chapter in the Young's former interest in the omnibus company was being concluded, a bitter twist had taken place for the new owner Henry Carter. No sooner had he moved the operation of the omnibuses to Rockey Knap and renamed it 'The Weymouth & General Omnibus Company' than he was forced through ill health to dispose of his entire business interests; the sale of his haulage business and

THE GOODWILL & PLANT OF THE WEYMOUTH & GENERAL OMNIBUS COMPANY, comprising three pair horse omnibuses, with garden seats (recently overhauled and in good running order) as now plying from the Dorchester Road and Westham to the Town Hall Weymouth.

According to the auctioneers records, there was no purchaser for Lot 133 'The Omnibus Company'. However, four horses (not bus horses) and various haulage wagons were purchased by Caleb Young. Apparently the Young family intended operating a haulage business from Holly Road Mews.

The bus service was taken over by Mr Henry Jesty, a livery stable proprietor of Crescent Street, Weymouth, who also ran various horse-drawn char-a-bancs. It appears that the omnibus operation returned to the Holly Road premises, the rate books showing that the stables and coach house for omnibus were rented from Mrs Young by Henry Jesty. The service continued until the end of September 1912, when it ceased. The *Southern Times* for 21st September noted,

Westham people, and indeed residents on both sides of the water will hear with regret that the service of omnibuses which has been in existence so long is to be abandoned. For some time it has been known that the service was running on a precarious tenure, but it was hoped that means would be found to preserve this convenient and useful means of communication. Apparently the owners have got 'tired' and as there is no possibility of its being taken over or subsidised by the local authorities, Westham people will now have to foot it.

A letter in the same paper suggested a novel idea which bears the hallmarks of the modern Mini-Bus service! Based on a system he had seen 20 years previously in Grimsby, a Mr Charmbury suggested that

. . . if you wanted to ride in any direction you simply waited a minute or so when a small wagonette holding about 12 people or so would pass. You simply got on, and however near or far you wished to go the fare was the same. The vehicles were drawn by one horse. Now if a person were to run one from the Statue to the Waverley Hotel every half hour it would pay. It is the cumbrous vehicles that take it out of the horses. Others could ply to other parts of the town.

Although himself a businessman neither Mr Charmbury or anyone else took up the idea.

In October 1912 a sale of Contractors Stock took place at the Holly Road Mews, which brought to an end the era of horse-drawn transport from the premises. The following month an auction of furniture and effects of Overdale House took place when Mrs Annie Young retired and left the neighbourhood. The sale of these premises closed the first chapter in Weymouth's omnibus history.

Bus Horses Owned by the Weymouth Horse Bus Company, September 1907

Name	Type	Age	Hands	Notes
BREDY	Brown Mare	5	15.3	C
TERROR	Brown Mare	6	15.2	A
BESSIE	Brown Mare	9	15.2	A C
GERRARD	Brown Horse	8	15.2	
MAGGIE	Piebold Mare	7	15.2	A C
NANCY	Piebold Mare	8	16.0	
BRILLIANT	Black Mare	7	15.3	C
KITTY	Black Mare	7	15.3	C
PUNCH	Bay Horse		15.2	
BONFIRE	Brown Entire	4		B D E

Notes
A in foal to Bonfire.
B Hackney bred Brown Entire by Denglat, (Sir W. Gilbeys Sire) rising four years, a sure
    foalgetter, has been ridden a few times.
C sold to Henry Carter 21st October, 1907.
D sold to Hayne 21st July, 1907.
E Being a stallion, it is unlikely this horse would have operated the horse buses in case
    he came into contact with a mare whilst on the highway!

A Hand = 4 inches measuring up to the top of the front shoulders.

Tramway Proposals

The first proposals for a tramway in Weymouth were put forward in May 1882, when there was discussion concerning a tramway to the brewery, situated in Hope Square. The second scheme was for a tramway from Lodmoor Hill, Dorchester Road, along the Esplanade to the pier, the chief proposer being Dr Joseph Drew a Director of Messrs Cosens & Company the local paddle steamer operators.

The 'Weymouth District Tramway Provisional Order' was obtained to construct a 3 ft gauge system, the means of propulsion not being specified. Following much disagreement concerning tramcars on the sea-front and certain objections in detail by the Board of Trade the scheme faded away.

Following the decision in 1902 to build a Council-operated power station, electric trams again came to the fore. In March 1904 Weymouth Council considered the tramway question, resulting in the Electric Lighting Committee being authorised to obtain full information and an expert report on a tramway scheme for both inside and outside the Borough - including a scheme for an electric tramway running from Upwey through Weymouth and Wyke Regis to Portland in conjunction with Portland UDC, who it was hoped would extend it to the Tophill district! It appears that Portland was not interested, or were playing a waiting game! In September 1905 they were worried by someone who wanted to supply electric light on the island, the Council opposing the application. Portland had a council owned-gasworks and was in the business of selling gas, whereas Weymouth was in the business of selling electricity!

No decision had been made on whether it should be a municipal or private enterprise! Several interested parties approached the corporation with various schemes, including the management of the Cheltenham & District Light Railway Co. At the same time a letter was received from the GWR expressing its disapproval of the tramway proposals, as it had only recently provided the road motor service and opened railway halts at Radipole, Upwey Wishing Well and Came Bridge, and there were veiled references to other forthcoming improvements.

To put matters into perspective, at that time the Borough boundaries were at Two Mile Copse, on Dorchester Road, (now Manor Roundabout) and at the top of Rylands Lane on the south side, Wyke Regis being then in the rural district. The report into the viability of a tramway, emphasised that a line between Wyke Hotel and the Spa Hotel at Radipole was the best financial proposition, but detailed as the report was, there was no mention of how the trams would cross the Town bridge. This being a swing bridge, some complex arrangements would be required to carry the overhead wire and rails! Neither was there any mention of the gauge, although most provincial systems of that period were 3 ft 6 in.

In December 1905 the National Electric Construction Company, which was at the time promoting a Bill for tramways in Folkestone, offered its services to Weymouth. At the February 1906 Council meeting a letter from Mr F. Chaunter, former resident engineer for the construction and maintenance of the Easton & Church Hope Railway, was read, in which he stated that he would be shortly going into partnership with a Mr A.H. Gibbings, and they were desirous of obtaining the support and co-operation of the council in securing powers to construct an electric tramway in the Borough. To mention one's connections with the construction of the hapless Easton line was not a wise move (see *Isle of Portland Railways Vol. II*) and nothing else was heard of Chaunter's scheme!

Councillors were already having doubts about the scheme, and agreed to call a public meeting so the views of the townspeople could be heard. It was agreed to put the matter to a town poll held on 18th June, in which - out of the 4,077 voters on the register - only 1,518 voted, 559 for, and 959 against.

Following this defeat the tramway question was allowed to drop until November 1908 when it was decided to contact the Railless Traction Company, who were prepared to explain the advantages of the system and cost of construction, which was nearly one-quarter to one-third that of the average tramway per mile! The Electric Light Committee considered the trackless trolley system unsuited to the requirements of the Borough. At that time no other Corporation had accepted the system, which was looked upon as something of a novelty which still needed proving in practice, and it was therefore too great a risk for a town like Weymouth. In fact, none had yet opened in this Country.

Following the withdrawal of the GWR motor buses at the end of August 1909, there was desperation for a replacement. A leader in the *Southern Times* for 23rd April, 1910, asked whether the rejection of the trackless trams scheme had not been a little too hasty. Bradford Corporation had just applied for, and obtained, Parliamentary powers to introduce an experiment in the railless (or trolley) system of tramways. The leader concluded, 'It would almost seem that it is just the sort of experiment that Weymouth might embark upon with profit and advantage'.

By August the Council were considering four schemes to provide transport within the town, motor buses, petrol electric buses, railless electric traction and trams. There was much debate concerning the alternatives offered. Councillor Jackson said that extending the trams to Radipole would never be remunerative as railmotors stopped at the Halt 19 times a day, and as the railway buses had never paid between Lodmoor House and Spa Road he would like to see that section omitted from the scheme. He also objected to the idea of trams running along the Esplanade.

A deputation of councillors visited Plymouth by a cheap railway excursion to view the tramways operating in that City, and at a special meeting a scheme involving three miles of 3 ft 6 in. gauge track, eight single-deck combination cars, car sheds and switchgear at a total cost of £27,000 was given due consideration. There was, however, a lack of support both within the Council and from the townspeople in general, and this was the last serious attempt by the Town to entertain a tramway system.

The Trackless Trolley system became known in later years as the 'Trolleybus', Bradford and Leeds being the first towns to actually run such a system. Both opened on the same day in 1911. If the local authority had been slightly more daring, that honour could well have belonged to Weymouth!

Had the Upwey-Portland scheme proceeded, the spectacle of a tram and an 'O2' with gate set racing each other across Chesil Beach would have been a joy to behold! In 1934 a suggestion was made that Weymouth Council should operate its own municipal bus service, but there was little support for this idea, and unlike the tramway schemes, it was never raised again!

DEPART FROM WEYMOUTH, Dorchester-road (Spa Hotel).					DEPART FROM WYKE REGIS. (Wyke Hotel).				
WEEK-DAYS AT			SUNDAYS		WEEK-DAYS AT			SUNDAYS	
A.M.	P.M.	P.M.	P.M.	P.M.	A.M.	P.M.	P.M.	P.M.	P.M.
9.0	1.0	5.0	2.0	6.0	9.31	1.31	5.31	2.31	6.31
10.0	2.0	6.0	3.0	7.0	10.31	2.31	6.31	3.31	7.31
11.0	3.0	7.0	4.0	8.0	11.31	3.31	7.31	4.31	8.31
NOON.									
12.0	4.0	8.0	5.0		P.M. 12.31	4.31	8.31	5.31	

Dorchester-road (Spa Hotel) ...dep.	as above	Wyke Hotel ...dep.	as above 32 minutes after
Westerhall-road (Six Turnings) ... ,,	5 minutes after	Wyke, Portland-road ... ,,	
G.W.R. Station ... ,,	9 ,,	Sandesfort House ,,	33 ,,
King's Statue, Thomas-street ... ,,	13 ,,	Clearmount-road ... ,,	36 ,,
Edmund-street, Town Bridge ... ,,	16 ,,	Clearmount ... ,,	37 ,,
Sidney Hall ... ,,	19 ,,	Rodwell-road ... ,,	38 ,,
Rodwell-road ... ,,	22 ,,	Sidney Hall ... ,,	41 ,,
Clearmount ... ,,	23 ,,	Edmund-street, Town Bridge ... ,,	43 ,,
Clearmount-road... ,,	24 ,,	King's Statue, Thomas-street ,,	46 ,,
Sandesfort House ,,	27 ,,	G.W.R. Station ... ,,	49 ,,
Wyke, Portland-road ... ,,	28 ,,	Westerhall-road (Six Turnings) ... ,,	53 ,,
Wyke Hotel ...arr.	29 ,,	Dorchester-road (Spa Hotel) ...arr.	58 ,,

THE FOLLOWING ARE THE FARES :—

FROM	Dorchester-road, Spa Hotel	Westerhall-road, Six Turnings	King's Statue, Thomas-street	Edmund-street, Town Bridge	Sidney Hall	Rodwell-road	Clearmount	Clearmount-road	Sandesfort House	Wyke, Portland-road
	d.	d.								
Dorchester-road, Spa Hotel	—									
Westerhall-road, Six Turnings	1	—	d.							
King's Statue, Thomas-st.	2	1	—	d.						
Edmund-st., Town Bridge	3	2	1	—	d.					
Sidney Hall	4	3	2	1	—	d.				
Rodwell-road	4	3	2	1	1	—	d.			
Clearmount	5	4	3	2	1	1	—	d.		
Clearmount-road	5	4	3	3	2	1	1	—	d.	
Sandesfort House	5	4	3	3	2	1	1	1	—	
Wyke, Portland-road	6	5	4	3	3	2	2	1	1	—
Wyke Hotel	6	5	4	3	3	2	2	1	1	1

Hand Luggage only will be Conveyed.

Above: Milnes Daimler No. 58, LC 1172 stands outside Stanton Court, Greenhill, prior to the tour of the route following the luncheon provided by the Mayor, Alderman T.J. Templeman on Friday 23rd June, 1905.
Author's Collection

Above: Timetable and fare chart published in the *Southern Times* at the opening of the GWR omnibus service between Wyke Hotel and Radipole Spa Hotel in 1905.

Right: Milnes-Daimler No. 50, LC 1171, awaits to depart from Stanton Court, Greenhill on a tour of the route. Seated alongside the driver is Alderman Templeman and his daughter.
Author's Collection

Chapter Three

The Great Western Railway Bus Service

During the early 1900s the railway companies were losing a vast amount of local traffic to the new tramway systems then opening up which, although not offering door to door transport, usually went nearer to one's destination than the local suburban station! This situation made them adapt a different attitude to their services, and very quickly halts were constructed and steam railmotors appeared on many local services. An alternative to the steam railmotor was to provide a railway-owned bus service. This was quicker to set up, and needed no infrastructure except the vehicles. It was also more flexible and could bring passengers from outlying areas to the nearest railway station.

The first railway-operated bus service in the British Isles commenced in February 1902 with a steam bus running between Whiteabbey and Greenisland Park, Belfast, operated by the Belfast & Northern Counties Railway.

The Great Western started to operate a motor bus service between Helston and The Lizard on 17th August, 1903, and before long routes were developed at many places throughout the company's system - mainly acting as feeders to their stations. By October 1905 it was calculated that Great Western buses had carried 1,456,071 passengers and covered 607,640 miles, and at the end of 1904 the GWR was the country's biggest operator with 36 motor buses; London could only muster about 20 such vehicles at that time!

Following previous experience, there is little doubt that the interest shown by Weymouth Council in tramways forced the Great Western's hand into providing a bus service at Weymouth. At the time both the main line to Dorchester and the Portland branch lacked intermediate Halts, and were vulnerable to competition.

To counteract this, between Weymouth and Dorchester railmotor Halts were opened at Radipole, Upwey Wishing Well, and Came Bridge on 1st June, 1905. Radipole served a growing suburb, whilst Upwey Wishing Well Halt was situated on Ridgeway Hill where the railway crossed the main Weymouth-Dorchester road. It was actually 1½ miles walk to the Wishing Well! Came Bridge, south of Dorchester was remote from Came Park and the Golf Club, or indeed anywhere else, except the nearby hamlet of Winterborne Monkton! Unfortunately the upgrading of the Portland branch was not such a simple matter. Struggling to carry the existing traffic, major improvements involving great expense and taking some time to complete were necessary, the bus being an easy solution. The first public announcement of the proposed bus service appeared in a supplement to the *Weymouth Telegram* on 3rd February, 1905.

GREAT WESTERN RAILWAY ENTERPRISE
MOTOR SERVICE FOR WEYMOUTH & WYKE
Commencing 1st May the Great Western Railway Company with characteristic enterprise propose to start a local bus service at Weymouth.

The motor bus that will be of the latest and up to date pattern will each carry we believe about 35 passengers and will run from the limit of the Borough on the Dorchester Road to Wyke Regis.

There will be two buses employed for the service which will be a half-hourly one, at popular penny fares for intermediate stages.

The net result of this great boon to Weymouth and Wyke will be that local residents will have constant, regular, and convenient means of access to and from the growing and populous district of Wyke at a cost of 1*d.* per journey. The intention of the GWR company is to make it an all the year round service.

Of one thing we are quite sure, it will meet a long felt want, and it ought to prove a good investment.

The *Telegram* went on to mention the 'possibility of the Company organising a motor train service with not less than four intermediate stations on the Portland branch as soon as the railway station and bridge have been built at Melcombe Regis'. However, this was not going to happen in the immediate future. The opening of the railmotor service to Dorchester and along the Abbotsbury branch on 1st May was received well by public and press alike. The May meeting of Weymouth Council was full of praise for the new service, but questions were asked because the bus service promised for the 1st May had failed to materialise! On the 18th May the Town Clerk said:

With regard to the question of railway facilities which came up at the last meeting, I saw Mr Kislingbury as arranged, with regard to the motor cars, and that gentleman assured me that the GWR Company had been hoping to place them on this month, but unfortunately the builders were so glutted with orders that they could not be obtained. They hoped however to have them next month. They would be put on directly they could be got from the builders.

The *Southern Times* for 10th June reported that the Town Clerk had been informed by Mr Kislingbury that the motor buses would be ready by 1st July. The two buses actually arrived in Weymouth by Friday 23rd June, and to celebrate the event the Mayor of Weymouth, Alderman T.J. Templeman, had a marquee erected in the grounds of his residence, Stanton Court, in which he gave a luncheon to officials of the GWR, members of the Town Council, and other influential residents of the area. The object of this convivial event was to give the Great Western's new bus service a good send-off. During lunch the Municipal Orchestra played a choice selection of music, and following the usual loyal toasts and various speeches, the guests were invited to partake of a ride on the two vehicles. It was noted in the local press that several gentlemen who sat on the nearside seats of the open top deck had trouble with their hats, 'and their ears and cheeks were lashed with the overhanging branches of trees along the route'. It further remarked that the offending trees were pruned the following day!

Commencement of the Service

The service commenced to operate on Monday 26th when over 800 people were conveyed along the route, and for the remainder of the week an average of 700 passengers per day were carried. This crowding caused complaints because it resulted in the late running of the buses. The service operated between the Spa Hotel at Radipole and the Wyke Hotel on the Portland road at Wyke Regis, via Dorchester Road to the Jubilee Clock, where a short detour was made down King Street to the railway station before proceeding to the King's Statue, thence down St Thomas Street, over the Town bridge, along North Quay, up Boot Hill and along Buxton Road to Wyke Hotel. The fares were Spa-Statue 2*d.*, Spa-Wyke 6*d.*, and Statue-Wyke

4*d*. The initial service was on the hour from the Spa Hotel, and 31 minutes past returning from Wyke, commencing at 9 am and finishing with the 8.31 pm from Wyke Hotel.

Although the new service was generally received with enthusiasm by the press, within days dissatisfaction was noted in the *Weymouth Telegram*:

> Much surprise is felt in Wyke at the heavy tariff and inadequate service in connection with the new system of motor buses, but it must be borne in mind that the innovation is only in the experimental stage at present, and no doubt in time both fares and distances will be adjusted to meet local requirements. Wherever these vehicles have been introduced the same objections have been evident at first, and when the requirements of the travelling public have been gauged, suitable alterations have been made. There has been evidence of this accommodating spirit already, and there is no reason to doubt that the GWR Co. will in time perfect the services to suit the popular demand.
>
> Consideration must be given, however, to the nature of the roads which are traversed and which cannot reasonably be compared with the populous thoroughfares through which these buses travel in larger towns. Rumour has it that the service is to be extended to Ferry Bridge and a considerable reduction effected in the fares next week, concessions which cannot fail to popularise the buses with Wykeites.

Despite the optimism raised in the *Telegram* the service was not extended to Ferrybridge. The Clerk of Wyke Regis Parish Council wrote to the GWR in the August raising the question, to which the GWR replied:

> The kind remarks of the Council were fully appreciated by the Company, who were giving consideration to the Council's request with regard to the later bus that would probably be granted, but as to running the service to the Ferrybridge the Company find themselves unable to grant the concession without making considerable changes in the times of running, and that would necessitate the abolition of the present hourly service.

In July the Weymouth branch of the Free Church Council, the Sabbatarians and the Latitudinarians, complained to the Council over the

> . . . intended running of the GWR Company's motor buses on Sundays, and earnestly hope the corporation of Weymouth will in the interest of the residents oppose these arrangements as leading to the increase of Sunday traffic and being prejudicial to the best interests of the town.

The Council was divided on the matter, Councillor Honeybon said:

> We have received a document from the representative ministers of the town and the matter was seriously considered. The Town Clerk went thoroughly into the matter. There were only two alternatives - either to refuse the licence or to grant it. We have power under the Hackney Carriage Bylaws to refuse a licence to anyone, but this Company also have the power to require us to show the just reason for refusing the licence. We see ourselves face to face with a big law case.

The whole affair became a matter of personal opinions, and as the buses did not intend to run before 2 pm the Council, not wishing to upset the GWR, let the matter proceed.

The buses had become the 'Plaything of the Hour', the new experience having to be tried by all. It was reported that on the August Bank Holiday they ran an half-hourly service and were crowded. During that period the timetable had been issued as a local handbill, the buses not appearing in the GWR timetable until 1st October, 1905.

It was at that point alterations were made to the service in the light of operating experience, the *Weymouth Telegram* noting:

> The abridged winter timetable of the motor omnibus service introduced last Sunday has been a source of disappointment to a large number of residents of Wyke, not only on account of the longer intervals, but more particularly because of the rearrangement of the fares and stages.

Although the service of 12 buses each way was maintained, buses only departed on the odd hour from the Spa Hotel going through to Wyke Hotel, the hourly departure from Wyke Hotel at half past the odd hour terminating at the top of Lodmoor Hill, from where they returned at three minutes past the even hour to Buxton Cross Roads, before returning at 36 minutes past the even hour to the Spa Hotel. This also applied to Sunday services, and the detour to the railway station from the Sea Front was also cut out.

The first serious accident involving a bus took place on 7th October between the top of Sandsfoot Hill and Foord's Corner, when for reasons not fully explained there was a problem with the vehicle, and whilst attempting to rectify it the driver had the rear wheel of the bus run over him, fracturing his left thigh and inflicting a serious wound below his right knee. Given first aid by people nearby, he was transported to hospital in the next bus. It was later reported that driver William Wright, who had transferred to Weymouth from Paignton, had his right leg amputated at the knee. However, he would be supplied with a wooden leg by the GWR and employed on light duties!

At the December Wyke Parish Council meeting Mr Jones said he had noticed that the bus service had been discontinued during the last few days. On enquiring, he was informed that the road between Sandsfoot Hill and Foord's Corner was in such a bad condition it was impossible to run buses over it. Indeed the timetables clearly stated that 'The road motor car and omnibus services are run subject to the condition of roads prevailing and the times are liable to alteration'. The condition of the roads was to be the main difficulty with the motor bus in Weymouth during the next few years, and the cause of many complaints and discussion at Council meetings.

Typical was an incident on 21st December, which the *Southern Times* reported thus:

MOTOR BUS HELD UP

The exceedingly slippery state which St Thomas Street was in on Tuesday morning had troubles in store for the GWR motor bus. Just before eleven o' clock, as the bus was coming over the bridge into St Thomas Street, there was a nasty side slip and the motor swerved into the pavement, smashing the overhead lamp outside Messrs Targett & Wiseman's shop. In a very short time the bus was righted, and proceeded on its journey.

January 1906 saw several of the short workings extended to Wyke Hotel and the Spa Hotel, and by July one service was extended to Whitehead's torpedo factory, departing for Radipole at 5 pm. Not exactly what the people of Wyke had requested the previous year, but it was something!

Private hire work was also undertaken. On 6th January, 1906, 200 children of Whitehead's employees were transported from Wyke Regis to the Sidney Hall for a party. On Good Friday two journeys were made to Putton Lane Chapel, Charlestown, in connection with special religious services, the local press immediately jumping to the conclusion that a regular extension of services was forthcoming! There were also other private hire operations and special workings over the coming years, typical being the special buses laid on for the annual horticultural show held at Radipole Manor.

At the May Council meeting the bizarre matter of the bus stop signs was discussed. Owing to the position in which they were fitted to lamp posts the top bracket of the sign cast a shadow and they could not be read after dark! Again slight alterations to the timetable took place for the summer months, the *Weymouth Telegram* reporting that

> . . . from the 1st June the GWR motor bus service will be extended and the fares reduced. There will be two cars in the afternoon by which passengers may travel from the Spa Hotel to Wyke Hotel and vice versa at the reduced fare of 4*d*.

On Whit Monday 4th June, 1906 the first fatality involving a motor bus in Weymouth took place, although through no fault of either the vehicle or the crew. As the bus was descending Boot Hill, Henry Gill, who was sitting on the upper deck, had his hat blow off. He ran down the stairs and jumped from the moving bus, falling onto the road and receiving a fractured skull from which he later died.

In August 1906 Wyke Regis Parish Council wrote to the GWR requesting that the latter place a seat at Foord's Corner for the convenience of its passengers. The GWR replied that 'They had motors running in many different places, but had never had such a request', and suggesting that if the Council wanted seats placed in the district they should 'do it themselves!' It would appear that the matter was then dropped, although for reasons never explained there was a GWR station seat at the Foord's Corner bus stop for many years - in fact well into the 1960s!

From the beginning of August two buses were run from the Alexandra Gardens after evening concerts. One ran to Radipole, the other to Wyke Regis. The latter brought forth letters, the *Weymouth Telegram* reporting that

> . . . some of the residents of Clearmount do not appreciate the buses. Some strongly worded letters, we believe, have been sent to the powers that be, protesting against this service and talking of the harm they will do the neighbourhood.

There is little doubt that these complaints were from people who simply did not want late night buses passing their property.

The Dust Problem

A letter to the council in July was the beginning of many complaints concerning the state of the roads and the buses. Mr R.A. Rogers of Handel House - a music shop in St Thomas Street - complained of the dust nuisance caused by the motor bus traffic which was doing a considerable amount of damage to his stock. He suggested the greater use of Corporation water carts.

In August the Borough Surveyor reported that the tarmacadam crossing near Hill House, Dorchester Road, had been damaged by the motor buses turning at that point, and it would be necessary to take it up and replace with stone pitching laid on Portland cement concrete. By the end of the year the Council were trying to obtain a contribution towards the road upkeep from the GWR, needless to say without success!

Right: No. 43, T 490 a Milnes-Daimler 20 hp forms an ideal prop for this family group photographed between 1907-1908 as driver Thomas gives his grandson his first driving lesson. The child's mother reticently faces the camera, whilst the family pet appears to have other attractions in view.

John Cummings Collection

Below: No. 13, BH 09, a Milnes-Daimler 16 hp photographed in the departure side yard of Weymouth station. The presence of traffic inspector Brooker, (standing alongside with white cap cover) suggests a special working such as one of the local horticultural shows. The bodywork of the vehicle at the time is of the char-a-banc variety with a roof, the rear windows being to protect the passengers from dust.

John Cummings Collection

On 6th November the bus due at Whitehead's at 5 pm was descending the slope past Ferrybridge Cottages when it skidded violently on the greasy surface and was almost overturned. Of the four inside passengers one was injured, his head and shoulders being forced by the shock clean through one of the windows, but fortunately despite the broken glass he suffered only abrasions to the legs.

By the end of the year the many complaints from shopkeepers and residents of St Thomas Street about the amount of dust thrown up by the buses were again being discussed by the Council. The *Southern Times* also took up the question of noise in an editorial during November, which expressed favour for the Darracq-Serpollet steam bus which was considered noiseless.

A motor bus that does not start with a jolt that shocks the passengers, does not leave a trail of smoke which well-nigh poisons hapless pedestrians, does not vibrate, and does not give vent to a loud bang which gives nervous people a severe shock is the very type the citizens of Weymouth have long been demanding. After their two years experience of the clumsy buses which tear up and down Weymouth Front with such thunderous noise, the prospect of some day having a noiseless and odourless bus is certainly pleasing, and while grateful to the GWR for the present buses it is fervently hoped that before long Weymouth may have the advantage of the wonderful strides that have been made in automobilsm [sic] since the present service, which is far from perfect and has many objectionable features, was installed.

There was no improvement to the roads during 1907, very few surfaces being tarred at that time, thus causing a dust problem in dry weather and a sea of mud when it was wet. The main complainants remained the shopkeepers of St Thomas Street. It would be puerile in many ways to compare the road conditions with those of later years, as modern tarmac surfaces and the equipment for laying it had not been developed. Readers over the age of 60 will remember the condition of the many 'un-adopted' roads that still existed into the 1950s! The buses themselves contributed to the problem, vehicles of the period being of crude construction compared with later models. The solid tyres, the springing, and the suspension were nothing like the equipment of later years. A ride on a pre-1925 vintage bus even on today's roads clearly shows up the inadequacies of early design. How these early buses and other vehicles proceeded along the roads without falling apart was a miracle!

An editorial in the *Southern Times* for 21st September, 1907 under the title 'Blundering Buses', remarked:

Noisy as the Great Western motor buses were when they were first brought to Weymouth, they are infinitely worse now, and the houses shake and nerves quake when the lumbering cars go by. Their usefulness is unquestioned, their punctuality is quite admirable, and with all their ugly defects we would not be without them. However we think the time has now come when the Great Western considering how remunerative the service has become might give us something better. We say nothing of the dust which the motors create, and which has doubled and trebled the labour of tradesmen and housewives along the line of route. If we enjoy the advantages of the service we must also put up with some of the inevitable drawbacks.

At the October Council Meeting the question of a noisy motor bus was raised by Councillor W.H. Bolt who was in trade as a jeweller and optician in St Thomas Street, and often made his anti-bus feelings known. Asked if any reply had been received from the GWR re the noise caused by their motor buses the Town Clerk

A line up of the Weymouth fleet between 1907-1908. Milnes-Daimlers No. 43, T 490; and No. 61, AF 148, and No. 8, CO 70, with char-a-banc body. Standing by the front wheel of No. 61 is leading driver Bailey.   *Author's Collection*

The same vehicles as in the view above but from a different angle showing the raised seats on the char-a-banc body of No. 8, CO 70. Leading driver Bailey is again standing between the two double decks, standing behind the engine of the centre vehicle is driver Cherry, who moved to New Quay, Cardiganshire, and later became Mayor of the town.   *Author's Collection*

Great Western Railway.

WEYMOUTH & WYKE REGIS MOTOR OMNIBUS SERVICE.

REDUCED FARES. Commencing October 1st, 1908, and until further notice.

Motor Omnibuses will run on Week-days and Sundays (condition of roads permitting) as under :—

WEEK-DAYS.

	a.m.	a.m.	a.m.	a.m.	p.m.	p.m.	p.m.	p.m.	p.m.	p.m.	p.m.	p.m.	p.m.
Dorchester Rd. (Spa Hotel) .. depart	8 30		10 30		12 30	1 30	2 30		4P30		6 30		8 30	9Y30
Top of Lodmoor Hill .. dep. about	8 33	9 33	10 33	11 33	12 33	1 33	2 33	3 33	4 33	5 33	6 33	⎰7 33	8 33	9Y33
Buxton's Cross Roads .. arrive	8 53	9 53	10 53	11 53	12 53	1 53	2 53	3 53	4 53	5 53	6 53	⎱7 53	8 53	9Y53
Wyke Hotel (Wyke Regis) .. ,,	8 59		10 59		12 59		2 59		4 59		6 59		8 59	9Y59

	a.m.	a.m.	a.m.	a.m.	p.m.	p.m.	p.m.	p.m.	p.m.	p.m.	p.m.	p.m.	p.m.
Wyke Hotel (Wyke Regis) .. depart	9 0		11 6		1 0		3 0		5R9		7 0		9 0	10Y0
Buxton's Cross Roads ,, dep. about	9 6	10 6	11 6	12 6	1 6	2 6	3 6	4 6	5 15	6 6	7 6	8 6	9 6	10Y6
Top of Lodmoor Hill ,, arrive	9 23	10 23	11 23	12 23	1 23	2 23	3 23	4 23	5 32	6 23	7 23	8 23	9 23	10Y23
Dorchester Rd. (Spa Hotel) .. ,,		10 25		12 25		2 25		4 25		6 25		8 25	9 25	10Y25

P This trip is extended to the Torpedo Works, Wyke Regis, Saturdays and Sundays excepted.
R This trip starts from the Torpedo Works, Wyke Regis, shortly after 5.0 p.m., Saturdays and Sundays excepted.
Y Saturdays only.

SUNDAYS.

The Service on Sundays will commence as follows : Dorchester Road (Spa Hotel) depart 2.30 p.m., running thereafter as on week-days.

The Cars will also call at the following intermediate stopping-places as shown below :—

Dorchester Road (Spa Hotel) ...depart	As above.		Wyke Hotel ...	... ...	As above.
Top of Lodmoor Hill ... ... ,,	about 3 mins. after.		Wyke, Portland Road ... ,,	about 2 mins. after.
Westerhall Road (Cross Roads) ,,	,, 5 ,,		Sandesfort House ... ,,	,, 4 ,,
Lennox Street ... ... ,,	,, 6 ,,		Buxton's Cross Roads... ,,	,, 6 ,,
Jubilee Clock (for G.W.R. Station) ,,	,, 8 ,,		Clearmount ... ... ,,	,, 8 ,,
King's Statue, St. Thomas Street ,,	,, 9 ,,		Rodwell Lodge ... ... ,,	,, 10 ,,
St. Edmund Street, Town Bridge ,,	,, 11 ,,		Sidney Hall ... ... ,,	,, 11 ,,
Sidney Hall ... ... ,,	,, 13 ,,		St. Edmund Street, Town Bridge ,,	,, 13 ,,
Rodwell Lodge ... ... ,,	,, 17 ,,		King's Statue, St. Thomas Street ,,	,, 16 ,,
Clearmount ... ... ,,	,, 21 ,,		Jubilee Clock (for G.W.R. Station),,	,, 17 ,,
Buxton's Cross Roads... ... ,,	,, 23 ,,		Lennox Street ... ,,	,, 19 ,,
Sandesfort House ... ... ,,	,, 26 ,,		Westerhall Road (Cross Roads) ,,	,, 21 ,,
Wyke, Portland Road ... ,,	,, 27 ,,		Top of Lodmoor Hill... ... ,,	,, 23 ,,
Wyke Hotel ... ... arrive	,, 29 ,,		Dorchester Road (Spa Hotel) arrive	,, 25 ,,

The above times do not apply to trip marked R.

THE REDUCED FARES ARE:

FROM	Dorchester Road (Spa Hotel).	Top of Lodmoor Hill.	Westerhall Road (Cross Roads).	Lennox Street.	Jubilee Clock for G.W.R.	King's Statue.	St. Edmund Street, Town Bridge.	Rodwell Lodge or Clearmount.	Buxton's Cross Roads.	Sandesfort House.	Wyke Hotel.	Torpedo Works.
	d.	d.	d.	d.	d.	d.	d.	d.	d.	d.	d.	d.
Dorchester Road (Spa Hotel) ...		1	1	1	2	2	2	3	3	4	4	5
Top of Lodmoor Hill ...	1		1	1	1	1	2	2	3	3	4	4
Westerhall Road (Cross Roads) ...	1	1		1	1	1	1	2	2	3	3	4
Lennox Street ...	1	1	1		1	1	1	2	2	3	3	4
Jubilee Clock (for G.W.R.) ...	2	1	1	1		1	1	1	2	2	3	3
King's Statue	2	1	1	1	1		1	1	2	2	3	3
St. Edmund Street, Town Bridge ...	2	2	1	1	1	1		1	1	2	3	3
Rodwell Lodge or Clearmount ...	3	2	2	2	1	1	1		1	1	2	2
Buxton's Cross Roads... ...	3	3	2	2	2	2	1	1		1	1	2
Sandesfort House	4	3	3	3	2	2	2	1	1		1	1
Wyke Hotel	4	4	3	3	3	3	3	2	1	1		1
Torpedo Works	5	4	4	4	3	3	3	2	2	1	1	

Passengers must join and alight from the Motor Omnibuses at the recognised stopping-places shewn in the Time Table above, or at the following places where the Motor Omnibuses will call if required: KINGSTHORPE, CARLTON ROAD, BOND STREET, CARINGTON CLOSE.

PASSENGERS will only be conveyed conditionally upon there being room in the Motor Omnibus.

TICKETS will be issued on the Motor Omnibuses, and must be retained until completion of journey. Full Fares to be paid for all Seats occupied.

BOOKS OF TICKETS.—Books containing fifty-five penny coupons can be obtained on application at the Booking Office, Weymouth Station, at a charge of four shillings each. Coupons should be tendered to the Conductor equivalent to the fare for each journey made, who will issue a ticket in exchange.

TIME TABLES.—The Directors give notice that the Company do not undertake that the Motor Omnibuses shall start or arrive at the time specified in the Bills; nor will they be accountable for any loss, inconvenience, or injury which may arise from delay or detention.

Through Railway Tickets will not be issued on, nor by, these Motor Omnibuses.

The Company reserve to themselves the right to decline to convey by their Motor Omnibuses any article of luggage or any parcel, but, subject to their being able to do so without inconvenience, passengers' hand luggage will be carried free.

DOGS.—Dogs are not carried on the Motor Omnibuses.

NEWSPAPERS.—Single Newspapers will be conveyed by the Cars at a charge of ½d. each.

For any further information respecting the arrangements shewn in this bill, application should be made to Mr. C. Kislingbury, Divisional Superintendent, Temple Meads Station, Bristol, or the Weymouth Stationmaster.

PADDINGTON, September, 1908.   JAMES C. INGLIS, General Manager.

(6000—12" x 10")   Arrowsmith, Printer, Quay Street, Bristol.   (B 821)

Timetable poster displayed locally for GWR Weymouth omnibus services, commencing 1st October, 1908.

A scene that is the epitome of an Edwardian seaside resort, people in their best clothes stroll along the Esplanade, and children are on their best behaviour. The Royal Hotel and other properties form a backdrop to this view, the peace being disturbed by a GWR Milnes-Daimler heading towards Radipole. *Author's Collection*

GWR Milnes-Daimler No. 11, AF 74 is stationary on Boot Hill with passengers alighting; has the vehicle come to what was politely called an 'involuntary stop' (which in plain English meant the vehicle had failed), or were the over obliging crew going to punish the cone clutch after letting passengers off on a steep hill? *A. Hutchings Collection*

said, 'Yes, the bus has been taken off the road for the past fortnight or three weeks, Mr Bolt. We have got another one on'. Mr Miller added, 'this is a healthy bus we have on now sir'. The Town Clerk remarked that he had not heard this one, agreeing that Mr Bolt was quite right - the old one had been perfectly awful.

The condition of the road could well have been a contributing factor in an accident on Sandsfoot Hill in January 1908. A young conductor named Holmes who had only recently commenced work was walking alongside the bus as it was climbing the hill. It is presumed he was carrying a scotch to place under the wheel in the event of the vehicle running back. He slipped and fell under the bus, which passed over one of his legs. He was taken to hospital in the bus. Again, like the earlier accident just along the road, it demonstrated how dangerous the work was in the early days.

Despite the dislike of the buses by Mr Bolt and several other members of the Council, they were popular with the general public. During the summer of 1908 there were reports on many occasions of overcrowding. At the September 1908 Council meeting the Town Clerk was instructed to ask the GWR for the half-hourly service to be continued during the winter months. However this was not granted. The summer service of 22 buses each way, with an extra late one on Saturdays, reverted to 13 each way again with a late bus on Saturdays. This Summer and Winter pattern was continued until World War I.

Again the subject of noise and dust was raised, a section of the community and some members of the Council still being against the buses. Dr De Meric said that he knew there was a great objection to the buses by some people. His own complaint was that they covered his gates with mud! However, he was very careful to tell the company that although his gates were very dirty when the buses passed he did not wish them to imagine that he opposed the running of the buses. He only called their attention to the fact that in London and some places they had splash boards! He was told that there was a financial difficulty, the boards being rather more expensive than the company was prepared to countenance. Councillor Bolt handed the Town Clerk a written question in which he asked what remedy the ratepayers had in abating the serious nuisance caused by the motor buses. He asked especially on behalf of shop-keepers and residents of St Thomas Street, but no doubt the nuisance was felt all along the route. The buses were about the worst that could be used. In reply, the Town Clerk said that 'the motor industry and motor traction is a very big industry, and it is an industry that had come to stay. The Council has licensed these buses, and they are entitled to run upon the roads'. Mr Bolt retorted that they were a nuisance to the town. They shook the houses, and people with weak nerves could scarcely stand the noise. He thought the less these buses ran the better it would be for the public generally. Whether the buses in use were right for the purpose was for the ratepayers to decide. Although other Councillors were in favour of the buses, stating what a great value they were to the inhabitants of Rodwell and Wyke Regis, Mr Bolt reiterated that they were a nuisance. They splashed the premises with mud, and ladies had to take shelter in shops while they passed.

The problem of the buses was highlighted by Councillor Honeybon, who said that he was aboard one on August Bank Holiday, and 'we stopped three times on the bridge, 20 times on Boot Hill, five times on Longhill, and seven times on Sandsfoot Hill'. The Town Clerk said he had written to the company, and they had admitted that the motors did go wrong sometimes. In fact that was an understatement! The records show that on Bank Holiday Monday 3rd August, three Weymouth vehicles failed and there was a suspension of the service. On No. 3 the engine was knocking, No. 11 had the 3rd speed bottom shaft give out, and No. 43 suffered from a broken

Milnes-Daimler No. 61, AF 148 stands outside the Spa Hotel at Radipole before returning to Wyke Hotel. The lack of traffic at that period is demonstrated by the fact the vehicle is waiting on the wrong side of the road. *John Cummings Collection*

End of the journey at Wyke Hotel, Milnes-Daimler No. 58, LC 1172 has turned into the entrance to Williams Avenue, passengers alight in the centre of the road. The bus will then reverse into the main Portland Road to park outside the Wyke Hotel before the return journey. This sort of manoeuvre may have been safe enough pre-1914. A similar manoeuvre made by a Southern National vehicle during World War II caused the death of a passenger who had just alighted from the vehicle. *M.J. Towzer Collection*

back spring. Indeed, No. 43 was incapacitated on the following two days when brake pins on a bracket sheared off and with timing problems respectively, whilst on the 20th and 21st of the month the magneto failed. Of the four cars allocated to Weymouth at that time, car No. 50 had many problems during the year, including a broken petrol pipe on 16th February, a broken gear rack on 5th March and a blocked petrol pipe the following day. She was stopped again on the 19th when the perch pole and pinion were dropping. Two cases of gearbox failure occurred in March, and there were differential main shaft problems in May. This was followed by two stoppages through spark plug problems, then bolts sheared off a distance plate, and a blocked petrol pipe caused stoppages in July. On 25th August spark plug failure and clutch spring problems caused a 2½ hour delay to the service, gear rack teeth were stripped on 5th September, and the second speed shaft broke on the 26th adding to the 12 failures of this vehicle which had already taken place during the year!

As with the earlier 'Tramway Question', there were those in favour and those against the motor buses. Indeed, as trams and other forms of transport were at the time being discussed by the Council, the GWR buses were fair game in the argument. From research of local papers of the period, it appears that the buses always took the blame, there being no reports of traction engines and other motor vehicles causing such mayhem! However, it was not only at Weymouth where complaints against the buses were being made. The *Commercial Motor* in November 1908 reported that Slough UDC had requested the GWR 'to take the necessary steps to lessen the noise produced by their motor omnibuses'.

A letter published on 26th September in the *Southern Times* just signed 'Ratepayer', was typical of the sentiments of a section of the community.

THE MOTOR BUS NUISANCE
When will our Town Council awake and put pressure on the GWR to compel them to abate this terrible mud-splashing and noise of the motor buses? One cannot walk down the street without having one's clothes spoilt, and to see the disgraceful state of the shop windows bespattered with mud certainly does not add to the beauty of Weymouth's streets. Have the Council no sympathy with the already heavily-rated tradesmen whose business must suffer from the nuisance? Or have they an interest in the GWR?

Withdrawal of the Service

Matters failed to improve the following year, and on Tuesday 31st August, 1909 the service was suddenly withdrawn, causing many complaints from local people. The GWR claimed that the service had lost money. Back in 1903 Lord Cawdor, Chairman of the GWR, had said of the company's motor buses: 'It is not a heavy expenditure, and the convenience will be that if the motor car does not succeed at one place we can take it to another'. The true facts of whether the buses lost money, or the improvements in local railway facilities caused the GWR to consider the buses unnecessary will never be known, but there was also the threat of the Council's various tramway schemes. The *Southern Times* for 28th August thought the GWR small-minded, saying:

That the Great Western Railway Company are susceptible to any continuous pin pricking which concerns any of their private interests may be taken as an accepted fact after the announcement just made that the motor bus service between Wyke Regis, Weymouth and Radipole is to be suspended after August 31st. The St Thomas Street tradesmen who have protested about the everlasting and much exaggerated dust nuisance have got their way , and the people residing in the suburbs of the town who regard the buses as a God-send in winter, have to suffer for it. In the meantime a petition is going around for signatures that will be sent to the Great Western Company praying them to revoke their decision.

The opening of both Westham Halt and Wyke Halt in that July and the improved service over the Portland branch could well have had an effect on the buses. However, Wyke Regis Halt was situated at Whitehead's torpedo factory, Ferrybridge, for which purpose it served admirably, but it was almost a mile from the centre of Wyke Regis. At that time the land along the Portland Road between Wyke Hotel and Ferrybridge was open fields. Rodwell station was almost a mile from Wyke Regis in the Weymouth direction.

On 4th September the *Southern Times* again spoke out:

The railmotors certainly do not meet the need that the buses have supplied, and though the lumbering, evil-smelling, dust creating machines were anathema to a certain section of the community, there can be no question that they were a valuable means of communication to the people of Wyke and Radipole. The company cannot be expected to continue to run them at a loss - which is bound to increase with the competition of the railmotors - but whatever the cause, the great cars have packed up and gone home. It is a swift and sardonic answer to the prayer of the St Thomas Street petitioners, who were recently praying for mitigation of the dust and noise which the cars created in that thoroughfare.

A letter published in the *Southern Times* on 11th September also disapproved of the buses:

I am a visitor to Weymouth for the first time, and came intending to stay for two or three weeks if I liked the place. This I did very much, and found my apartments most comfortable; but in a day or two I found the noise from the motor buses so irritating and annoying that I made up my mind to leave at the end of a week. However, I saw by the papers that these buses were to be discontinued on September 1st, and as you know this decision has been carried out, and I only hope they will never again be put upon the road, for I cannot tell you what a relief it is to myself and family to be able to sit with the windows open free from the perpetual noise we had endured. I have no doubt that numbers of other visitors could endorse what I have said.

The Town Council expressed regret at the withdrawal of the service, but apart from some remarks to the effect that Wyke Halt was a good ten minute walk from the main village whereas the buses were much closer, little else was said. Weymouth was now without buses.

Perhaps a note taken from the *Weymouth Telegram* on 10th September summed up the situation. The Town Clerk reported that

. . . as instructed by the Council I communicated with the District Superintendent of the GWR the petition of numerous inhabitants as to the noise caused by the motor buses, and urged that smaller and less noisy vehicles should be used. Mr Kislingbury promised to give the matter consideration. But since then the buses have been taken off the road.

If it had not been serious, the application by Messrs Alexander Masters & Co. to 'Run Rickshaws' in Weymouth - a quite novel proposal - could well have been taken as sarcasm. However this exotic transport never arrived!

In July 1910 the *Southern Times* returned to the subject of the missing buses,

There is suspicion that the buses were withdrawn in pique. The GWR were irritated by the complaints of the noise and dust that the vehicles made, and the mischievous petition got up by certain residents in St Thomas Street, some of whom left with the motors, was the last straw. If the buses were withdrawn to punish the malcontents, we would suggest it has gone far enough, and we hope Mr Kislingbury will see his way to advise a speedy restoration of a service which, though far from perfect, was exceedingly useful.

At a Council meeting the same month Councillor Watts said:

The other day I had an interview with a prominent official of the GWR, who appeared very sick at the petition that had been sent to the Company against the buses, and as a result of which the buses were taken off the roads last season.

Despite all the talk of various schemes, including Mr Watts' 'Light Motor Buses', there was no replacement service until June 1911, when Messrs Motor Coaches Ltd commenced a service between Radipole and Wyke Regis, and also to Westham and Chickerell. Unfortunately, as described in Chapter Four, their stay was short, and Weymouth was again without buses!

Reinstatement of the Service

In an age before excessive bureaucracy, arrangements could be quickly brought into operation if needed. On Friday 19th July, 1912 the GWR made application to Weymouth Council to operate three buses, which having been duly considered by the licensing committee, was granted. Indeed, so quick was the response that just three days later (Monday 22nd July) railway buses again commenced to operate in Weymouth on their original route between Radipole and Wyke Hotel. This time it was a joint venture involving the GWR and LSWR. It was agreed that the GWR provide and run the vehicles and provide the necessary staff, garage accommodation and equipment on the joint account of the two companies, the vehicles being treated in all respects as jointly owned. In the event of the service being discontinued they were to be taken over wholly by the GWR at an agreed valuation. The working accounts were to include the proportionate cost of vehicles in temporary replacement of those taken off for overhaul and repair, together with the interest on capital to be made up half-yearly on 30th June and 31st December. Any profit or loss was to be shared equally by the two companies, and any claims arising from accidents, etc. would be paid in equal shares. The agreement concluded: 'It being understood that the service is to be put on as an experiment, either company to be at liberty to discontinue it at short notice in the event of the results not proving satisfactory'. At the same time the Joint Committee decided to have a telephone connected to Weymouth station installed at Rocky Knap garage, the installation cost of £12 being borne by the joint account.

Considering that at the time the town had been without any regular transport, the *Southern Times* was not exactly over-enthusiastic over the return of the service.

WYKE REGIS AND WEYMOUTH.

ROAD MOTOR CAR.   **WEEK DAYS.**

	A.M.	A.M.	A.M.	P.M.	P.M.	P.M.	P.M.	P.M.	P.M.	P.M.	P.M.	P.M.	P.M.
Wyke Regis (Wyke Hotel) ...... dep.	9 0	....	11 0	....	....	1 0	1 30	....	....	3 0	3 30	....	
Buxton's Cross Roads .. dep. about	9 6	10 6	11 6	12 6	1236	1 6	1 36	2 6	2 36	3 6	3 36	4 6	
Top of Lodmoor Hill .... arr.	9 23	1023	1123	1223	1253	1 23	1 53	2 23	2 53	3 23	3 53	4 23	
Dorchester Road (Spa Hotel) .. ,,		1025		1225		1 25	1 55	2 25			3 55	4 25	

	P.M.	P.M.	P.M	P.M.	P.M.	P M.		P.M.	P.M.	P.M.	P.M.	P.M.
Wyke Regis (Wyke Hotel) ...... dep.	....	5 9	5 30	....	....	7 0	....	7 30	....	....	9 0	9S30
Buxton's Cross Roads .. dep. about	4 36	5 15	5 36	6 6	6 36	7 6	..	7 36	8 6	8 36	9 6	9S36
Top of Lodmoor Hill .... arr.	4 53	5 32	5 53	6 23	6 53	7 23	....	7 53	8 23	8 53	9 23	9S53
Dorchester Road (Spa Hotel) .. ,,			5 55	6 25			..	7 55	8 25	8 55	9 25	9S55

S Saturdays only.

Special Notice.—A Car will leave the Pier and Alexandra Gardens after the perform-ance at the Pavilion Theatre each evening and run to Dorchester Road.

ON SUNDAYS the Service will commence as follows :—Dorchester Road (Spa Hotel) depart 2.30 p.m., running thereafter as on week-days.

The times are liable to alteration.

Timetable for the joint GWR & LSWR Weymouth omnibus service published in the GWR public timetable. October 1912.

Milnes-Daimler No. 50, LC 1171, waits on the wrong side of the road at the Spa Hotel before departing for Weymouth. The driver and conductor are dressed in Winter uniform, the massive oil headlights and primitive front mudguards are prominent, whilst the gent on the right is intent on being in the photograph.   *Author's Collection*

The buses were put on Monday, and they are now running with the scrupulous regularity which is characteristic of the railway services. This gives them their real value, and without it no buses or trams could ever succeed. In coming to the help of the town in the present emergency, the railway companies have done Weymouth a good turn. We could have wished for a smarter and lighter bus, but on the principle that one must not look a gift horse in the mouth, Weymouth is grateful for anything on wheels that will run regularly and keep time.

The *Weymouth Telegram* for 26th July expressed the following sentiment;

No doubt it is with mixed feelings that the inhabitants of Weymouth looked upon the inauguration of the new motor omnibus service. Although the last service proved a great convenience to many, there were those who thought that the buses were more nuisance than a use to the town.
But the new buses which have already been extensively patronised are of a type in which all the latest improvements are embodied, and the service should prove to be a boon to the residents and visitors alike. In addition to which a special bus leaves the Pavilion and the Alexandra Gardens at the conclusion of the performance at the former each evening and makes numerous stops all the way to the Spa Hotel. We would like to add that many expressions of delight have been passed by those who have used the vehicles.

The new service, although to the same pattern as before, did not have a journey extended to Ferrybridge for the torpedo works, as the opening of Wyke Regis Halt on the Portland branch in July 1909 made this unnecessary.
Two weeks later on 3rd August the *Southern Times* raised the question of a bus service to Chickerell, stating what a success Motor Coaches Ltd had made of that route the previous year! The request appeared to be ignored. Meanwhile the reinstated Radipole-Wyke Regis service was proving successful, the *Great Western Magazine* reporting that in the first three weeks the route had carried 18,927 passengers.
Although the Council were pleased to have the buses back, there was a little unease at the January 1913 meeting when the Town Clerk produced a copy of the LSWR's new Parliamentary Bill and drew attention to section 33:

The company may provide, own, work, and use in connection with or in extension of their railway system or otherwise in any district to which their system affords access, road vehicles to be drawn or moved by animal power or electrical or other mechanical power.

The Council were worried that the company could obtain powers under this Act of Parliament overlapping local bylaws and their powers!
The condition of the roads that had caused so many problems was hardly mentioned, perhaps the traders of St Thomas Street and others had learned their lesson. Although water-bound macadam roads were still in place improvements had been carried out on the Esplanade and certain main roads, but it was not until the end of September 1913 that work commenced on relaying St Thomas Street with wooden blocks, which was to be a vast improvement.
History does not record the details of the buses used on the service at that period. The allocation in 1912 and early 1913 consisted of two Milnes-Daimlers and a Dennis single-deck vehicle. Later this was changed to one Milnes-Daimler and two Dennis vehicles.
Although the LSWR was involved in the service, there seems to have been little enthusiasm to publicise the facilities. The LSWR Summer timetable for 1914 gives no

Right: Milnes-Daimler No. 116, AF 544, stands with her crew at an unidentified location. The lack of protection for the driver is clearly shown in this view, the canopy being of little help in driving rain.

Author's Collection

No. 58, LC 1172, poses for the camera in Buxton Road shortly after the service commenced in 1905. What appears to be a long leaf spring under the vehicle is actually the suspension unit for the rear gear shafts. The brake block which acts against the tyre was only to be used for parking; the destination boards read 'WEYMOUTH Dorchester Road, GWR STATION & WYKE REGIS'. Photographed at what is now the junction with Clearmount Road the poor condition of the highway is shown, the building in the background was the residence of F.J. Barnes a Portland Quarry owner, the strip of land behind the bus is today occupied by a filling station.

Author's Collection

Milnes-Daimler No. 66, AF 192, stands outside Wyke Hotel before returning to Radipole. The variation of body styles and paintwork on the different vehicles is clearly shown, note the ornate side window.

D.F. Hollings Collection

No. 64, AF 647, waits by the Wyke Hotel to return to Weymouth, it must be the day the drayman calls, the barrels are out! It appears there has been a snowfall looking at the roofs and the state of the road. The trees in the distance was where old Wyke ended until the 1930s developments.

M.J. Towzer Collection

Above: Dennis 20 hp single-deck No. 158, AF 717. Although this photograph was taken outside the 'Red Lion' at Avebury, Wilts, it clearly illustrates the class of Dennis vehicle that worked at Weymouth just prior to World War I. *Phillip J. Kelley Collection/ex-BR (Western Region)*

Below left: A view taken at the Spa Hotel during World War I period. Standing alongside the Milnes-Daimler is a lady conductor, one of the many who kept bus services going through two World Wars. *Author's Collection*

Below right: A Naval parade passes the King's Statue at Weymouth at some time between 1912-1914. Note the GW & LSWR bus stop sign on the gas lamp alongside the statue. *C.L. Caddy Collection*

details of motor buses except the Exeter-Chagford service, a list of coaches, horse buses, and motor buses running to and from the company's stations. For Weymouth-Wyke Regis it just stated 'Motor Bus frequent service, see special handbills'.

World War I

The war put a stop to any further expansion of the bus service; indeed, it was a miracle it survived! By August 1916 it had been reduced to such an extent that there was no bus to Wyke Regis between 11 am and 5 pm, and the last bus on Saturday nights was discontinued. Furthermore, owing to the shortage of staff, ladies were employed as conductors.

With the publication of the July 1916 GWR public timetable, the Road Motor timetables were discontinued and replaced by a list of places served, and noting 'For particulars see special handbills'. Also printed in bold type was the warning that 'The services are liable to withdrawal or alteration without previous notice', a situation that continued for over four years.

Because of the petrol shortage, by late 1917 the GWR was conducting experiments in converting vehicles to run on coal gas stored in inflatable bags strapped to the upper deck, it being estimated that approximately 250 cubic feet of coal gas gave the equivalent output of one gallon of petrol. The *GWR Magazine* for March 1919 gave a list of road motor services that had cars fitted to run on coal gas, this including Weymouth. However the *Southern Times* throughout the period made no mention of the GWR buses being fitted for gas operation, whereas they did mention a coal merchant's lorry and a large char-a-banc serving one of the local army camps as being converted.

The only other official reference to affairs at Weymouth was in a General Manager's report dated March 1918, which stated that, owing to the fuel shortage, the Weymouth-Wyke Regis road motor service was suspended on two days a week. Known vehicles employed at the time were Milnes-Daimlers Nos. 64 (AF 647) and 169 (AF 652), the latter having departed by November 1921, but no records exist of their means of propulsion whilst in the town. The railway strike of October 1919 was reported by the local press in a low key approach, the *Southern Times* mainly mentioning what train services were running and the views of the general public, there being no mention of the road motors. A report of a packed strike meeting stated 'one or two women employees attended', but whether they were bus conductresses or other railway staff is not stated!

Restoration and Expansion

The Road Motor Services first reappeared in the public timetable for July 1920, when a service of 10 journeys each way was provided on weekdays only. Although the short workings to Lodmoor Hill had ceased, the 11.10 am, 3.10 pm and 5.10 pm services from the Spa Hotel terminated at Buxton Cross Roads. However the first departure from the Spa Hotel at 9 am, and Wyke Hotel at 9.35 am, as in pre-war days still did not allow workers to take advantage of the services.

In July 1920 Weymouth Council granted the GWR permission to extend its road motor service from Radipole Spa Hotel to the Borough boundary at Mount Pleasant

An unidentified GWR Maudslay double-deck runs along Weymouth Esplanade past the Burdon Hotel. In the background, Dorchester Road curves away left past St John's church.

A. Hutchings Collection

A GWR Maudslay single-deck departs from Preston heading towards Weymouth, during the short period GWR omnibus services were extended outside the Borough.

A. Hutchings Collection

(now Manor roundabout), resulting in the service being extended to Upwey from 4th October. With the introduction of this extended service there were 17 journeys over the middle section of the route, 11 going through to Wyke Hotel, and six to Upwey, with short workings over principal parts at suitable times, a glance at the timetable showing that operating procedures were improving.

In October the Council made representations to the GWR with a view to the provision of a motor bus service from the Town bridge to Westham during the reconstruction of the Backwater bridge (Westham bridge). This immediately brought forth a letter of protest in the *Southern Times*, in which the writer - who signed himself 'Safety First' - expressed concern about double-deck buses passing through the archway under the Portland branch railway in Newstead Road, owing to the narrow 2 ft pavement and the large number of children who passed that way to school.

The service, which ran through to Chickerell, commenced in January 1921. The route was from the King's Statue via the Town bridge, North Quay, Newstead Road, turning into Abbotsbury Road at the Rock Hotel, and proceeding to Westham Cross Roads and into Chickerell Road. The route at that time adequately covered Westham, the main housing estate having yet to develop.

Initially five journeys each way served Chickerell, whilst the other rural terminus at Upwey was served by four. There were 14 departures from the Spa Hotel into town, albeit the first departure was not until 9.30 am, whilst there were only five departures from Wyke Hotel, the earliest being at 10.35 am! The introduction of the summer timetable in July saw the elimination of the short workings terminating at Buxton Cross Roads (the junction of Buxton Road and Cross Road). Eleven journeys ran to Chickerell, and 12 to Upwey, with two extra short workings as far as the Spa Hotel, whilst Wyke Hotel had eight departures and a later start time of 9.40 am. However, there was now a late bus departing from the Statue at 10 pm for the Spa Hotel. With the opening of the new Westham bridge in that July the Westham/Chickerell service was diverted over the direct route via Westham Road, the new bridge and Abbotsbury Road. Finally on 11th July, 1921 GWR buses started to run to Preston.

The October 1921 timetable again saw service reductions, and a 9 am departure for the first of 13 journeys to and from the Spa Hotel, whilst the first of the seven journeys to Chickerell departed the King's Statue at 9.15 am, returning from the village at 9.45 - the same time as the first departure took place from the long established terminus at Wyke Hotel. Preston had a token service of two buses a day, the first returning from the village at 11 am.

The July 1922 timetable again reflected the summer variations required in a holiday resort, Preston being served by four journeys, Chickerell and Upwey both having five. Eleven reached Wyke Hotel, whilst 17 served the Spa Hotel, although the late bus was removed, the last departure from the King's Statue being 8.30 pm (on Saturdays only). The great improvement for the Summer of 1922 was the reintroduction of Sunday services, the first bus departing from the Spa Hotel at 1.15 pm. Services were again reduced on 2nd October, and the Sunday buses withdrawn.

Within two years of the war ending the railways found themselves in a different situation. The motor vehicle had become a reliable machine, and not only were the many new private operators a threat to the railway buses, they also broke the monopoly of railway travel in general. In Weymouth several small operators commenced services to various outlying districts, whilst on Portland several char-a-banc proprietors operated a service from Easton station to Portland Bill during the summer months.

WEYMOUTH, CHICKERELL, PRESTON, UPWEY, WYKE REGIS.

	a.m.	a.m.	a.m.	a.m.	a.m.	a.m.	no n	p.m.	p.m.	p.m.	p.m.	p.m.	p.m.	p.m.	p.m.	p.m.	p.m.	p.m.	p.m.	p.m.	p.m.	p.m.
Upwey (for the Wishing Well and Ridgway Hill) . . . . . . dep.				11 0					2S15		3 25			5S55						7 45		
Grey's Road . . . . . . dep.abt.				11 3					2S18		3 28			5S58						7 48		
Swan Inn . . . . ,, ,,				11 6					2S21		3S1			6S 1						7 5		
Redlands Farm . . . . . . ,, ,,				11 10					2S25		3 35			6S 5						7 52		
Radipole (Spa Hotel) . . . . ,, ,,	9 0	9 30	10 0	11 (	11 15		12 0	1 0	1S15		2S30	3S30	3 40		4S30	6S10			6 30	7S30	8 (	8S30
Westerhalls . . . . . . ,, ,,	9 5	9 35	10 5	11	11 20		12 5	1 5	1S20		2S35	3S35	3 45		4S35	6S15			6 35	7S37	8 (	8S35
Preston . . . . dep.						11 50				1 50				4 15				5 55				
Cross Roads . . . . . . dep.abt.						11 55				1 55				4 20				6 0				
Coast Guard Station . . . . ,, ,,						12 0				2 0				4 25				6 5				
Greenhill . . . . ,, ,,						12 5				2 5				4 30				6 10				
Weymouth (King's Statue) { arr.abt. {	9 9	9 39	10 9	11 9	11 25	12	12 9	1 9	1S25	2 9	2S39	3S39	3 50	4 34	4S39	6S19	6 15	6 33	7S39	8 1(	8S39	
	9 10	9 40	10 10	11 10		12 10	12 10	1 10		2 10	2S40	3S40		4 35	4S40	6S20		6 40	7S40		8S40	
Adelaide . . . . arr.abt.		9 45				12 15				2 15				4 40				6 45				
Westham Cross Roads . . . ,, ,,		9 50				12 20				2 20				4 45				6 50				
Charles Town . . . . . . ,, ,,		9 55				12 25				2 25				4 50			7 0	6 55				
Chickerell . . . . ,, ,,		10 0				12 30				2 30				4 55								
Town Bridge . . . . . . dep.abt.	9 12		10 12	11 12			12 12	1 12			2S42	3S42			4S42	6S22			7S42		8S42	
Rodwell . . . . arr.abt.	9 17		10 17	11 17			12 17	1 17			2S47	3S47			4S47	6S27			7S47		8S47	
Buxton Cross Roads . . . . ,, ,,	9 22		10 22	11 22			12 22	1 22			2S52	3S52			4S52	6S32			7S52		8S52	
Wyke Regis . . . . ,, ,,	9 30		10 30	11 30			12 30	1 30			3S 0	4S 0			5S 0	6S40			88 (		9S 0	

	a.m.	a.m.	a.m.	a.m.	a.m.	a.m.	a.m.	p.m.	p.m.	p.m.	p.m.	p.m.	p.m.	p.m.	p.m.	p.m.	p.m.	p.m.	p.m.	p.m.	p.m.	p.m.
Wyke Regis . . . . dep.	9 35		10 35		11 40	12 40		1 35		3S 5	4S 5		5S 5			6S45		8S 5		9S 5		
Buxton Cross Roads . . . dep.abt.	9 40		10 40		11 40	12 40		1 40		3S10	4S10		5S10			6S50		8S10		9S10		
Rodwell . . . . ,, ,,	9 43		10 43		11 43	12 43		1 43		3S13	4S13		5S13			6S53		8S13		9S13		
Town Bridge . . . . . . ,, ,,	9 46		10 46		11 46	12 46		1 46		3S16	4S16		5S16			6S56		8S16		9s16		
Chickerell . . . . dep.abt.		10 0				12 45			2 35					5 10			7 5					
Charles Town . . . . . . ,, ,,		10 5				12 50			2 40					5 15			7 5					
Westham Cross Roads . . . ,, ,,		10 10				12 55			2 45					5 20			7 10					
Adelaide . . . . ,, ,,		10 15				1 0			2 50					5 25			7 15					
Weymouth (King's Statue) { arr.abt. {	9 45	10 19	10 49		11 49	12 49	1 4	1 49	2 54	3S19	4S19		5S19	5 29		6S59	7 19	8S19		9S20	9S35	
	9 50	10 20	10 50	10 50	11 50	12 50	1 5	1S50	2 55	3S20	4S20	3 50	5S20	5 30	6 15	7S 0	7 20	8S20	8 30	9S20	9S35	
Greenhill . . . . dep.abt.				11 28				1 28				3 53		5 33								
Coast Guard Station . . . . ,, ,,				11 33				1 33				3 58		5 38								
Cross Roads . . . . . . arr.abt.				11 38				1 38				4 3		5 43								
Preston . . . . ,, ,,				11 45				1 45				4 10		5 50								
Westerhalls . . . . . . abt.dep.	9 55	10 25	10 55		11 55	12 55	1 10	1S55	3 0	3S25	4S25		5S25			6 20	7S 5	7 25	8S25	8 35		9S40
Radipole (Spa Hotel) . . . ,, ,,	10 0	10 30	11 0		12 0	1 0	1 15	2S 0	3 5	3S30	4S30		5S30			6 25	7S10	7 30	8S30	8 40		9S45
Redlands Farm . . . . . . ,, ,,		10 33						2S 3	3 8				5S33					7 33				
Swan Inn . . . . ,, ,,		10 36						2S 6	3 11				5S36					7 3(				
Grey's Road . . . . . . ,, ,,		10 40						2S10	3 15				5S40					7 40				
Upwey (for the Wishing Well and Ridgway Hill) . . . arr.abt.		10 45						2S15	3 20				5S45					7 45				

S—Also runs on Sundays.

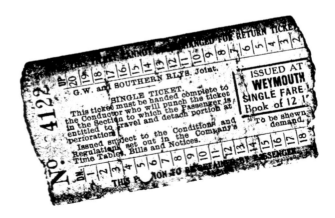

Timetable for joint GWR & LSWR Weymouth omnibus services published in the July 1922 GWR public timetable and showing the extended services to Chickerell, Preston and Upwey.

A ticket from a book of 12 obtained in advance from stations at discount prices. This particular ticket, issued for use at Weymouth, was a 'GWR and Southern Rlys Joint' issue.

A Luton-based company, Messrs Road Motors, commenced to operate a service between Upwey and Portland Victoria Square during 1921. Ten years before there had been a distinct lack of buses in the town, but now everybody wanted to run a service! The principal contestants - the GWR and Messrs Road Motors - fell out of favour with the Council Watch Committee in March 1922, the Town Clerk being instructed to arrange a meeting between the manager of Road Motors, the GWR, and the Committee in an attempt to provide a more efficient bus service.

During the summer of 1922 buses of the National Omnibus & Transport Company made their first appearance in Weymouth, but the Council allowed them to operate only during the summer months on services from Bridport and Yeovil where they had already become established. In 1924 The Weymouth Motor Company - a small local concern operating a char-a-banc fleet - sold out to the 'National', which meant that for a modest outlay the National acquired the fleet, the Edward Street premises, and the all important Hackney licences, thus casting the mould for all future bus services in the area. The following year Road Motors of Luton was also acquired by the 'National', these two purchases firmly establishing the company in the town with two garages and the necessary route licences.

Whilst all the additions and alterations to local bus services were taking place, the railways themselves had gone through the upheaval of the Grouping of the various companies. Although the Great Western was not unduly affected and kept its old name, the LSWR became part of the newly-formed Southern Railway, this resulting in the lettering 'GWR & LSWR' on the sides of the railway buses operating at Weymouth being replaced by 'GWR & SR'. With the withdrawal of the Exeter-Chagford service in September 1924, the last remaining road motor service of the former LSWR, Weymouth became the sole motor bus involvement of the Southern Railway, albeit only from a financial standpoint.

Retrenchment of Services

Although between 1920 and 1928 the GWR had opened up over 100 services, including the purchase of several small businesses, the post-war extensions at Weymouth were to be short-lived. From 7th July, 1923 the extension from Radipole to Upwey, and the services to both Preston and Chickerell, were withdrawn owing to strong competition from Road Motors and other small operators, who were themselves to be shortly taken over by 'National'.

At that time Chickerell, Upwey, and Preston were well outside the Borough, and apart from a certain amount of summer trade, could not support a regular service. It was not until the late 1930s that ribbon development would change the situation. Indeed the words of the Tramway Report 19 years earlier that 'the profitable portion was between Spa Hotel and Wyke Hotel' were still proving correct.

The competition from other operators also gave good reason for the GWR to bring their service more to the attention of the public. At the September 1925 Watch Committee meeting, the Weymouth station master, on behalf of both the Great Western and Southern Railways, asked if the committee would agree to the companies fixing their timetable boards to lamp standards, similar to those provided by the National Omnibus & Transport Company. This was agreed subject to payment to the Council of 1s. per board.

During the General Strike of 1926 the crews of the GWR buses, being NUR members, stopped work, whereas the 'National' continued to run normally, as did

RADIPOLE, WEYMOUTH AND WYKE REGIS.

WEEK DAYS.

	a.m.	a.m.	a.m.	a.m.	a.m.	a.m.	a.m.	a.m.	noon	p.m	p.m	p.m	p.m	p.m
RADIPOLE (Spa Hotel) .. dep.	8 0	8 30	9 0	9 30	10 0	10 30	11 0	11 30	12 0	12 30	1 0	1 30	2 0	2 30
WESTERHALLS .. ,,	8 5	8 35	9 5	9 35	10 5	10 35	11 5	11 35	12 5	12 35	1 5	1 35	2 5	2 35
WEYMOUTH (King's Statue) {arr. dep.	8 9	8 39	9 9	9 39	10 9	10 39	11 9	11 39	12 9	12 39	1 9	1 39	2 9	2 39
TOWN BRIDGE .. ,,	8 10	8 40	9 10	9 40	10 10	10 40	11 10	11 40	12 10	12 40	1 10	1 40	2 10	2 40
RODWELL or CLAREMOUNT ,,	8 17	8 47	9 17	9 47	10 17	10 47	11 17	11 47	12 17	12 47	1 17	1 47	2 17	2 47
BUXTON CROSS ROADS .. ,,	8 22	8 52	9 22	9 52	10 22	10 52	11 22	11 52	12 22	12 52	1 22	1 52	2 22	2 52
WYKE REGIS .. arr.	8 30	9 0	9 30	10 0	10 30	11 0	11 30	12 0	12 30	1 0	1 30	2 0	2 30	3 0

WEEK DAYS—continued.

	p.m.	p.m.	p.m.	p.m.	p.m.	p.m.	p.m.	p.m.	p.m.	p.m.	p.m.	p.m.	p.m.	
RADIPOLE (Spa Hotel) .. dep.	3 0	3 30	4 0	4 30	5 0	5 30	6 0	6 30	7 0	7 30	8 0	8 30	9 0	..
WESTERHALLS .. ,,	3 5	3 35	4 5	4 35	5 5	5 35	6 5	6 35	7 5	7 35	8 5	8 35	9 5	..
WEYMOUTH (King's Statue) {arr. dep.	3 9	3 39	4 9	4 39	5 9	5 39	6 9	6 39	7 9	7 39	8 9	8 39	9 9	..
TOWN BRIDGE .. ,,	3 10	3 40	4 10	4 40	5 10	5 40	6 10	6 40	7 10	7 40	8 10	8 40	9 10	..
RODWELL or CLAREMOUNT ,,	3 17	3 47	4 17	4 47	5 17	5 47	6 17	6 47	7 17	7 47	8 17	8 47	9 17	..
BUXTON CROSS ROADS .. ,,	3 22	3 52	4 22	4 52	5 22	5 52	6 22	6 52	7 22	7 52	8 22	8 52	9 22	..
WYKE REGIS .. arr.	3 30	4 0	4 30	5 0	5 30	6 0	6 30	7 0	7 30	8 0	8 30	9 0	9 30	..

WYKE REGIS, WEYMOUTH AND RADIPOLE.

WEEK DAYS.

	a.m.	a.m	a.m.	a.m.	a.m.	a.m.	a.m.	noon	p.m.	p.m.	p.m.	p.m.	p.m.	p.m.
WYKE REGIS .. dep.	8 30	9 0	9 30	10 0	10 30	11 0	11 30	12 0	12 30	1 0	1 30	2 0	2 30	3 0
BUXTON CROSS ROADS .. ,,	8 35	9 5	9 35	10 5	10 35	11 5	11 35	12 5	12 35	1 5	1 35	2 5	2 35	3 5
RODWELL or CLAREMOUNT ,,	8 38	9 8	9 38	10 8	10 38	11 8	11 38	12 8	12 38	1 8	1 38	2 8	2 38	3 8
TOWN BRIDGE .. ,,	8 41	9 11	9 41	10 11	10 41	11 11	11 41	12 11	12 41	1 11	1 41	2 11	2 41	3 11
WEYMOUTH (King's Statue) {arr. dep.	8 45	9 15	9 45	10 15	10 45	11 15	11 45	12 15	12 45	1 15	1 45	2 15	2 45	3 15
WESTERHALLS .. ,,	8 50	9 20	9 50	10 20	10 50	11 20	11 50	12 20	12 50	1 20	1 50	2 20	2 50	3 20
RADIPOLE (Spa Hotel) .. arr.	8 55	9 25	9 55	10 25	10 55	11 25	11 55	12 25	12 55	1 25	1 55	2 25	2 55	3 25

WEEK DAYS—continued.

	p.m.	p.m.	p.m.	p.m.	p.m.	p.m.	p.m.	p.m.	p.m.	p.m.	p.m.	p.m.	p.m.	
WYKE REGIS .. dep.	3 30	4 0	4 30	5 0	5 30	6 0	6 30	7 0	7 30	8 0	8 30	9 0	9 30	..
BUXTON CROSS ROADS .. ,,	3 35	4 5	4 35	5 5	5 35	6 5	6 35	7 5	7 35	8 5	8 35	9 5	9 35	..
RODWELL or CLAREMOUNT ,,	3 38	4 8	4 38	5 8	5 38	6 8	6 38	7 8	7 38	8 8	8 38	9 8	9 38	..
TOWN BRIDGE .. ,,	3 41	4 11	4 41	5 11	5 41	6 11	6 41	7 11	7 41	8 11	8 41	9 11	9 41	..
WEYMOUTH (King's Statue) {arr. dep.	3 45	4 15	4 45	5 15	5 45	6 15	6 45	7 15	7 45	8 15	8 45	9 15	9 45	..
WESTERHALLS .. ,,	3 50	4 20	4 50	5 20	5 50	6 20	6 50	7 20	7 50	8 20	8 50	9 40	10 10	..
RADIPOLE (Spa Hotel) .. arr.	4 0	4 30	5 0	5 30	6 0	6 30	7 0	7 30	8 0	8 30	9 0	9 50	10 20	..

Timetable for joint GWR & LSWR Weymouth omnibus services published in the July 1927 GWR public timetable.

the many small operators who no doubt made capital out of the situation. The GWR service continued until noon on 4th May when the staff of one leading driver, four drivers, four conductors, and one cleaner joined the strike and the service was suspended. Volunteers were engaged and a partial service with one bus commenced on the 9th, a full service being run from the 11th when a non-striking driver from Marlborough and a supernumerary conductor manned a second vehicle.

The Watch Committee, ever vigilant, discussed the matter at their next meeting and decided that 'licences need not be issued in respect of the volunteers driving and conducting the omnibuses of the Company during the recent strike'. On 9th September the Watch Committee were told that conductor Furness of the GWR was inside his bus talking to a passenger instead of being on the bottom step with a scotch whilst the bus was ascending Sandsfoot Hill, and the Hackney Carriage Inspector was instructed to interview the offender! This was not the first complaint against the company, the Watch Committee receiving a letter about the very fast speed of the GWR omnibus which left the King's Statue for Radipole at 9.35 pm on 17th December, 1924. One can only conclude that this was the driver's final trip of the day!

Following the withdrawal of the Upwey, Chickerell and Preston services, the Spa Hotel-Wyke Hotel route was concentrated upon. The Summer service from 1925 onwards consisted of 27 journeys each way daily, providing a half-hourly service. Sundays commenced with the 2 pm departure from the Spa Hotel and provided 15 round trips. On weekdays the first departure from the Spa Hotel was at 8 am, returning from Wyke Hotel at 8.30 am. Although this was better than the service in the early days, it still failed to cater for workmen who mostly started work well before 8 am in those days - and shop and office staff would have been 'pushed'! This remained the general pattern of the service during its final years.

With the rapid decline in GWR-operated bus services during the late 1920s Road Motor Car services ceased to be published in the general timetable, the July-September edition of 1928 having the following note. 'The Road Motor Car services are omitted from this timetable, but particulars of the services will be forwarded to those publishers who require the information'. By the Summer of 1932 seven pages of comprehensive details of services operated by omnibus companies associated with the GWR appeared in the timetable. However there was no mention of the Southern National, or indeed any Weymouth-based services!

Rail Replacement Scheme

The serious financial position of the Portland branch (*see Isle of Portland Railways Vol. II*) reflected the success of the bus services provided by the 'National' and the private operators. In February 1927 'National' acquired Smith & Hoare, which was running a local service between Victoria Square and Easton. The 'National' had also purchased a plot of land and some tea rooms in Victoria Square in order to provide an office and waiting room, and later an operational depot was built. Having bought out the local operators, 'National', who up until then had only ventured as far as Victoria Square from Weymouth, commenced to operate to Easton offering a choice of 22 journeys each way daily and 10 on Sundays, whilst from Victoria Square to Weymouth, Radipole, and Upwey, 27 journeys were operated. The fares on the buses were not only cheaper than those on the railway, but the omnibus company issued blocks of 50 tickets at 25 per cent discount.

It was difficult for the railway to compete. By road the distance between Portland and Easton stations was barely two miles, whereas the railway made a detour of over 3½ miles around the cliffs, and steep gradients ruled out speed. It was calculated that to provide a railway bus service between Portland and Easton would cost £2,850, this sum providing two Guy 32-seat single-deck buses and converting the disused goods shed at Portland into a garage. The weekly working expenses of two drivers, two conductor/cleaners, fuel and other items would amount to £25 15s. to operate a daily service of 10 journeys each way between Victoria Square and Easton, with five journeys extended to Southwell.

The Joint Committee were of the opinion that any road service introduced by the railway companies would represent a considerable improvement on the former conditions, but any attempt to match the service operated by the local operators would be unprofitable. It would also have the disadvantage of requiring passengers to change from bus to train at Portland station, whereas the 'National' ran direct to Weymouth. There had already been some questioning of the railway's position in the operation of buses, and the Joint Committee feared that the National Omnibus & Transport Company might raise further questions as to the railway company's powers to run them. The idea was therefore shelved, but had it been pursued it would have been a very early example of a 'Railway replacement' road service.

The Vehicles and Operation

The buses employed at the commencement of the Weymouth service were two 20 hp Milnes-Daimler vehicles, fleet Nos. 50 & 58, LC 1171 and LC 1172. There were frequent changes of vehicles at the various depots, No. 58 being replaced by No. 61 (AF 148) by February 1906, and a third bus added, No. 66 (AF 192), which had arrived by June. Both these vehicles were Milnes-Daimler double-deckers. No. 66 was replaced by No. 43 (T 490) around July of 1907, this vehicle having the distinction of operating the first service between Paignton and Totnes on 17th April, 1905.

No. 61 was also transferred away later in the year , No. 8 (CO 70) arriving in the town for the Summer, no doubt making her presence known when she knocked a big end bearing out on 25th June!

There were several changes of vehicle during 1908. No. 43 departed towards the end of the year, and Nos. 4, 11, 45 and 49 - all double-deck Milnes-Daimlers - operated the services for various periods during the summer. Just as there were frequent changes of vehicle at the depots, the bodies on the vehicles were also subject to change, No. 43 having been fitted with at least three different types of body within as many years. No. 116 was fitted with an observation car body for operating 'Shakespeare Country' tours in the Stratford-upon-Avon area when new.

Transferring the vehicles between the widely spaced depots was not easy, both the chassis and bodies were often moved around the system by rail on bogie crocodile wagons, the goods yard crane usually being sufficient to carry out any lifting work required.

Breakdowns were an accepted occurrence in the early days. In fact, any involuntary stop of less than eight minutes was not classed as a breakdown, but any time lost in excess of that was recorded in a ledger maintained by the Road Motor Department. The entries between 1905 and 1908 make interesting reading over 90 years later, but they belong to an age almost before garages, and there was no recovery service! The driver was also the mechanic, having to do the best he could with local facilities. Even the telephone was uncommon, so obtaining the spare car to continue the service was fraught with difficulties.

From the commencement of the service in June 1905 until the end of the year there were eight recorded breakdowns - not bad when one considers that in August alone the cars covered 2,915 miles. The whole of 1906 saw 21 failures, the average failure for the GWR fleet being one in every 1,000 miles covered! The following year there were only 18 failures at Weymouth, but in 1908 a total of 32 breakdowns was recorded. From the beginning of 1909 the breakdown reports were simplified to pure statistics, and for the four weeks ending 31st January, 1909 the two Weymouth cars covered 2,071 miles, with two failures exceeding eight minutes!

During this period of change the older vehicles were going out of the fleet. During the 1912 period several of the Dennis 20 hp 16-seat single-deckers worked in the town, this batch of 10 vehicles, Nos. 153-162, having been purchased during 1911. The Milnes-Daimlers still operating in Weymouth during 1919 were replaced by Maudslays from other depots, Weymouth being one of the few depots to keep double-deck vehicles. It is reputed that three ex-London General 'B' type double-deck bus bodies had been purchased and fitted to the Maudslay chassis involved.

On 12th January, 1920 the first AEC - No. 241 - arrived in the Town, complete with a Dorset registration FX 5203, the only GWR railway bus registered in the county. Departing on the 9th May, it was transferred to Paignton and received a Devon registration, T 9124. In 1929 it was converted into a lorry.

Early in 1925 the Maudslays - except No. 209 - were withdrawn from Weymouth, being replaced by AEC 45 hp single-decks including No. 247 (AX 1416) arriving on 30th September, 1925 and No. 286 (XM 9791) in November. No. 274 (LU 9326) arrived at Weymouth on 24th March, 1926, departing that November with No. 286 following the arrival of the two new Maudslay ML3s. The AECs did not survive long as buses, both 274 and 286 being converted into lorries during 1927, and No. 247 likewise the following year.

The last double-deck vehicle in the GWR fleet, No. 209 (T 4350) a Maudslay 40 hp, was withdrawn from Weymouth during 1926. In October the same year Nos. 1209 and 1210 (YR 6217 and YR 6218), both Maudslay ML3 chassis fitted with Buckingham 32-seat rear-entrance bus bodies, arrived at Weymouth, these new vehicles representing the very latest in road transport and the introduction of pneumatic tyres. In July 1927 No. 1244 (YH 6817), a Guy FBB with a 32-seat Hall Lewis body, arrived, allowing No. 247 - the last of the old vehicles - to be withdrawn. The Guy did not stay long, transferring to Abergavenny in 1928, and entered the Western Welsh fleet in April 1929, but retained its original fleet number. The Guys, which were disliked by the Great Western drivers, were also disliked by Western Welsh. Within a short while they were sold back to their makers in part exchange for new vehicles, it being recorded that No. 1244 had been converted to a goods vehicle in June 1931.

The Guy was replaced at Weymouth by Maudslay ML3 No. 1230 (VC 7504), but her stay was brief. She was replaced by ML3 No.1212 (YR 6412). In four weeks over the March/April period of 1930 two Thornycroft BC vehicles with Vickers 26-seat bodies, Nos. 1606 & 1607 (UV 4080 and UV 4081), operated at Weymouth. The most luxurious vehicles to operate in the resort, their seating capacity of only 26 coach-type seats allowed good leg room, whilst overhead luggage racks, curtains at the windows, and a clock on the front bulkhead added to the high-class finish. Referred to as 'Pullman Coaches', between August-October 1929 they had been based at Wolverhampton to operate an express service to Aberystwyth, via Bridgnorth and

Ludlow. The reason for these two vehicles appearing at Weymouth for such a short period is unclear, refits or repairs to other vehicles seeming to be a possible reason.

Both vehicles moved to Swindon, 1607 remaining there until joining the Bristol Tramways fleet in January 1932 as No. X124 (renumbered 110) in 1937. She was broken up by Bristol Tramways in March 1938. No. 1606 later moved to Slough, where on 10th April, 1932 the GWR Slough area services were taken over by London General Country Services Ltd. Owing to the Taplow route being outside the LCGS operating area, the route and three buses, (including No. 1606) were transferred to the Thames Valley Traction Company, where No. 1606 took the fleet No. 257 and was allocated to Wantage to operate the Reading-Wantage service. The vehicle was actually kept at Wantage railway station, an appropriate arrangement in view of its previous ownership! She remained there until early 1938, being transferred to the Ledbury Transport Company fleet from 1st January as No. 56.

The Ledbury Company of Reading was a Thames Valley subsidiary which could not be wound up for licensing reasons. As it was necessary to maintain this 'paper fleet' many transferred vehicles never turned a wheel on Ledbury licensed routes. Still active in May 1938, No. 56 was reported as sold on 11th November, and was broken up in August 1940 by G.C. Cook, scrap merchants of Kennington, London SW8. She was the last GWR Weymouth vehicle to survive.

During 1929 the fleet consisted of Nos. 1209, 1210, and 1212, these later being joined by No. 1523 (YW 3354) for a brief visit, to be replaced in June by No. 1595 (UU 4822) - a new Maudslay ML3B with a Vickers 32-seat body. These buses served the Town until the withdrawal of the service.

The Maudslays all passed to Western National, 1230 and 1523 in January 1929 when the majority of services in the West Country came under its control. Vehicles 1209/10/12 and 1595 were the last four at Weymouth - and indeed the last four GWR vehicles in operation - and were transferred to Western National on 16th February, 1934, there being no arrangements with Southern National. The buses had a book value of £800, and Western National agreed to purchase them for £400. Of the remaining balance of £400, the Southern National Company was to pay the joint railway companies one half (£200), the other half being regarded as a loss on realisation to be shared between the two railway companies. It is doubtful that they ever operated for their new owners, being advertised for sale in *Commercial Motor* on 16th January, 1935. Nos. 1210/12 were sold on 16th May, 1935, 1209 on 8th July, and 1595 on 4th January, 1936.

The livery of the fleet varied over the years. In the early days most vehicles were brown whilst others were brown and cream, and some single-deck vehicles had red or cream bonnets. For the most part the Weymouth vehicles were in a brown livery with cream window bars, various amounts of gold lining being employed, whilst a black band edged on both sides with gold was used around the engine bonnets. Most of the interiors were varnished woodwork. It appears that the wheels were also painted brown. The letters 'GWR' in plain gold block were displayed along the lower body sides, and at times adverts for businesses in the area were carried on the upper deck sides and front. When adverts were not carried the words 'Great Western Railway' were displayed in full on both sides of the upper deck and the letters 'GWR' on the front and rear upper panels. Sometimes these initials were also shown on the lower side panels as well. Destination boards giving the principal places on route were displayed above or below the lower-deck windows.

In 1908 much of the elaborate lining was dispensed with, and in 1913 new vehicles and those just overhauled were painted in Brunswick green - the same as the company's locomotives. With the outbreak of war, repainted vehicles appeared in plum livery, as did railway passenger rolling stock. At the end of the war green livery again appeared, although by late 1922 brown and cream became the standard for the remaining years, applied in various styles to suit the type of vehicle, some of the later Maudslays having polished metal engine bonnets when new. Likewise, with the latter vehicles, the destination boards (by now reduced in length) were carried in clips just below window level, whilst advertising was restricted to the sides of the luggage rack towards the rear of the bus. In later years it appears that the repainting of Weymouth buses was carried out under contract by Mr Dennis, a local painter.

In most places a garage for the railway buses was erected on the station premises, and often took the form of a corrugated iron shed in the goods yard, but at Weymouth the vehicles were kept in a rented garage at Rocky Knap about ½ mile north of Radipole Spa Hotel. The depot was in the charge of a leading driver who was also responsible for a daily report which had to be forwarded to the department headquarters at Slough, giving an account of the vehicles working, spare, and undergoing maintenance and repair, plus details such as tyres put on and taken off vehicles - this being important as tyres were usually purchased and paid for on a mileage basis. By 1904 the company had a tyre contract at 3.0576d. per mile. All this detail, and much more, was kept on a card system at Slough.

In later years a lad cleaner was also employed, his day starting at 6 am. It was his first job to fill the buses with petrol from cans kept in a nearby store which was licensed to hold 300 gallons. The cans of petrol were sent from Swindon stores packed in wooden cases, but this arrangement ceased in March 1929 when a 1,000 gallon tank and petrol pump were installed in the station yard at Weymouth.

After refuelling the buses, the next job for the cleaner was to clean the outside of the vehicles. The conductors were responsible for sweeping the insides of the buses and cleaning the internal brasswork. Until the arrival of the new Maudslays, which were fitted with electric light (they also carried oil lamps as back-up), the cleaner had to clean out and refill the acetylene tanks situated on the rear platforms. Pipes from these tanks led to the carbide lamps on the bus. Maintenance at small depots like Weymouth was the responsibility of the leading driver assisted by anyone else willing to learn the complexities of early buses, and must have been an ordeal given the primitive garage conditions of the time. Although spare parts could be sent quickly by passenger train from Slough stores, the only other resources available to the local staff were ingenuity, the local blacksmith, or perhaps the workshop staff at the local engine shed!

The Milnes-Daimlers and the early Maudslays required a vast amount of maintenance just to keep them running, and one suspects the early Dennis and AEC chassis were little better.

The road conditions of the time caused damage to both wheels and the solid rubber tyres, resulting in the company specifying a built-up steel wheel of their own design which stood up better to the rigours of the roads. In later years the early pneumatic tyres were susceptible to many punctures. The Maudslay ML3 was usually fitted with single rear wheels, whereas the ML3B had twin rear wheels, although there is evidence on occasions that ML3s ran with twin rears.

Even the Maudslay ML3 required much maintenance compared with later vehicles. They needed complete engine oil changes every 2,000 miles, gearbox and differential oil every 5,000 miles (but topped-up weekly), cleaning of the petrol filters every two weeks, and there were numerous grease points to attend to, and some points required oiling daily. Added to this it was recommended that the engine be decarbonised every 6,000 miles.

No means of clutch adjustment was provided, and only the following very interesting details were given on the subject.

> If the clutch is fierce or is slipping, it can usually be cured by holding it out of engagement (a wooden strut placed between the pedal and some convenient point works well) and cleaning the leather lining with paraffin. Then with a stiff feather a little colon or castor oil (mineral oil must not be used) should be applied to the leather, and if possible it should be allowed to soak in by keeping the clutch disengaged over night.

Driving staff were under the control of the Road Motor Department, whilst the conductors, who paid their takings into the booking office, came under the jurisdiction of the station master.

The wages for a driver in the early days ranged from between 21s. to 29s. per week, to which was added 2d. mileage money for every 10 miles run in service plus a petrol bonus of 1d. per gallon for every gallon saved above a consumption of four miles per gallon. Some drivers would secure this economy by adding a little paraffin, which was issued for the lamps and cleaning parts of the bus, to the petrol. Conductors earned 16s. a week. There was double pay for Sunday work, and the working week was 60 hours spread over seven days. By 1933 the wages for a six-day week had risen to £3 3s. for a driver and £2 14s. for a conductor.

Up to at least the Great War it was not uncommon for drivers to teach their conductor to drive on quiet trips. One is left to wonder who suffered the greatest ordeal - the learner driver or the passengers! Once the would-be driver was proficient he would be sent to the GWR Road Motor headquarters at Slough, where he would have to take a practical test on dealing with engine failures, followed by having to answer many questions, and concluding with a written examination. Once passed as a driver, in true railway tradition he would be the

Great Western Road motor staff photographed outside Rocky Knap garage, Radipole. Extreme left is conductor George Priest, second left driver Taffy Williams, and fifth left, leading driver Scriven. Note the superior cap badge worn by the drivers compared to the conductors.   *George Priest Collection*

'junior hand' and spend some time on the relief staff covering duties at various places - often at very short notice - including the driving of lorries in the cartage fleet. When not required for driving duties he would return to Slough to assist in the workshops thus gaining mechanical knowledge, until a vacancy occurred at a depot for a regular driver.

To start with the Road Motor Department had few precedents to draw on for the recruitment of staff. An article in the September 1910 *Great Western Railway Magazine* described the company's method of dealing with the situation.

> The collection and training of sufficient and suitable driving and repairing staffs were matters of some difficulty. In the early days a good deal of sifting had to be done to eliminate men who, either from not being used to railway discipline and standards of duty, or from a too-exalted idea of the status of a motor driver, proved unsuitable for public service work. With the lapse of time, however, it has become possible to train the driving staff from youths and passenger car drivers now graduate through the respective steps of conductor, cleaner and goods lorry driver.
>
> A comprehensive rule book has been compiled, in which are embodied regulations respecting restrictions of speed, instructions for dealing with small defects, duties of the various grades, etc. Before a man is promoted to the position of passenger driver he has to pass a written and oral examination as to his mechanical knowledge and acquaintance with the rules of the road, as set out in the rule book.

As early as 1904 it was decided to issue a rule book for motor staff. Little was left to chance, the explicit instructions including, 'The driver should practice working the brakes, and learn to estimate distances. It is also important that great care must be exercised in descending hills'. Also that

> Conductors must obtain fares for all passengers, luggage, parcels, and goods carried; to ensure that the car is kept to its advertised schedule; to ensure that the vehicle is kept clean; and to tell the driver if the car is giving off an objectionable smoke. Conductors must take with them on every journey Bell Punch, tickets, pouches, small change, and to ensure that the vehicle also had lamps, destination boards, seat aprons, dusters, hand brushes and two lengths of strong cord.

Staff were also warned of their conduct to both passengers and the general public, including the 'Absolute avoidance of profane or indecent language', and employees were warned not to enter into an altercation with anyone.

The rules covering passengers were just as thorough! After the usual disclaimers clearing the company of just about everything, came,

> The cars will call to pick up and set down passengers at the intermediate places shown in the timetables. Passengers may also join the car at any other point *en route*, on payment of the fare from the previous stage, provided there is sufficient accommodation and the car is not ascending a steep hill. Intending passengers are requested to give a clear and distinct signal to the driver of their desire for the car to stop, at a sufficient distance to enable it to be stopped gradually.

Given the brakes of the period, a cynic would take the last request as giving the driver a very substantial distance in which to stop!

Smoking was prohibited inside enclosed cars, as was 'spitting in or on the cars', and 'Ladies are not allowed to ride on the front seats of cars'. These were the two seats up front alongside the driver, the fear being that female company would be a distraction. To enforce this they were quickly made 'Smokers Only' seats, a move defeated when some ladies took up smoking, so a surcharge of 3*d.* was made for these seats. As this still failed to deter certain ladies from wanting to sit next to the driver, a 'Gentlemen Only' notice was displayed above these seats.

Even man's best friend could not travel without rules!

Small lap dogs carried by passengers will be conveyed provided no objection is raised by other passengers, charge 6*d.* for each distance up to 12 miles. Dogs packed in baskets or boxes will be conveyed at ordinary parcel rates which are parcels up to 14 lb. = 2*d.*, 28 lb. = 3*d.* and 56 lb. = 4*d.*

With these rules one can imagine some miserly individual conveying 'Rover' from Wyke to Radipole wrapped in brown paper! Furthermore, the exact definition of a 'lap dog' is to this very day a bone of contention with bus crews.

Fourteen years later - in 1927 - although dogs in baskets and boxes still travelled at parcel rates, small dogs carried by passengers and other dogs which could be carried without inconvenience could travel up to 10 miles for 3*d.*

It was not until 4th May, 1914 that half fares for children up to the age of 14 were introduced; previously they had paid full fare, those under three years of age travelling free if carried in arms.

Originally standard Edmondson-type railway tickets were issued, but they were quickly superseded by the bell punch bus ticket, although the Williamson system was used. It appears that in the early days of the joint service a geographical type of ticket was in use on which the various stage points were named, this later reverting to the conventional fare stage numbering down the sides of the ticket, and as with many bus tickets of the period they carried adverts on the reverse side. An interesting feature of many GWR tickets was that, in addition to the normal serial letters and numbers printed at the top of the ticket, there was a second printed number in the centre. It is assumed that this was the conductor's or ticket box number to whom that particular stock was issued, Weymouth tickets showing the numbers 108-112.

Passengers could also obtain books of tickets from stations at discount prices, 24 2*d.* tickets = 3*s.* 6*d.*, 24 3*d.* tickets = 5*s.* 3*d.*, 24 6*d.* tickets = 10*s.* 6*d.*, or 24 1*s.* tickets for £1 1*s.*

By 1928 the ticket system had become somewhat complex, not assisted by the fact that each conductor used an individual stock of tickets each numbered in a separate series, involving the storage of a vast stock. This was replaced by a system where conductors were supplied from a common stock held at their home station. A further reduction in stock was gained by the removal of return tickets, a single ticket of the return fare value being issued and punched accordingly to denote 'return'. These arrangements also allowed the conductors' waybills and accounting to be simplified, although again separate stocks had to be printed for the Weymouth area showing 'Great Western & Southern Rlys Joint Motor'.

Prior to the Great War five inspectors covered the system and supervised the services, as well as making surprise visits to buses *en route* to check tickets and the collection of fares. They also assisted the local station master in arranging special traffic and private hire work, this being charged at 2*s.* a mile at that period. Parcel traffic was also canvassed for and they generally looked after the interests of the Road Motor Department.

Uniforms changed over the years. In the early days when the driver had no protection from the elements he wore a heavy leather coat in bad weather, breeches and gaiters, and on his cap band was embroidered 'Motor Driver'. Conductors wore ordinary porters' suits and an overcoat in Winter, 'Conductor' being embroidered on their cap band. These styles were still in use during the Great War, when the uniform of a conductress was a two piece suit, consisting of jacket and skirt, in the style of a Salvation Army uniform! All staff were issued with a long dust coat for use during the Summer months.

A Technical Description of the Vehicles

When the first Great Western buses ran in Weymouth the road transport industry was still in its infancy, and the Milnes-Daimler was more advanced than many other early vehicles. Indeed, it was not until the introduction of the famous London General 'B Type' in 1911 that major improvements were made and standards set. The Milnes-Daimler was of German descent, the German Daimler company - having developed what was basically a goods vehicle chassis - came to an agreement with the Birkenhead tram car builders G.F. Milnes & Company to assemble and body the Milnes-Daimler at Hadley Shropshire, the first models entering service in January 1902. Within five years there were more than 600 in service.

Weymouth's first two vehicles were of the three-ton variety, which was common for double-deck buses, and had a wheelbase of 11 ft 3 in. and track of 4 ft 11½ in. The chassis was constructed of strong channel section with riveted cross members, the front end of the frames being shaped inwards allowing the front wheels a good lock, and both the front and rear axles were supported from semi-elliptic springs.

Milnes-Daimler No. 58, LC 1172, stands at King's Statue before departing for Radipole, the conductor is collecting fares on the upper deck, the driver seated behind the wheel, and another uniformed official points the lady in the direction of the bus behind which is the junction of Westham Road. In this pre-1910 view Frederick Place is shown to the left, the first part of the building on the right was demolished as part of the Westham Road widening scheme.   *Author's Collection*

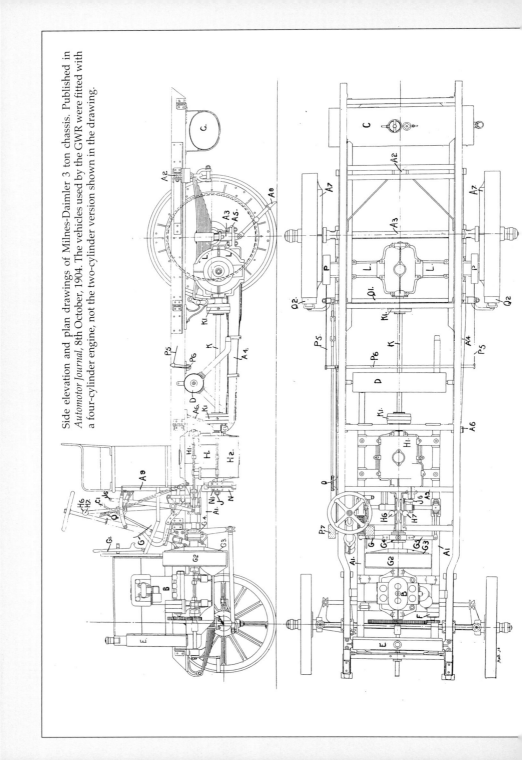

Side elevation and plan drawings of Milnes-Daimler 3 ton chassis. Published in *Automotor Journal*, 8th October, 1904. The vehicles used by the GWR were fitted with a four-cylinder engine, not the two-cylinder version shown in the drawing.

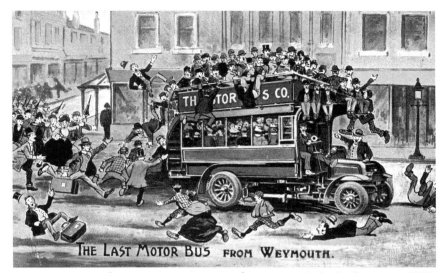

THE LAST MOTOR BUS FROM WEYMOUTH.

Posted in Weymouth on 21st September, 1912 this comic card clearly illustrates a GWR Milnes-Daimler, not suggesting the GWR would overload its buses to the degree shown here. *Author's Collection*

As with many four-cylinder engines of the period the cylinders were divided into sets of two, the cylinder bore being 105 mm with a stroke of 130 mm, developing 18/20 hp at 800 rpm. Two cam shafts operated the inlet and exhaust valves, the right side the inlet, and the left the exhaust, the latter also actuating the rods which worked the ignition plugs. These were supplied by low tension current from the magneto via a distribution board bolted to the cylinder tops, the insulation fitted to the push rods consisting of soap stones (marble) which by its brittle nature caused many irritating failures.

Although a shaft-driven water pump supplied a copious supply of water to cool the engine, the lubrication of the engine left much to be desired. Oil was contained in a tank situated on the rear engine bulkhead which supplied lubricant to the engine via 10 sight feeds. In addition the driver could force oil into the crankshaft area from a hand pump situated on the dashboard, and via a series of cocks the pump could be used to remove surplus oil from the crankcase! The oil tank was pressurised from the exhaust system, as was the petrol tank situated at the rear of the vehicle to force fuel through to the carburettor, another dashboard-mounted hand pump giving assistance. Exhaust was also used to force water to cool the transmission brake.

The flywheel and clutch cone spokes were constructed so as to act as a fan and draw air through the radiator and across the engine. The inner rear flange of the flywheel was tapered to accept the leather-faced clutch cone, this being controlled by the left-hand pedal in the cab which had a dual function. When depressed a short distance it operated the clutch, further depression applying the transmission brake which projected from the front of the gearbox. The brake drum was of cast steel, whilst the external brake shoes were of cast iron, water being induced onto the drum from an exhaust pressurised tank when required.

The gearbox was a simple four speed and reverse unit, giving speeds of 3, 5½, 7, and 12 miles per hour. However gear changing was not so simple, involving three gear levers mounted in a frame in the centre of the cab. When the lever nearest the

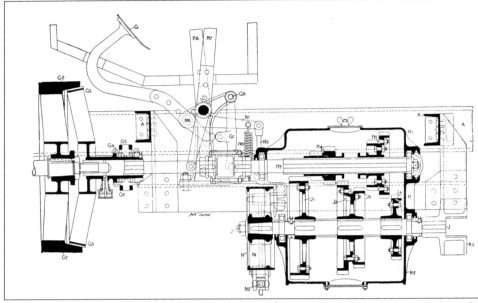

Details of the cone clutch (*to the left*) and gearbox of the Milnes-Daimler.   *Automotor Journal*

View showing attachment of rear axle to the main frame and the position of the differential countershaft and the small cog of the star and planet drive system.   *Automotor Journal*

driver was pushed forward, first gear was engaged. Second gear was selected by moving the lever to the back position, and to engage third gear the lever was moved to the centre position, and then the central lever was pushed forward, this being moved backwards to engage fourth gear. With both these levers in the centre position, the third lever could be moved forward for reverse gear.

From the gearbox to the differential the drive was via a conventional propeller shaft. However, as with many vehicles of the period the rear axle had no means of driving the rear wheels, the accepted method being sprocket wheels and roller chains driving from a combined differential and countershaft which was situated forward of the rear wheels. The Milnes-Daimler was unusual for the period, as instead of the roller chain method, cogs at the end of the drive shafts engaged with internally toothed rings bolted to the spokes of the rear wheels. Although this 'Star & Planet' system undoubtedly worked, wear in service caused a high level of noise which probably accounted for many of the complaints.

The differential shaft was supported by two long wooden radius bars which, although armoured with steel strips, gave a considerable amount of elasticity to absorb many of the road shocks. The differential shaft also carried two cast steel brake drums at the outer ends, the external brake shoes being of cast iron and applied by means of a cable operated by the right-hand pedal in the cab. The third brake was a spoon or block brake operating on the face of the tyres of the back wheels and controlled from a handbrake lever in the cab. It was purely a parking brake; application whilst the vehicle was in motion would have severely damaged the tyre. If all else failed, and to prevent the vehicle running back on a hill, a pair of sprags under the back of the vehicle could be released by a cord from the cab!

The gearbox and differential shafts were mounted in ballraces, whereas the road wheel bearings were not. To reduce friction, perforated bronze bushes, free to revolve, were inserted between the steel hubs and the steel axles, lubricated by screw-down grease cups. The perforations helped retain the lubricant. The wheels were shod with Shrewsbury-Challiner solid rubber tyres, the front wheels being 32 in. diameter and 4 in. wide, the rear 40 in. diameter with twin 4 in. wide tyres. Illumination was by oil lamps, with acetylene lamps in globes for the interior.

Having digested this brief description on the mechanics of the vehicle one cannot but sympathise with the driver, a hand throttle adding to the already complex and temperamental controls. These men were the true pioneers of motoring!

Technical advancement and lessons learned in service brought about an almost continuous stream of modifications to successive vehicles, so much so that the first two Weymouth buses were quickly dated. An advanced chassis had been introduced by early 1907, when modifications to the engine included an engine-operated plunger pump for lubrication purposes, and the three gear change levers were replaced by a single one operating through a gate. Many modifications were also carried out by the GWR to these chassis over the years - with great success.

For all its faults the Milnes-Daimler served the GWR well, many ending their days as lorries in the cartage fleet. No. 58, LC 1172, one of the first buses at Weymouth, survived World War I as a bus, working at Saltash in Cornwall, for a time running on coal gas.

Many bodies for the Milnes-Daimlers were built under contract by various companies like Christopher Dodson Ltd, who in turn often sub-contracted the work, this accounting for the many variations in detail which only allows a general description of the bodywork used on the Weymouth Milnes-Daimler double-decks. Constructed of good quality timber, finished and painted to the high standards of

Edwardian workmanship, the body had many traces of horse bus ancestry, and many features that were to be basic bus body design for many years.

The average vehicle was 22 ft long and 6 ft 6 in. wide. The lower saloon was fitted with bench-type side seats, upholstered in leather, seating seven passengers each side. The floor down the centre was fitted with wooden slats. In the centre of the front bulkhead, either a window that could be lowered by a leather strap, railway carriage fashion, or a hatchway was usually provided. Straps hung from the ceiling for the convenience of standing passengers, and the interior lighting was provided by acetylene lamp, the equipment to produce the gas being fitted to a small platform under the stairs.

The upper deck accommodated 18 passengers on wooden garden bench-type seats, four pairs on the off side, five pairs on the nearside, aprons being provided to protect the seats and passengers during inclement weather. On some vehicles a bell plunger fitted on top of the front screen allowed communication with the driver below. The entire upper deck was very basic, like the earlier horse bus it was in fact a single-deck body, with a slightly curved watertight roof, to which the seats were fixed. Rails, decency boards and a set of stairs completed the arrangements.

The mudguards were no more than curved strips of metal, and were the most primitive part of the vehicle. Two passengers were allowed to sit on the bench seat alongside the driver who had no protection whatsoever. A later railway modification to some vehicles provided a raised screen with an angled back top placed at the rear engine bulkhead, although the angled top would appear to force wind and rain into the driver's face! Added to this, the massive oil lamps fitted to the front of the vehicle - although looking very impressive - failed to give much illumination for the hapless driver.

The 10 Dennis chassis purchased during the Summer of 1910 were vastly different from previous vehicles in the fleet. They were powered by a 20 hp four-cylinder petrol engine with a conventional four-speed gear box and live back axle. The 16-seat Swindon-built bodies had, for the period, a very modern look about them, with three large windows each side with six hammered glass opening toplights above them.

Entrance was by way of two well-placed wide steps alongside the driver on the near side, access to the saloon being via a sliding door. If one man operated buses had been allowed in those days the little Dennis would have been the perfect choice. A wire framed luggage rack was mounted on the roof, reached by a ladder on the rear of the body. The only crude parts of these vehicles were the front mudguards which were again simply curved steel sheets. Unfortunately, with the pressing needs of the Great War, these useful vehicles were converted into parcel vans during 1915.

The AEC single-decks were of the 'Y' type (by 1921 also known as the 'AEC 501') first introduced in 1915. There were many variations by the end of production in 1920, being given chassis letters YA-YE. Many were fitted with a 'Tylor JB4' four-cylinder petrol engine of 5 inch bore and 6 inch stroke, developing 40 hp, claimed to give 45 hp at 1,000 rpm. Transmission was via a four-speed gear box and worm-driven back axle. The chassis were of a rugged construction, as proven by many in War Department service. Of the Weymouth vehicles, Nos. 274 and 286 were 'YA' types built during 1917 and bought ex-War Department, whilst Nos. 241 and 247 were new chassis in 1919 of the 'YE' type, each costing approximately £1,100.

The ex-War Department chassis were overhauled at Slough workshops and, with others, were sent to Swindon where bodies were fitted in No.17 Road Wagon shop, and this is where the first problem arose. The bodies were heavily built like a railway carriage, one long-service driver describing the vehicle as feeling 'fully loaded before the first passenger stepped aboard'. As with the pre-war Milnes-Daimler and

Maudslay chassis it was a simple matter to exchange bodies. For example, No. 286 had been recorded with a char-a-banc body in May 1924.

The second problem was that the chassis was basically that of a lorry so the body was pitched high, making boarding and alighting a little difficult. With the introduction of the low frame bus chassis, the AECs quickly reverted to lorries or were disposed of.

In later years the name 'Maudslay' became synonymous with Great Western Railway buses; indeed, there were historical connections, as Maudslay had supplied the engines for Brunel's steamship *Great Western* in 1838. The company had been founded in 1797, quickly entering the marine engineering business and supplying many engines for ships of the Royal Navy.

In 1899 the heavy marine business closed, the company moving from London to Coventry and established a factory to develop internal combustion engines. Again successful, its engines had many marine and gas engine features in their solid construction, with ample inspection doors allowing for easy repairs and maintenance. A variety of cars and commercial vehicles were also produced.

In 1913 a new range of commercial chassis was introduced, a 3 ton and a 4 ton model being suitable for omnibus bodies, the GWR purchasing 15 chassis. The 3 ton version had a 32 hp engine, whilst a 40 hp was fitted to the 4 ton model. The transmission was via a cone clutch and four-speed gear box to a bevel-drive rear axle. It was the introduction of the live back axle, abolishing the previous chain drive methods, that added to the success of the new chassis.

Both models were fitted with four-cylinder engines, the 32 hp having 4½ inch cylinder bores and the 40 hp 5 inch bores - both with a 5 inch stroke. The 3 ton model had a 13 ft wheelbase, the 4 ton 13 ft 6 in., the chassis prices being £692 and £764 respectively. A feature of the chassis was that the frame members had the top and bottom edges facing outwards - a Maudslay feature well into the 1930s. Another feature was the Maudslay overhead camshaft, which was housed in a box above the cylinder heads, and could be hinged back to allow easy access to the valves, which it was claimed could be cleaned in two minutes. The camshaft was driven by a vertical shaft from the crankshaft, whilst the magneto was driven off the opposite end of the camshaft, and large inspection doors made the big ends accessible. As with most chassis of the period, changing bodies was no problem.

Maudslay, which had always been innovative with its products, was one of the first companies to produce a proper low-level passenger chassis, as distinct from a modified goods model. The new models introduced in 1925 were the ML2, ML3, and ML4. The ML3 was a forward control version with a wheelbase of 16 ft 6 in. intended for bus bodies catering for up to 37 passengers. The first order for 18 ML3 chassis was given to Maudslay in April 1926 at a price of £777 15s. per chassis, the advertised price in the trade press at the time being £925!

The ML3 - later known as the Maudslay 'Masta' - was powered by a Maudslay 4.94 litre four-cylinder petrol engine with a bore of 110 mm and stroke of 130 mm developing 30 hp. The engine was of standard Maudslay design with a detachable cylinder head and overhead valves worked from a single camshaft along the top of the cylinder head, and rotated by a bevel gear from a vertical shaft placed at the back of the engine and driven from the crankshaft. The vertical shaft also powered a cross shaft for the magneto and water pump, which were fitted to the 'off' and 'near' side respectively. A downward extension of the vertical shaft operated the gear-type engine lubrication pump.

The Zenith carburettor was fed by an autovac, and the induction pipe between the carburettor and engine was fitted with a water jacket. A GWR requirement was that a thermostatic control be fitted into the water circulation system.

Maudslay ML3 No. 1212, YR 6412, stands outside the Southern National garage at Radipole before departing for Wyke Hotel. Standing in front are driver Williams and conductor Priest, the railway type ventilators on the bus roof are interesting. The photograph was taken shortly after the formation of Southern National, one of its vehicles appears to the right, but the wall of the garage still has the cast concrete 'National' sign on display.   *Author's Collection*

Driver George Norley stands alongside Maudslay ML3 No. 1109, YR 6217, outside the Post Office in Portland Road after arriving at Wyke Hotel. Of particular note is the fact that the vehicle is running with single rear wheels. The railway carriage roof ventilators and the combined electric/oil lamps add an antique effect to this vehicle.   *Author's Collection*

Transmission was via a large inverted leather-faced cone clutch, gear changing being assisted by a clutch brake for the four-speed gearbox, final drive being via an underslung worm drive differential incorporated into the back axle.

One of the most important parts of any vehicle is the brake system, and here again Maudslay was one of the first to provide brakes on all four wheels - albeit not in the form developed in later years - but it was an advance on the 'Back Wheels only' brakes of old. With the ML3 the brakes on the rear wheels were only operated by the handbrake lever, the footbrake operating the transmission brake situated behind the gearbox. It consisted of a 12 inch diameter drum with internally expanding brake shoes. These brake shoes were attached to a torsion bar which partially rotated when the brakes were applied, so actuating the front brakes via a suitable linkage.

The driver's cab layout was simple, with both the handbrake and the gate-operated gear lever situated next to each other on the right. The GWR still believed in getting its pound of flesh out of the bus crews, so electric self-starting motors were not fitted! Although of progressive design at the time, rapid developments quickly overtook the ML3. It was, however, one of the more successful vehicles of the period. The GWR owned 151 ML3s and variations.

The 32-seat bodies for the first 18 chassis were supplied by John Buckingham of Birmingham, each one costing £350 net. Again, as with the chassis, both the design and construction methods were different from that of later years, very little aluminium being used. The body frames were constructed of timber, usually ash, the structure being strengthened with mild steel plates and brackets, whilst the body panels were usually of 20-gauge silver-finished steel. As can be deduced, the weight compared with modern all-aluminium bodies was much greater. Unfortunately these timber-framed bodies quickly suffered from distortion and deterioration - one of the main reasons why pre-war buses were often re-bodied!

Returning to the Buckingham bodies of 1926, extracts from the remaining records of the specification clearly show that the GWR was not content to accept a standard product!

Seats to be fitted with best quality spring cases, stuffed with hair and covered with leather of an approved colour. 7 inch padded squab with back mounted on spring frame and filled in with three ply wood.

Painting, Body and chassis to be painted in Great Western Railway standard colours, and lettered on sides and rear as required. Instructions as to smoking, number of passengers, emergency door and Hackney Carriage plates to be painted in as required. Transfers will be provided by the GWR.

As few sizes of glass as possible to be used throughout. Body contractor to supply full dimensions so that replacements can be easily obtained.

An approved form of ventilator to be fitted in front and on the roof clear of luggage space. Sufficient ventilation to be supplied for the driver's cab.

With the above item it appears from various photographs that a standard railway carriage roof ventilator was used, and some of the door handles look suspiciously like railway fittings! However the following item has that true ring of railway operation in wording and deed.

Lighting, Interior to be illuminated with eight electric lamps complete with all necessary wiring to GWR standard diagram. Electric tail lamp at back of body showing red light behind, white light into the body and illuminating registration number.
Bracket for GWR standard oil tail lamp to be provided.

Of the Guy FBB chassis purchased by the GWR only one - No.1244 - is recorded as operating at Weymouth. It could well have been sent for trial runs at Portland where it had been suggested these vehicles be used. History does not record if it ever reached the island, as many of the bodies fitted to the Guy chassis proved too heavy, resulting in engine overheating and other problems. They would not have been successful on a service to Easton!

The FBB was the first forward-control bus chassis produced by Guy in 1926. It had a wheelbase of 16 ft 5 in. and was powered by a 4.5 litre four-cylinder petrol engine developing 38 bhp at 1,000 rpm, with a cylinder bore of 108 mm and a stroke of 140 mm. The bore was increased to 115 mm by 1927. The valves were placed on the left side of the engine and, like the cylinder head of the Guy, they had an inclined arrangement, it being claimed that this gave ease of adjustment like a side-valve mechanism with the efficiency of overhead valves.

Transmission was via an adjustable fabric-faced cone clutch and a four-speed gear box to a conventional differential and back axle. Brakes were to the back wheels only, an extra £50 being charged for front wheel brakes. Fortunately for both drivers and passengers, the GWR opted for the expedient of having front brakes fitted, but not the luxury of a self-starter!

A variety of builders supplied bodies for the Guy chassis, the Weymouth vehicle having a Hall Lewis body at a cost of £375. The vehicles supplied to the GWR all had 32-seat bodies, and like many larger Great Western buses of the period, opposite the entrance door was a pair of rear-facing seats. These and the back seats were of the tip-up type, which allowed space for extra luggage. The rear section of the vehicle was screened off from the forward part, which allowed it to be used as a smoking section. Again surviving records describe some of the features of the bodywork, such as the emergency door being of sliding pattern fitted to the front bulkhead, so that in the event of an emergency passengers could leave the vehicle via the driver's cab. Other specifications were:

Windows, Seven windows to be fitted on the near side of the body, five of which are to drop, eight windows to be fitted on the off side, and five of these to drop. Drop windows are actuated by means of approved mechanical winders. All drop glass to be ¼ inch polished plate, and fixed windows 32 oz. sheet.

Roof, Constructed of Ash hoopsticks, suitably strengthened by steel bracket plates and covered with ⅜ inch lapped slats. The whole covered with waterproof canvas coated with white lead before and after canvassing, weather moulding fitted around roof.

It was also specified that the roof had to be strong enough to support 10 cwt of luggage on the luggage rack. The electrical specifications were the same as those for the Buckingham bodies,with an added stipulation for 'Combined Lucas (or other approved make) electric and paraffin side lamps'.

The last statement may appear odd to the modern motorist, but during the 1920s not everybody had complete faith in electric lights, including railway companies! With most combined lamps the electric fitting came as an attachment, all that was required being to unscrew the back light and screw the electric bulb holder in its place. The oil burner remained in position while the electric light was used, and it was not necessary to remove the bulb when burning oil!

The Guy was certainly not the best purchase the GWR made. Being overbodied, it lacked the required power. Ironically, the GWR could have specified a six-cylinder engine at £964 per chassis, or a year later they could have obtained an improved model, but in those fast-moving times yesterday's racehorse quickly became tomorrow's donkey!

The most modern vehicles to operate at Weymouth were Nos. 1606 and 1607 - two of a batch of 11 Thornycroft BC single-decks purchased by the GWR in July 1929. A low frame forward-control chassis originally introduced in late 1927, it had been refined by the time of the GWR purchases. The wheelbase was 16 ft 6 in. and the vehicle was powered by a Thornycroft ZB/6 6.9-litre six cylinder side valve petrol engine, the cylinders having a bore of 105 mm and stroke of 133 mm, developing 85 bhp. A four-speed crash gearbox and twin plate dry clutch drove an underslung worm drive back axle.

The braking systems had improved by this time. The footbrake worked Westinghouse vacuum servo-operated brakes on both front and back wheels through a series of rods. In the absence of the later developed triple-servo system the front brakes were applied through steel pins passing down through the centre of the king-pins, so as not to be affected by steering movements. The handbrake worked only the propeller shaft transmission brake, in effect making it only a parking brake!

Both front and rear tyres were 36 in. x 6 in. pneumatics, the rears being twin. The complete chassis weighed 3 ton 6 cwt. The advertised price was £915, but electric light and starter motor were extra.

The GWR selected Vickers' bodies for these vehicles and were not disappointed in the result, and although not arriving until nearly the end of the railway bus services, the Thornycroft buses were very successful. At that time the company also operated well over 70 smaller Thornycroft buses and numerous Thornycroft lorries in their cartage fleet, and many of the later models lasted into the early 1960s.

The Final Years

The reconstruction of the Weymouth Town bridge between late 1928 and July 1930 was to cause problems for bus operators. Unfortunately Westwey Road had not then been built, resulting in the GWR buses having to travel from the King's Statue via St Thomas Street, School Street, Westham Road, and Westham bridge to Abbotsbury Road, thence via Ilchester Road to Newstead Road and under the railway arch to the Sidney Hall, regaining the original route at the foot of Boot Hill. On the inward journey buses travelled up Newstead Road to the Rock Hotel, turned right into Abbotsbury Road and proceeded directly to the King's Statue via Westham bridge and Westham Road.

A speed restriction of 6 mph applied in Ilchester Road and Newstead Road, and only buses up to a seating capacity of 32 passengers were allowed, with no standing passengers. Furthermore all buses had to run on pneumatic tyres.

Despite these precautions the operation of buses in these narrow roads was difficult. On 11th May, 1929, whilst crossing the road to buy some sweets on his tenth birthday, John Coleman of Newstead Road ran out from behind a bus proceeding from Ilchester Road towards the Railway Arch, straight into the path of a bus proceeding up Newstead Road, with fatal results.

The railway buses had originally been provided to combat the tramway proposals, an idea which by the mid-1920s was long dead and buried! The number of passengers who actually used the bus before or after a train journey was very small, the majority of passengers being quite divorced from normal railway operations, just using the bus for short journeys within the town! During the 1920s the whole question of road transport became a political matter for the

Thornycroft BC, No. 1607, UV 4081, viewed at Slough still on trade plates following delivery from the builders. The photograph shows the fine outline of the Vickers B26R body, note the small details, the combined electric/paraffin side lights the nearside one having a Pyrene type fire extinguisher above it (!) and the absence of a nearside mirror (not a common fitting pre-war). The outward opening rear door clearly indicates a vehicle not designed for fare stage work, whilst the legal lettering 'Speed 20 MPH' is an indignity on such a fine vehicle.

Phillip J. Kelley Collection/ex-BR (Western Region)

Interior view of No. 1607, UV 4081, clearly showing the high-quality finish of the Vickers B26R body. The coach seats, curtains at the windows and clock on the front bulkhead all indicate a vehicle intended for long distance rather than short fare stage duties. Note the sliding emergency door, slightly open in the rear of the driver's cab.

Phillip J. Kelley Collection/ex-BR (Western Region)

railways. The 'Fair Deal Campaign' of the GWR, followed by the report from the Railway Clearing House on 'Road Motor Transport in Relations to the Railways' published in July 1925 and the Royal Commission on Transport in 1929, raised many questions that had been irrelevant a few years before. The rights of the railways in general to operate buses were challenged by rival operators - although the matter was not really pursued until 1925 when the London & Provincial Omnibus Owners Association officially disputed their rights. After that the whole set-up gradually changed. In August 1928 the railways were granted an Act of Parliament to enable them to operate bus services in their own right, but this was not pursued in the broadest sense. The Great Western, like the other railway companies, took a 50 per cent interest in the large omnibus companies that had been developing in its own territory. The National Omnibus & Transport Company was split into three - Eastern National, Western National, and Southern National. The Western National was formed in January 1929, Southern National following in July, and on 1st January, 1929 GWR bus services in the West Country were absorbed into the National Omnibus & Transport undertaking (later the Western National).

Even at that late stage some new services were commenced in the South Midlands, and long distance routes on the principle of those later worked by Associated Motorways were proposed early in 1929, including Bristol-Weymouth.

With the passing of the 1930 Road Traffic Act and the subsequent licensing of services by the Traffic Commissioners, the GWR applied in 1931 for a Road Service licence to continue the service of stage carriages operated between Radipole, Weymouth and Wyke Regis, this being granted that October and renewed the following year. A second renewal was granted on 29th September, 1933, at which point the service had only three months to run!

Of greater interest was the application made in October 1931 for a Road Service Licence to run excursions starting from Portland railway station. On the outward journey passengers travelled by rail throughout to various destinations. On the return journey passengers travelled by rail to Weymouth Town station, thence by road to Portland station. All passengers were to hold rail tickets throughout issued at inclusive return fares, and the maximum number of vehicles to be used on these excursions were two on any one day. The excursions were to run approximately 20 times during the year on dates not specified. This was clearly a method of returning excursionists to Portland without running an additional train, thus greatly reducing operating costs.

A renewal application was granted on 26th February, 1932 to operate a service of express carriages for the purpose of running a group of excursions and tours at inclusive fares only, starting from Portland railway station. Not more than one vehicle could be used in connection with any particular excursion. It is assumed that there were plans to operate tours for passengers arriving by train, and it would appear that both licences were obtained by the railway to safeguard its options, as there is no evidence to suggest these operations ever took place.

In January 1934 this licence was renewed for a further year, but in late March it was cancelled as 'the service had not been operated'. In fact, the railway bus service had ceased altogether! Owing to this, a short period licence was granted to Southern National on 19th February, 1934 'To operate a service of express carriages on an excursion from Weymouth to Portland', shortly after which both Western and Southern National were issued with licences giving blanket cover for associated railway operations.

By the end of 1932 the remaining GWR bus services had been handed over to various companies, but the joint Weymouth service survived - albeit only working a section of the major route in the Town (although a very profitable section), mainly because the joint railway companies could not agree on the capital value and the proportions for the division of revenue. They also disagreed over a proposed Salisbury-Yeovil service jointly operated by Wilts & Dorset and Southern National, and a route between Bodmin and Wadebridge. Ironically it had been dissension between the joint companies that had delayed the opening of the Portland branch 66 years previously!

Eventually agreement was reached, the *Dorset Daily Echo* on Friday 29th December, 1933 carrying a notice that:

The omnibus services operated by the Southern National Omnibus Co. Ltd, and the G.W. and S.R. jointly, will as from Monday January 1st 1934, be operated by the Southern National Omnibus Co. Ltd to a revised timetable, particulars of which may be obtained from all conductors and local offices of the Company.

A short piece on the front page announced,

WEYMOUTH'S REVISED BUS SERVICE. CHANGES COME INTO FORCE ON MONDAY. A revised bus service between Radipole and Wyke Regis will come into force on Monday, consequent on the withdrawal of the GWR buses. Buses will be travelling along that route approximately every 15 minutes with additional buses during the rush hours. One bus will proceed via Boot Hill and the other along Rodwell Avenue. Buses will be passing through these thoroughfares on an average every half an hour.

The service will be continuous from about 7 am until after 10 pm. The dozen drivers and conductors of the GWR buses were interviewed yesterday by GWR officials from London. They will be taken on by the GWR Road Goods Services which operate in some parts of the country, by the Southern National in Weymouth or by the Western National. The men have to give their decision in a few days.

On an inside page the *Echo* noted the 'disappearance of the familiar GWR chocolate and cream buses from the Wyke Regis and Radipole route on Monday', and mentioned the pioneering days of GWR railway bus services.

The final day of GWR bus services was Sunday 31st December, 1933, the following note appearing in the Monday *Dorset Daily Echo*, stating that a reporter was

. . . one of the last passengers to take a ride in a GWR bus at Weymouth last night. The vehicle carried a black flag at half mast on a miniature pole erected at the rear of the bus. Busmen were their usual cheery selves, and as courteous as users of the fleet have always found them.

Services commenced to be operated by Southern National on Monday 1st January, 1934, but as the first Short Period licences were not granted by the Traffic Commissioners until 6th January, it has to be assumed that legal etiquette was observed until that date, Southern National buses so employed displaying 'On Hire to GWR' notices as their licences were still valid.

In March, Southern National applied to the Traffic Commissioners for two licences to continue the services previously operated by the GWR, and to extend them from Radipole Spa Hotel to both Upwey Wishing Well and Upwey Royal Oak - and during the Summer months from Wyke Regis to Portland Bill - and also to issue season tickets. With these licences granted, the service became incorporated into the Southern National's Upwey-Portland service. It was agreed that four of the vehicles used by Southern National on the Portland-Upwey service display the letters 'GWR and SR.' under the Southern National fleet name. The profits from the combined services were apportioned between the two railway companies and the Southern National. From the gross receipts the omnibus company was allowed to deduct its cost per mile, based on all its services for the financial year, plus 5 per cent interest on the capital employed in the pooled service. The profit from the pooled service was then divided between the railway companies and the Southern National on the basis of mileage run by each company for 1932. This worked out at 82.22 per cent to Southern National, and 17.78 per cent to the two railway companies who then had to divide it again.

The railway companies were thus receiving a steady income from their bus interests by having a 50 per cent share in the company, giving them a healthy share of the profits in general, and the 1933 agreement also gave them a particular interest in Radipole-Wyke Regis service, the best route in Weymouth! During 1934 the railway companies share of the profit was £963, in 1939 they received £2,373, and for the year ending 30th September, 1945, £5,175. Although during the war years and after there were exceptional circumstances, including fuel rationing and virtually no private motoring, it has to be noted that bus fares had not increased greatly during that period, certainly not compared with the massive increased inflicted later.

One matter that should not be forgotten is the fate of the staff employed on the GWR buses. As there was no agreement with Southern National, many of them went to the Western National, where they were treated as 'loan staff' - an arrangement that allowed them to keep their railway privileges. Conductors Furnace and Hart went to St Austell, conductor Priest to Penzance, driver Little to Kingsbridge, and driver Norley to Totnes. Others remained in the employment of the GWR. Driver Zealey and conductor Masters went to the Road Motor workshops at Paddington, conductor Summers to the workshop at Lostwithiel, Cornwall, and leading driver Tomkins, who had been in charge at Weymouth, moved to the Road Motor workshops at Exeter. Those not wishing to leave the town, drivers Williams and Goodman, took employment with Southern National at Weymouth.

Thus we come to the end of a very interesting chapter in the history of both local transport and the bus operation by the Great Western Railway, of which it has been said that it did most things differently from other railways, and usually did them better. It could rightly claim to be the pioneers of railway owned bus services in mainland Britain, and possessed a far larger fleet than any other railway company. The decision to divest its bus operations was taken in a fast changing world, and as on other railways, investment in the associated bus companies proved to be a wise move in the ensuing years.

Locally the railway buses had been the precursors of future operations within the Weymouth and Portland area, and also held the historical distinction of being the last GWR bus service to operate. It also saw the end of the GWR Road Motor Department in the town, as goods cartage was carried out by contractors and railway goods delivery vehicles were not employed. Ironically it was not until after nationalisation that the Road Motor Department returned in October 1949 under the control of British Railways, Western Region, but that is another story.

Great Western Railway known Weymouth Fleet

No.	Reg No.	Chassis	No.	Body	Type	No.	Built	Acq.	Sold	Notes
4	AF 61	M/Daimler 16hp			DD		16/1/04			
8	CO 70	M/Daimler 16hp			B22R		17/8/05			5
11	AF 74	M/Daimler 16hp			DD		25/3/04			
13	BH 09	M/Daimler 16hp			CB		17/7/05			6
43	T 490	M/Daimler 20hp			DD		19/4/05			
45	CA 126	M/Daimler 20hp			B36OT		7/3/05			7
	CO 125	M/Daimler 20hp			DD					
50	LC 1171	M/Daimler 20hp			16/18		6/6/05*			
58	LC 1172	M/Daimler 20hp			16/18		26/6/05*			
61	AF 148	M/Daimler 20hp			DD		27/7/05			
64	AF 647	M/Daimler 30hp			DD		30/3/11			
66	AF 192	M/Daimler 28hp			DD		22/3/06			
116	AF 544	M/Daimler 30hp			DD		9/5/10			
169	AF 652	M/Daimler.30hp	9279		DD		6/4/11			
		Dennis 20hp			B16F		1910			1
209	T 4350	Maudslay 40hp			DD		10/7/14			
241	FX 5203	AEC 45hp	15051	GWR			12/1/20*			2, 8
247	AX 1416	AEC 45hp	15057	GWR	SD		28/10/19			2
274	LU 9326	AEC 45hp	11442	GWR	SD		9/5/23 *			3
286	XM 9791	AEC 45hp	10644	GWR	SD		22/2/23*			3
1209	YR 6217	Maudslay ML3	3946	Buckingham	B32R		4/10/26		6/2/34	
1210	YR 6218	Maudslay ML3	3948	Buckingham	B32R		4/10/26		16/2/34	
1212	YR 6412	Maudslay ML3	3950	Buckingham	B32R		29/10/26		2/34	
1230	UC 7504	Maudslay ML3	4227	Buckingham	B32R		7/3/28		1929	
1244	YH 6817	Guy FBB	22371	Hall Lewis	B32R		6/27		4/29	
1523	YW 3354	Maudslay ML3	4303	Buckingham	B32R		27/6/28		8/29	
1595	UU 4822	Maudslay ML3B	4685	Vickers	B32R		28/6/29		2/34	
1606	UV 4080	Thornycroft BC	18816	Vickers	B26R		18/7/29*		4/32	
1607	UV 4081	Thornycroft BC	18821	Vickers	B26R		29/7/29*		2/32	

Notes
* denotes date into service.
1. fleet numbers of vehicles operated at Weymouth unknown. Converted to parcel vans 1915.
2. New chassis built 1919.
3. Ex War-Department chassis built 1918
4. Ex No. 476. until 8/23.
5. Originally AF 153.
6. Originally A 5013.
7. Re-registered as AF 86.
8. Re-registered as T 9124.

Disposals
241	To lorry 1929 scrapped 1933.
247	To lorry 5/28 scrapped 1933.
274/286	To lorry 4/27 scrapped 1933.
1209	To WNOC 16/2/34 sold 8/3/35 purchaser unknown.
1210/1212	To WNOC 16/2/34. sold 16/5/35 purchaser unknown.
1230	To WNOC 1929 sold 30/9/34 to Seddon of Arscott as a lorry.
1244	To Western Welsh 4/29, later returned to Guy Motors. To goods vehicle 6/31.
1523	To WNOC 30/8/29 sold 16/5/35 purchaser unknown.
1595	To WNOC 16/2/34 sold 4/1/36 purchaser unknown.
1606	To London General Country Services 4/32, to Thames Valley 4/32 as No. 257. To Ledbury Transport 3/38 as No. 56. To G.C. Cook Kennington London, SW8 scrap merchants. Scrapped 8/40.
1607	To Bristol Tramways 2/32, as No.X124, No. 110 1937. Scrapped by Bristol 3/38.

Chapter Four

Weymouth Independent Operators
Pre-1914

Joseph Edwin Turner

Joseph Edwin Turner is regarded as the first local operator of a motor char-a-banc. Unfortunately the story of Turner's life is littered with contradictions, particularly through interviews he gave in later years.

Turner had been employed as an engine driver on the Great Western Railway, leaving in 1898 owing to eyesight problems. He set himself up as a firewood and metal merchant at 17A King Street, Weymouth, and his involvement with motor transport commenced about 1906 with the running of excursions from the Alexandra Gardens to both Upwey Wishing Well and Sutton Poyntz. With his Upwey excursion he pointed out in his advertising material that the railway halt was over a mile distant!

The only recorded detail of his operations was a report in the *Southern Times* following a collision on 4th August, 1908, when *The Tourist,* a char-a-banc, belonging to Mr Turner and driven by a man named Williams, returning from Preston was in collision with a trap at Greenhill. The only surviving photograph of Turner shows him at the King's Statue with a Coventry-Daimler motor wagonette.

The Coventry-Daimler was amongst the earliest motor vehicles on the road, and therefore even less refined than the early Milnes-Daimlers of the GWR! The vehicle operated by Turner was powered only by a 4½ hp two-cylinder engine with a cylinder bore of 90 mm and stroke of 120 mm. The engine was water cooled, but as the radiator had not yet been developed, a large water tank was fitted between the rear frames of the chassis. Electric ignition was also still developing so the 'Hot Tube' system was employed, this being operated by what could best be described as a small petrol blowlamp which heated the platinum tube. Pressure to operate the blowlamp was obtained from the exhaust system. To start the system the blowlamp had to preheated in the time honoured way by creating a small fire!

The drive from the engine to the four-speed gearbox was via a double-faced leather cone clutch, reverse being obtained by shifting the cross shaft to engage the other bevel gear of the differential. The final drive was roller chain from the cross shaft to the rear wheels. The brake system consisted of a foot brake operating a band on a drum fitted to the cross shaft, the handbrake being a simple block application to the tyres of the rear wheels. All four wheels were of the normal carriage type of the period, having wooden spokes and rims onto which solid rubber tyres were fitted, the wheels being the weakest point of the whole design. The chassis frame was constructed basically of wood, reinforced by steel plates, and the rear springs were elliptic as were most carriages of the day. Ackermann steering was employed, controlled through a vertical shaft and tiller, a steering wheel being fitted to vehicles constructed after 1900! The engine and gearbox was carried on a sub frame.

The whole machine was little more than a motorised wagonette, but when first introduced in 1897 it represented the forefront of automobile engineering!

It was the wooden spokes of the rear wheels of a Daimler wagonette that caused Britain's first fatal motor accident in February 1899. Descending a steep hill in Harrow, the normally ineffectual brakes suddenly jammed, the force wrenching the spokes out of the rear wheels, the driver and passenger being thrown onto the road!

Joseph Turner sat at the controls of his Coventry-Daimler wagonette. Seven passengers was the full pay load for a trip on this very early form of motor char-a-banc. The similarities to the previous horse drawn vehicles are very clear. On this early model even the steering wheel was an item of the future, tiller steering being employed.   *Author's Collection*

Motor Coaches Ltd vehicles lined up at the King's Statue, Weymouth before the commencement of the service on Whit Monday 5th June, 1911. At the ends the two 'Thames' double-decks FX 910 and FX 911, next to them two 'Hastings' type 'Thames' single-decks. Two taxi-stand in the centre.   *Author's Collection*

Unfortunately no details or registration of the actual machine operated by Turner survive, it being assumed that he purchased it second-hand away from Dorset. Turner also owned a 15 cwt 10 hp Durkopp, and a Panhard 7 hp Landau. At his bankruptcy hearing in March 1911 he stated that he had purchased three motor cars and ran them at Weymouth, but admitted that in the end he lost money over it. Two obsolete Daimlers were sold for £23, and for a third car (which was burnt) he received £90!

Turner had also engaged in speculative house building, an advert in the August 1906 *Weymouth Telegram* stating: 'Turner & Son, Firewood, scrap iron and Metal merchants, Kings Street, has for sale several new freehold houses in Alexandra Road'. Unfortunately he overstretched himself in 1909 when he became a shareholder in a Poole-based tugboat venture, this bringing about his bankruptcy.

Turner's two brothers took over the business, J.E. Turner becoming manager. In December 1913 the Weymouth Diving & Towage Company was formed, Turner, who described himself as a metal merchant, was a Director and Secretary to this company. His salvage exploits are a story in their own right, being totally unsuccessful! His son-in-law William Torrance was drowned whilst diving on a wreck in December 1921, and within a year two of Turner's tugs sank in unusual circumstances, this terminating the salvage company! The King Street premises passed to Waterman, and later Restorick, the coal merchant.

Not being one to give up easily, by 1924 Turner was back in business as a taxi driver, a trade he continued until he was 92, passing away in April 1955 aged 95 years. During the 1970s his great-grandson was a driver for Southern National, often driving on the Upwey and Sutton Poyntz routes Joseph Turner had pioneered.

Motor Coaches Ltd

Motor Coaches Ltd was one of the companies that submitted proposals to Weymouth Corporation to operate a bus service following the withdrawal of the GWR service in 1909.

Motor Coaches of London was formed in July 1910 with a capital of £20,000 divided into 31 shares. The original head office was at 17 Philpot Lane in the City of London, although this had moved to 29/31 Piccadilly by the following June. The new company was part of the Thames Ironworks Shipbuilding and Engineering Company Ltd, the motor vehicles being produced in the workshops of the former John Penn Marine Engine works at Blackheath. Penn had amalgamated with Thames in 1899, and the motors - built alongside marine engines - were marketed under the name 'Thames' (no relation to the later Ford Thames). By early 1911 Motor Coaches were operating services at Hastings, Bexhill, Eastbourne, Folkestone, and other places, one purpose of this exercise being to stimulate interest in the products of the Thames Ironworks.

A letter to Weymouth Town Council on 27th January, 1911 offered to provide a motor bus service:

In the event of Weymouth Town Council being willing to give Messrs Motor Coaches privilege in monopoly say for five years, we on our part will undertake to establish a first class service for motor omnibuses, coaches and char-a-bancs for the benefit and convenience of the town. Also, in return for the privileges granted, to pay a sum equal to 10 per cent on any profits that may be earned by the Weymouth service into the town exchequer, the amount to be certified annually by the auditors of Motor Coaches Ltd. If

MOTOR COACHES, LIMITED.

Busses Stop Here.

(BUSSES DO NOT STOP AT INTERMEDIATE PLACES.)

TIME TABLE.

SPA ROAD AND WYKE REGIS.

SPA ROAD	9 0	—	12 45	—	4 30	—	10 15S	10 15
LODMOOR HILL	9 3	10 35	12 48	2 30	4 33	6 45	10 18	10 18
LENNOX STREET	9 8	10 38	12 51	2 35	4 38	6 50	10 23	10 23
KING'S STATUE	9 13	10 43	12 56	2 40	4 43	6 55	10 28	10 28*
TOWN BRIDGE	9 18	10 48	1 1	2 45	4 48	7 0		
DORSET PLACE	9 23	10 53	1 6	2 50	4 53	7 5		
RODWELL AVENUE	9 26	10 58	1 11	2 55	4 58	7 10		
BINCLEAVES ROAD	9 30	11 2	1 16	3 0	5 3	7 15		
BUXTON CROSS ROAD	9 35	11 7	1 21	3 5	5 8	7 20		
WYKE	9 40	11 12	1 26	3 10	5 13	7 25		

WYKE	9 50	11 20	1 45	3 30	5 40	7 40		
BUXTON CROSS ROAD	9 57	11 27	1 52	3 35	5 45	7 43		
BINCLEAVES ROAD	10 2	11 32	1 57	3 40	6 0	7 48		
RODWELL AVENUE	10 4	11 35	2 2	3 45	6 5	7 53		
DORSET PLACE	10 6	11 37	2 4	3 50	6 10	7 58		
TOWN BRIDGE	10 11	11 42	2 9	3 55	6 15	8 3		
KING'S STATUE	10 16	11 47	2 15	4 0	6 20	8 8	10 30S	
LENNOX STREET	10 21	11 52	2 20	4 5	6 25	8 13	10 35	
LODMOOR HILL	10 25	11 56	2 24	4 10	6 30	8 18	10 40	
SPA ROAD	—	12 0	2 28	4 15	—	8 20	10 43	

S—Saturdays only.   * Leaves for Wyke after Pavilion Theatre Performance.

SPA ROAD WESTHAM, AND CHICKERELL.

SPA ROAD	8 0	10 0	12 0	3 0	5 0	—	8 15S	
LODMOOR HILL	8 3	10 3	12 3	3 3	5 3	—	8 18	
LENNOX STREET	8 8	10 8	12 8	3 8	5 8	—	8 23	
KING'S STATUE	8 13	10 13	12 13	3 13	5 13	6 35	8 28	10 45*
TOWN BRIDGE	8 18	10 18	12 18	3 18	5 18	6 40	8 33	10 30
WESTHAM	8 28	10 28	12 28	3 28	5 28	6 50	8 43	11 0
CHICKERELL	8 45	10 45	12 45	3 45	5 45	7 5	9 0	11 15

CHICKERELL	9 0	11 0	2 0	4 0	6 0	7 15	10 0S	
WESTHAM	9 15	11 15	2 15	4 15	6 15	7 30	10 15	
TOWN BRIDGE	9 25	11 25	2 25	4 25	6 25	7 40	10 25	
KING'S STATUE	9 30	11 30	2 30	4 30	6 30	7 45	10 30	
LENNOX STREET	9 35	11 35	2 35	4 35	—	7 50		
LODMOOR HILL	9 40	11 40	2 40	4 40	—	7 55		
SPA ROAD	9 45	11 45	2 45	4 45	—	8 0		

S—Saturdays only.   * Leaves for Westham and Chickerell after Pavilion Theatre Performance.

NO SUNDAY SERVICE—The Company do not guarantee to adhere strictly to the above times, but will always study the convenience of the public.

Timetable for the bus service of Motor Coaches Ltd.
Published in the *Southern Times* for 22nd July, 1911.

the necessary negotiations are completed in good time we shall be able to start such a service immediately after the coronation [of King George V].

In an interview with a Council committee the Manager, Mr R.D. Saunders, clarified the following points:

1. No Sunday service would be run unless the town desired one.
2. Local labour would be encouraged and employed.
3. The present Summer char-a-banc traffic would not be damaged, Motor Coaches proposing to run the long route services outside the Borough.
4. The cars would be especially constructed weighing about 4½ tons for the Radipole-Wyke Regis service, and 3 tons for the Westham service.
5. A service to the Town Council's wish would be maintained, and a guarantee given that this would be continued for a term of years.
6. The fares would be on the basis of one penny per mile or portion thereof, this estimate being subject to arrangement between the Company and the Corporation and
7. If negotiations are completed at once some coaches would be transferred from Hastings to Weymouth so that a temporary service could be started at the beginning of June.

The committee agreed to accept the offer, but pointed out that 'The monopoly cannot be granted legally, but it is understood that the moral support of the Council is sufficient guarantee'.

On Wednesday 15th February several councillors took a trial trip on a bus of a type similar to, but heavier than, those proposed to be used on the service. The route taken for the test was from the Spa Hotel to Wyke Hotel via Buxton Road, the return from Wyke being made along Wyke Road.

There was enthusiasm for the proposed new service, an editorial in the *Southern Times* on 4th March told of the need for a bus service, and that an important feature of the service would be long tours the company would offer during the Summer. These were not in any way to compete with the char-a-bancs that had served the town so well. The touring cars would go further afield and would run to many places of interest in Dorset and on the borders, which were now only accessible by train. The char-a-bancs referred to were the horse-drawn wagonettes operating to local beauty spots and villages on the edge of town.

Operations commenced on Whit Monday 5th June, the *Weymouth Telegram* giving a full account of the opening day. Before the services commenced, the two double-decks, two char-a-bancs, and two taxis were lined up at the King's Statue for the photographer to record the event.

The opening runs were completed without any hitch, and the two char-a-bancs were allocated to pleasure trips along the Preston Beach to Springhead. This was an immediately popular trip, and hardly a journey started with an empty seat. Throughout the day the cars were greatly utilised.

'Theatre goers were decidedly pleased on leaving the performance of *The Girl From Nowhere* at the Pavilion on Monday evening to find three buses awaiting them, two running to Wyke and the other to Radipole! The bus fares are exceedingly reasonable, being 1*d.* per mile'.

Getting the service started was not without difficulty, the management stating that they were 'unable to set the fares and times at the beginning'. The Chickerell part of the Westham journey did not commence until the second week in July, and the lightweight buses needed to cross the Backwater (Westham) bridge were not available, causing the

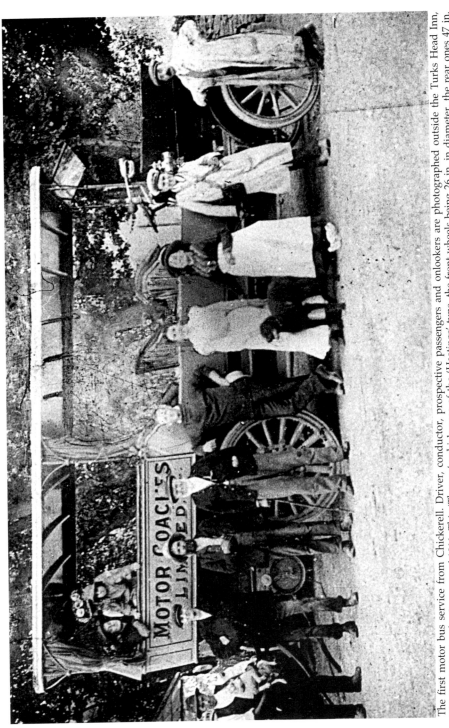

The first motor bus service from Chickerell. Driver, conductor, prospective passengers and onlookers are photographed outside the Turks Head Inn, Chickerell during the Summer of 1911. This 'Thames' vehicle was of the 'Hastings' type, the front wheels being 26 in. in diameter, the rear ones 47 in. diameter. The 27-seat body was divided into two compartments and was more on the lines of a coach than a bus, proving that coaches were used for fare stage work from the earliest days!

Turks Head Inn

Chickerell service to be routed via the Town bridge, North Quay, and Newstead Road, Passengers were charged 2*d*. to Westham instead of 1*d*., but the management assured the Council that it would revert to 1*d*. when the new vehicles arrived!

Motor Coaches were optimistic, a report in the *Southern Times* on 24th June publishing a letter from their Chairman, Arnold Hills:

The Company began operations at Hastings in August last, and now have cars running at Hastings, Eastbourne, Folkestone and Weymouth. It is the intention of the Company to place similar cars all along the South-West coast. They will run chiefly for pleasure, and I hope by next year they will get to Lands End. The object of Motor Coaches Ltd is to restore the glories of the road, and to bring back some of the ideas of the old coaching days. The coaches will be facsimiles of the old stage coaches, adapted to a six-cylinder 40-horse power chassis. These could run from London to Brighton, Windsor, Oxford, Cambridge etc. They also intend to develop the commercial side of motor traction, and have already completed contracts with the Post Office for a through parcel service around London. The next ten years will see an enormous transfer of traffic from the railways to the roads. It will thus be seen that Motor Coaches Ltd is a Company which has not only solid backing, but a good deal of public and patriotic spirit, and Weymouth must consider itself fortunate to have become one of the centres of its operations.

Despite these pronouncements of a successful future, at Weymouth affairs were far from well, and the *Southern Times* for 8th July noted: 'Owing to certain peculiarities which the residents have noticed in this company's local service and timetable, the latter is generally known here as 'The wait and see timetable'. This is a bit of folklore which may be worth preserving'. There was also a petition from cab and char-a-banc proprietors protesting that Motor Coaches Ltd were encroaching on their popular short trips! The Town Clerk visited the London offices to seek an explanation for the delays in setting up the agreed service, only to be told by the Chairman of his firm determination to spare no money and effort to make the running of motor buses in Weymouth a success, and pledging himself to allow a long period for the purposes of experiment, but at the same time he refused to seal the draft agreement - at present in his hands - between the Corporation and his company, until he was satisfied that experiment showed reasonable signs of success. He should not tie his company with an obligation to run coaches, perhaps as a serious loss, for five years. In a follow-up letter sent to the Town Clerk, the Chairman remarked:

Some of the difficulties have been entirely beyond our control. As I explained to you the vexatious non-delivery of bodies has prevented our placing our new type of motor coaches upon your service this summer. The order for building these coaches was given by myself to the Gloucester Wagon Works nearly three months ago with promise of delivery by the end of June. Meanwhile I am sending down shortly two new char-a-bancs similar to those you already have running, and I hope that we shall be able to give a good account of ourselves in dealing with your summer traffic.

The *Southern Times* for 22nd July reported on the state of affairs:

Mr McEwan, the General Manager of the Company, was at Weymouth and doing everything possible to organise and perfect the present system. The cars in use are temporary, and are clearing the way for a thoroughly efficient and regular service when the new cars are completed. Mr McEwen stated that the matter was being pushed forward with all possible speed and it was only the abnormal pressure of work at the Thames Ironworks that had hindered the building of the Weymouth cars.

It was also reported that:

Daily arrangements are being made in regard to the char-a-banc drives into the 'hinterland'. It has been found impossible to adhere to any set programme of motor tours, owing to the cars being chartered so frequently by private parties.

The timetable had been revised, giving a service of six trips daily between Radipole Spa Hotel and Chickerell, three between Radipole and Wyke Regis, and three between Lodmoor Hill and Wyke Regis. From reports it would appear that the Chickerell service was well patronised, not exactly what could be classed as a local beauty spot and in those days a small village, but conductors were reported as taking as much as £8 a day, although one suspects that a good proportion of that revenue was obtained from passengers travelling on the Weymouth end of the service!

The Revd G. Barrett, writing to the *Southern Times*, complained of a most unsatisfactory timetable,

. . . .that the buses failed to keep to, often departing from the King's Statue early and travelling along the route ahead of time, stopping at King Street and the crew disappearing, then arriving with petrol to put in the vehicle and cleaning the engine.

In the following edition further complaints of the same nature concerning the crew disappearing at King Street and oiling the machine, and general early running were reported. It must be admitted that looking at the timetable some of the journey times were long between points, even allowing for the vehicles and roads of the day! Whereas the GWR service had travelled from the Town bridge via North Quay and Boot Hill to Rodwell, the Motor Coaches vehicles travelled via Trinity Road, Hope Square and Rodwell Avenue, there being a booked timing point at Dorset Place (now the bottom of Newbury Road).

By that autumn it had become clear that Motor Coaches Ltd were in difficulties; indeed, the entire Thames Ironworks concern was failing. At the October Council meeting the Mayor said 'I do not consider that the Company has done any one single thing that they have promised to do. I could not blame the council if they did not give this Company any further sympathy'. Mr Clarke wondered how the buses could be expected to pay if they had no fixed time of running, as they could not be depended on!

At the November meeting there were further complaints that the promised vehicles had still failed to arrive, and that the service remained unreliable. A letter from the company made the following points:

I beg to inform you that we have some time since completed the design of the new cars, and the chassis are in the course of construction at our Greenwich works. We shall not, however, attempt anything in the way of a new service before next Spring; meanwhile we are principally concerned with the new Admiralty programme, and much will depend upon our success or failure in this competition whether we continue operations next year at all. I propose however, to run the two buses during the Winter so long as there is any reasonable traffic demand.

Unfortunately history does not fully record all the vehicles employed at Weymouth, the *Commercial Motor* for 15th June, 1911 stated that 'at present, six Thames machines are employed'. The opening day photograph shows double-decks FX 910, and FX 911, registered on 3rd June, 1911 to Motor Coaches of Rocky Knap, Weymouth. The only other available details show that they were 4 tons 4 cwt, with 2 ft 6 in. diameter front wheels, and 3 ft 2 in. rear wheels, and that the vehicles were painted red, white, and blue! No information was given as to whether they were new or re-registered - a frequent occurrence at that time. Also clearly shown are two taxis and two char-a-bancs known as the 'Hastings Type'. They were very advanced for their day, with bodies which seated 27 passengers, driver and conductor. A windscreen and fixed roof were provided, and canvas side curtains provided for inclement weather. *Commercial Motor* described them thus:

The luxuriousness and comfortable riding - the latter being due in a great measure to the large-diameter wheels which are employed - these vehicles are superior to any other public service char-a-bancs of which we have experience. They are fitted with four-cylinder engines which develop 40 hp, and the drive is transmitted through a leather-faced cone clutch, in which cork inserts are introduced, and a sturdy four-speed and reverse gearbox to a differential countershaft; the final drive is taken through roller chains to each of the rear wheels. The chassis is not unduly high, although the leading wheels are 26 in. diameter and the driving wheels are 47 in. in diameter, the latter being 8 in. larger than the generally accepted standard for a London motorbus. All wheels are shod with North British solid rubber tyres, 4 in. single being fitted to the front wheels and twin tyres of 3 in. to the back wheels.

In mid-November 1911 it was announced that a Receiver had been appointed on behalf of the debenture share holders of the Thames Ironworks, and another Receiver for Messrs Motor Coaches Ltd. It was clear the construction of HMS *Thunderer*, at 25,000 tons a far greater tonnage than any other vessel built by the yard and the largest warship ever built on the Thames, was the final straw for a hard-pressed company. Construction had commenced in April 1910, and was completed in June 1912, but on 21st December the yard closed. Of Motor Coaches Ltd, in December 1915 it was reported that Mr Ian M. Henderson, the only receiver, was a prisoner-of-war in Germany. Therefore there never was a formal winding up of the company, which was dissolved by December 1917.

Unfortunately, Weymouth had witnessed the final days of Messrs Motor Coaches, the victim of events within its parent company, Thames Ironworks. Thus also ended a major chapter in Thames ship building history. However, marine engines built by John Penn & Sons continued to propel the Weymouth paddle steamers, *Premier*, *Empress*, *Victoria*, *Monarch*, and *Consul*, for many years!

Motor Coaches Ltd

No.	Reg No.	Chassis	No.	Body	Type	No.	Built	Acq.	Sold	Notes
	FX 910	Thames			DD			6/11		1, 2
	FX 911	Thames			DD			6/11		1, 2

Notes

1. June 1911, the date both vehicles were registered with Dorset County Council little else known; both vehicles 4 tons 4 cwt, front wheels 2 ft 6 in., rear 3 ft 2 in. Vehicles painted red, white and blue.
2. Noted to Hastings 1912.

Other vehicles were employed at Weymouth, details unknown.

Weymouth Motor Touring Co., Edward William Puffett

The loss of the horse bus service, particularly to the inhabitants of Westham, was referred to in the *Southern Times* of 30th November, 1912: 'The need of a cheap light omnibus service for Westham is becoming increasingly urgent, and the genius of our city fathers if local enterprise is not equal to the emergency, ought to be able to find a means of supplying this great public want'. In the event it was local enterprise that took up the challenge. Following the sale of the former Weymouth Omnibus Company premises in Holly Road during November 1912 to Mrs Barge, they were rented by E.W. Puffett, resulting in the introduction of a motor bus service to Chickerell via Westham.

Puffett, who was a native of Risca, South Wales, came to Weymouth in 1891 as a fitter at the newly opened Whitehead torpedo factory. He became the landlord of the Royal Oak public house at Lodmoor Hill, Dorchester Road, in the latter part of 1907, and by early January 1913 he was operating a bus service between Weymouth and Chickerell via Westham - a venture the Great Western Railway had refused, despite requests from the Town Council.

The new service had created much interest, and on 29th January a meeting was held at the Queens Hotel, Weymouth, where interested parties from Weymouth and Chickerell met to discuss a proposal to form a company to run motor buses in the district. The *Southern Times* reported:

> Mr Puffett who is at present running a service between Weymouth and Chickerell, was present and gave the meeting the benefit of his experience in regard to the service which he had instituted. Mr Puffett produced photographs of light single-deck cars to carry 20 or 27 passengers, and approximately stated the initial outlay and the probable cost of running.
>
> There was a unanimous feeling that if the best interests of the town were to be served, and the outlying districts populated it was imperative that they should be linked up with an up to date service of cars. Seven gentlemen present guaranteed to subscribe the necessary sum of money to float a company, and it was decided that it should be styled the 'Weymouth & District Motor Service Company'. Mr Puffett estimated that for a commencement at least four cars would be necessary. Details in connection with the running of such cars were forthcoming, but the amount of capital required to be called up and the legal business was left over until Mr H.A. Huxtable who had promised to act as solicitor in the event of a company being formed could be present.

Despite the optimism of the meeting and the support offered, it appears that the matter was never pursued, as no further reports appeared in the local press. However Puffett did persevere with his service to Chickerell.

The vehicle Puffett commenced his service with has not been identified. However, in April 1913 he acquired a new Fiat omnibus weighing 1 ton 18 cwt., painted in a green livery picked out in white and black. In November a three-year-old Fiat 24 hp touring car was purchased, and like many operators of that period, hire cars were also operated.

The Council granted permission in February 1914 for Puffett to build a motor garage at the Holly Road site, and after the clearance of the original stable buildings, a corrugated garage and workshop were erected to the rear of the cottages forming 14-22 Holly Road, whilst the space behind Overdale House formed a parking yard. These arrangements lasted for the remainder of the garage's working life. In May 1914 the Council Licensing Committee asked Puffett if the hourly bus service he was operating to Westham could be increased to half-hourly, but whether this ever happened or not is unrecorded. However, the new business became sufficiently established to allow Puffett to vacate the Royal Oak by October 1914.

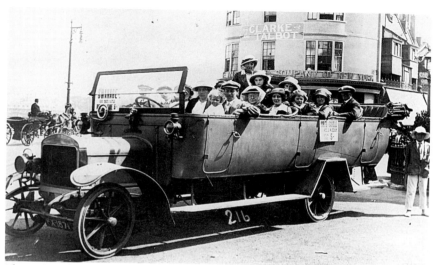

The only vehicle in the Puffett fleet for which a photographs has survived is his Thornycroft char-a-banc, FX 1871. New in September 1913, fare to either Corfe Castle or Swanage 5s., quite a trip in those days just before war was to change the lives of these passengers for ever. Even in those days drivers had their own decoration, note the teddy bear in the centre below the windscreen. *Author's Collection*

During September 1913 Puffett purchased a Thornycroft 'C' type 30 hp char-a-banc, FX 1871, weighing 2 tons 18 cwt. and painted in a grey livery. Discounting the previous attempt by Turner with his wagonette and the short-lived Motor Coaches Ltd affair, the Thornycroft could well have been the first proper motorised char-a-banc to operate in the area.

Details of Puffett's operations are vague, and it would appear that he took on any work going! Although World War I had commenced in September 1914, a timetable was published the following year giving six return journeys to Chickerell via Westham, two short workings to Westham during the late afternoon, and a 'special run' from the new Army camp at Chickerell at 8.35 pm.

The Weymouth Town Guide for 1916 still advertised Puffett trading as the 'Weymouth Motor Touring Company. Landaulettes, cabriolettes, and touring cars for hire, motor char-a-bancs for parties at special terms. Motor buses night and day, and automobile engineers'. Obtaining staff to carry out the work was also difficult. Twice during the 1916/17 period Puffett appealed to the Military Tribunal against two members of his staff, a mechanic and a driver, being required for war work and army service. During the same period two 17-year-olds employed as taxi drivers were involved in fatal accidents - in neither case any fault of theirs - whilst working at Chickerell Camp.

In February 1915 Puffett registered what the Taxation Registers described as, 'FX 2581 LCCO motor bus, 3 t 18 cwt with mahogany double-deck body, also noted as char-a-banc painted French grey'. It is considered that this vehicle was a former London General 'B' type bus. The next purchase also illustrates the complexities of vehicle registrations of the period. FX 1661 was a Seldon Lorry with a char-a-banc body weighing 2 tons 18 cwt and registered on 17th March, 1917 to John Bagg, Grosvesnor Gardens, Bournemouth. It was Registered to W.E. Puffett, Westham Garage, on 29th October, 1917. Bournemouth Police reported that the car had been converted into a lorry and was on hire to Weymouth, having been resold to Puffett on 17th October, 1917. It was cancelled in the register on 2nd April, 1918.

It is impossible to have an accurate account of Puffett's fleet, as he may well have acquired non-Dorset registered vehicles. The *Southern Times* for 4th May, 1918, referring to fuel shortages, stated: 'Gas-propelled vehicles are now quite a common sight in Weymouth, for besides the huge char-a-bancs that ply to the camps, several tradesmen are using them'. There is no evidence that any person other than Puffett was operating char-a-bancs at that time, so it has to be assumed that the vehicles mentioned were his!

Again, a complication that can confuse historians was the re-issue of registration numbers. The number of the Fiat bus FX 1661, appeared again during 1917 on a Seldon which had been acquired from the person who had purchased the Fiat. Despite a search of the taxation records, the matter of these two vehicles has never been fully resolved. In January 1920 Puffett registered an Austin char-a-banc using the number of his former Thornycroft vehicle FX 1871. Also during the latter years Puffett had been dealing in cars, there being records of a number of transactions in the County Taxation Records

In March 1920 Jack Radford took over the Westham garage and the Austin char-a-banc, and Puffett purchased the Criterion restaurant on Weymouth Esplanade and also went into the building trade. He later ran a cafe in King Street, which ironically later became the Southern National canteen! Puffett had departed from the transport industry at a point when many were entering it. Had Weymouth & District Motor Services actually started and survived World War I, the Weymouth transport scene could well have been different! Puffett passed away on 20th April, 1942 aged 70 years.

E.W. Puffett, Westham Garage

No.	Reg No.	Chassis	No.	Body	Type	No.	Built	Acq.	Sold	Notes
	FX 1661	Fiat 30 hp			B			4/13		1
	FX 1661	Seldon			CH		3/17	10/17	2/18	2
	FX 1871	Thornycroft			CH		9/13	9/13	3/17	3
	FX 1871	Austin 20 hp			CH		1/20	3/20		4
	FX 2581	LGOC			OT44RO			2/15	9/16	5, 6

Notes
1. Weight registered as 1 t. 18 cwt.
2. Note in Dorset Taxation records. Seldon lorry, char-a-banc body 2 t. 18 cwt reg 27/3/17 to John Bagg, Bournemouth. Registered Puffett , Westham Garage 29/10/17. Note in register 'Mr Bagg never completed the register on 17/3/17. Bournemouth Police reported that car had been converted to lorry and on hire to Weymouth, resold to Puffett Oct. 17th. Cancelled 2nd April, 1918'.
3. Registration cancelled 26/3/17.
4. Probably ex-WD chassis.
5. Re-registered vehicle.
6. Note in Dorset Taxation records 'LGOC motor bus 3 t. 18 cwt 2 q., mahogany double-deck bus, also noted as char-a-banc, French grey, reg 3/2/15, 1/9/16 cancel all correspondence'.

Previous Owners
FX 1661 (Seldon) John Bagg, Bournemouth

Disposals
FX 1661 (Fiat) to John Bagg, Bournemouth, date not recorded.
FX 1871 (Austin) to Jack Radford, Westham Garage 3/20. To T.J. Clarke, coal merchant, as lorry.

George Francis Bugler

George Francis Bugler was in business at Rodwell Garage, Boot Hill, Weymouth, from where he operated a high-class taxi service. In April 1914 he acquired his first char-a-banc, a second-hand Lacre 30 hp model which had been new in July 1912 to the Briant family of Exeter Road, Bournemouth.

Despite the difficulties of World War I, Bugler purchased two more vehicles in August 1915, this time British Ensign 40 hp chassis FX 3096 and FX 3132, and by January 1916 the Lacre had been sold. The *Southern Times* for July 1916 advertised attractive motor drives in the *White Heather* and *Empress* cars, described as 'powerful and well equipped 40-hp motor char-a-bancs', which included trips to Portland, Abbotsbury, Bridport, Sherborne, Milton Abbas, Cerne Abbas, Lulworth Cove, and Corfe Castle. By July the adverts had ceased; no doubt the Petrol Control Order and the worsening war situation brought the enterprise to an end. Before long both vehicles were sold and converted to lorries.

In February 1919 it would appear that plans were afoot to restart the char-a-banc business, and a British Ensign lorry - EL 2225 - was purchased from Poole owners. When re-registered with Bugler it was recorded as a flat-bed lorry painted dark green with red wheels. It is assumed that a body from one of the previous vehicles had been stored and was now mounted on this chassis. History does not record if operations actually started, as in June that year the vehicle was sold to Isle of Wight owners, only to be sold again two months later, clearly demonstrating the instability in the char-a-banc trade at that time.

A fourth British Ensign, EL 2250, was acquired in July 1919, again from Bournemouth owners. However, this vehicle was also sold very quickly, being purchased by a Yorkshire firm early in 1920.

George Bugler's Lacre, EL 874 stands at the King's Statue before departing on a tour, but where to? Notices on the side state, Upwey Wishing Well 1s. return. Lulworth Cove 4s. return. World War I caused this delightful vehicle to be converted into a lorry for a Bournemouth dairy in February 1916.   *Author's Collection*

The livery of Bugler's vehicles was white lined out in black, except the Lacre which had retained the scarlet lake and primrose wheels of the previous owner.

Bugler had the distinction of being the only local char-a-banc operator to use the British Ensign chassis. British Ensign, a London-based company, was formed in 1913, and by late 1914 the three-ton chassis were being produced at their Willesden Green factory. It was powered by a four-cylinder Tylor engine with a bore of 4½ in. and stroke of 6 in. Transmission was via a cone clutch, four-speed gearbox and live back axle, a transmission brake being fitted to the propeller shaft and brake drums to both back wheels. The chassis, complete with wheels, sold for £675 and was suitable for use either as a lorry or char-a-banc. Following World War I British Ensign concentrated on a design of luxury car and quickly faded from the scene.

Bugler's other unusual purchase was the Lacre, (a name derived from Long Acre, the London street in which the company's head office was situated). By 1910 this manufacturer had introduced a range of chassis up to three tons. The vehicle Bugler purchased was of the 32 cwt type with a 13 ft 6 in. wheelbase, powered by a four-cylinder engine. Following World War I, Lacre concentrated on the production of road sweeping equipment, a product for which they are better known!

The reason for the quick sale of the later vehicles could well have been that in May 1919 Bugler became a Director of the newly-formed Weymouth Motor Company Ltd, with a holding of fifty £10 shares. Early in 1920, for reasons never explained, he resigned from the company, also selling his own business and leaving the area. The Rodwell garage continued in the motor trade, being run by Chantry Bros. During World War II the premises were used by the National Fire Service, later becoming a garage and workshop for Messrs V.H. Bennett, the Weymouth department store. In recent years the garage part has been demolished and mews-type cottages built on the site.

ATTRACTIVE

MOTOR DRIVES.

WHITE HEATHER AND EMPRESS CARS.

THESE Powerful and Well-Equipped 40 Horse-power MOTOR CHAR-A-BANCS will MAKE REGULAR TRIPS during the Season, weather and other circumstances permitting.

BOOKING OFFICE: Mr. T. J. GUPPY'S FANCY BAZAAR, ST. MARY-STREET.

PROGRAMME :—

MONDAY.

Morning—Upwey and Bincombe. Grand Circular Drive—Return Fare, 1s. 6d. Portland. For the Chesil Beach, &c.—Return Fare, 1s. 6d. *Afternoon*—Abbotsbury, for the renowned Swannery and Tropical Gardens—Return Fare, 3s. Bindon Abbey, via Moreton Woods and Moreton Park, Highford and Wool—Return Fare, 4s.

TUESDAY.

Morning—Upwey, for the Wishing Well—Return Fare, 1s. Portland, for the Chesil Beach —Return Fare, 1s. 6d. *Afternoon*—Lulworth Cove, via Winfrith, Marley Woods, and West Lulworth, returning via East Lulworth's famous Castle—Return Fare, 4s. Osmington Mills, famous for Lobster Teas, and giving a magnificent Panoramic View of Weymouth and Portland—Return Fare, 2s.

WEDNESDAY.

Morning—Portland, for the Chesil Beach—Return Fare, 1s. 6d. Upwey, for the Wishing Well—Return Fare, 1s. *Afternoon*—Abbotsbury, for the renowned Swannery and Tropical Gardens—Return Fare, 3s. Lulworth Cove, via Winfrith, Marley Woods, and West Lulworth, returning via East Lulworth's famous Castle—Return Fare, 4s.

THURSDAY.

Morning—Upwey, for the Wishing Well—Return Fare, 1s. Sutton and Bincombe, for the White Horse, &c—Return Fare, 1s. 6d. *Afternoon*—Moreton and Dorchester, for the Rhododendron Forest—Return Fare, 4s. Milton Abbey, Grand Rural Drive to Milton Abbas, the ideal Village, the. grand old Abbey, and the seat of Sir Everard Hambro—Return Fare, 5s.

FRIDAY.

Morning—Portland, for the Chesil Beach—Return Fare, 1s. 6d. Circular Drive to Chickerell. Nottington, Upwey, Bincombe, a beautiful Country Drive—Return Fare, 2s. *Afternoon*—Cerne Abbas, passing Dorchester (the County Town), &c., to view Cerne Giant—Return Fare, 4s. Corfe Castle, beautiful Marine Drive to visit the Fine Old Castle, situate amid charming Country—Return Fare, 5s.

SATURDAY.

Morning—Upwey and Bincombe, grand Circular Drive—Return Fare, 1s. 6d. Sutton and Bincombe, for the White Horse, &c.—Return Fare, 1s. 6d. *Afternoon*—Osmington Mills, famous for Lobster Teas, and giving a magnificent Panoramic View of Weymouth and Portland—Return Fare, 2s. Abbotsbury, for the renowned Swannery and Tropical Gardens—Return Fare, 3s.

SUNDAY.

Bridport and West Bay, noted for some of the most beautiful Country in Dorset (this constitutes a lovely trip)—Return Fare, 5s. Sherborne, for the renowned Abbey and Public School, passing numerous Country Seats, charming Villages, &c., and giving unsurpassed views of North Dorset—Return Fare 5s.

The CARS may be HIRED for PRIVATE ENGAGEMENTS.   [4515

Despite the war situation, Bugler was still able to advertise tours for his char-a-bancs in July 1916.

George Francis Bugler, Rodwell Mews Garage, Weymouth

No.	Reg No.	Chassis	No.	Body	Type	No.	Built	Acq.	Sold	Notes
	EL 874	Lacre 30 hp			CH		7/12	4/14	b2/16	
	FX 3096	Brit/Ensign			CH		8/15	8/15	b10/18	
	EL 2250	Brit/Ensign			CH		7/15	7/19	b2/20	
	FX 3132	Brit/Ensign			CH		8/15	8/15	b8/18	
	EL 2225	Brit/Ensign			CH		5/18	2/19	6/19	

Previous Owners

EL 874   New 2/7/12 to Reginald William Albert Briant & Ernest Briant, executors of Mark Briant, Eagles Nest Lodge, Exeter Road, Bournemouth. Livery scarlet lake and primrose wheels.

EL 2225   New to William Greenslade, Fish Merchant, Poole, registered 9/5/18.

EL 2250   New July 1915 to A.W. Futcher & Co., Cranborne Mews, Tregonwell Road, Bournemouth. Blue livery by 4/16 painted white.

Disposals

EL 874   8/2/16 registered to Isaac & Co., Christchurch Road, Boscombe, Bournemouth, with lorry body, dark blue, white lettering.

FX 3096   1/10/18 registered to J.R.L. Walsh Engineering Works, New Barnet, with van body.

EL 2250   3/20 to A.E. Gelder, Central Garage, Slickstone near Barnsley. White livery as CH.

FX 3132   By 8/18 to R.C. Walsh Engineering Works, New Barnet, registered as a van 15/1/19.

EL 2225   6/19 to G. Fowler & Co., Railway Street, Cowes, IOW. 8/19 to Thomas Naismith, Cambridge Hotel, Shoeburyness.

Percy John A'Court, Gloucester Mews, Weymouth

Percy John A'Court was one of the early pioneers of motor transport in the Borough. His father owned riding stables, and Percy had assisted in the development of horse wagonettes and carriages in the town. With the arrival of the motor vehicle A'court established a garage in Gloucester Mews, situated behind both the Gloucester and Royal Hotels, then the two top class hotels in the town. A'Court quickly established a good reputation with the class of person who could afford to hire a vehicle and chauffeur. When HM King George V visited Weymouth in 1912 it was Percy A'Court who drove him from the harbour pier to the railway station, a photograph of this event appearing in his advert for the 'Royal Garage' in the Town Guide into the 1930s!

In July 1914 he purchased his first char-a-banc, a Maudslay 40 hp model with a 30-seat body. Not only had A'Court selected a good quality chassis, the seating capacity was quite high for the time! Unfortunately the outbreak of World War I curtailed expansion of the business, the Maudslay being taken over by the War Office, and A'Court volunteered for overseas service as an ambulance driver serving in France and Italy.

Following the war he purchased an Albion chassis in April 1919 and fitted the body of the pre-war Maudslay that had been removed and stored. On 26th April the first advert appeared in the *Southern Times* giving details of excursions operated by *The Wessex* 32 hp Touring Car, a rather gracious description for a char-a-banc. The first advertised excursion was to Sherborne on Sunday 27th April, departing at 2 pm and costing 7s. An afternoon tour of Portland was offered on the Monday at 3s. Other trips later advertised included Bournemouth for 7s. 6d. and Cheddar Caves for 15s., the latter being an 8.30 am start! Here for the first time we were to see serious competition to not only the Portland branch but to railways in general from the motor coach.

With the formation of the Weymouth Motor Company Ltd in May 1919, A'Court become a principal shareholder and Director. The following March the Albion was transferred to the ownership of the Weymouth Motor Company, and so ended A'Court's direct ownership of char-a-bancs

By that time the Gloucester Mews garage had been rebuilt, and the other aspects of the business continued. A'Court took an interest in many organisations in the town; he joined the Town Council in 1922, being elected Mayor in 1925-1926. Later he became an Alderman. Following failing health he died on 26th April, 1942, aged 63 years.

Prior to the invasion of Europe the Gloucester Mews garage was used in connection with trials conducted on Weymouth sands for waterproofing military vehicles. In 1946 the garage became a depot for Messrs Drake & Sons, wholesale fruit and vegetable merchants, the 'over the pavement pumps' set into the front wall of the garage continued selling Cleveland Petrol for many years. Drake's finally closed the depot in 1993, since when it has served several purposes, but its future is uncertain.

P.J. A'Court, Royal Garage, Gloucester Mews, Weymouth

No.	Reg No.	Chassis	No.	Body	Type	No.	Built	Acq.	Sold	Notes
	FX 2410	Maudslay 40 hp			CB30		7/14	7/14	1916	1
	FX 4525	Albion 32 hp			CB28		4/19	4/19	3/20	2

Notes
1. Body removed and stored then fitted to chassis of FX 4525.
2. Fitted with body of FX 2410.

Disposals
FX 2410 impressed by War Office 1916 as lorry.
FX 4525 to Weymouth Motor Company Ltd 3/20.

Percy A'Court proudly seated in his new Maudslay char-a-banc FX 2410 in August 1914. According to the wording on the back of the postcard it was the maiden trip, the passengers being other Hackney drivers and conductors. People named are Gregory, Seward, Parsons, George Reed, Jess Daw, George Way, Charlie Bateman and Tom Pope. A 30-seater it was a large vehicle for its day.   *Author's Collection*

Chapter Five

The Portland Independent Operators

The exact date on which the first motor char-a-banc made its appearance on the island is lost in time. There were, however, plans by Richard Lano to start a motor bus service on the island prior to 1910. In September 1913 the *Southern Times* reported that employees of a Portland firm had travelled to Wells by char-a-banc for their annual outing, the origin of the vehicle being unknown. The two points that are certain are that the first regular omnibus service to reach the island as far as Victoria Square commenced in October 1921, and the first to cover the island was commenced by Messrs Smith & Hoare in May 1924.

Before setting out the history of the individual operators, an outline of the general scene will clarify many points. The situations existing at Weymouth and at Portland for the Portland operators were exact opposites. Portland UDC were easy going over the interpretation of their Hackney regulations - at least as far as the local operators were concerned! Weymouth Corporation on the other hand, operated a strict regime, and would not grant the Portland operators licences to ply for hire within the Borough. In June 1925 Richard Smith had applied for a Hackney licence to operate a service between Castletown and Weymouth, an application Weymouth Council would not entertain. Likewise in April 1928 and May 1929 Saunders Brothers applications to ply for hire within the Borough were refused.

The Weymouth Hackney Inspector also kept an eye on the Portland operators who brought parties into town. In October 1927 there were complaints that Messrs E. Way and Saunders had plied for hire outside the Regent Theatre, and later in the year F.C. Hoare was fined £1 for plying for hire within the Borough with a motor coach. In January 1928 the National Omnibus Company reported Frank Saunders for picking up passengers outside the Regent Theatre and at the north end of St Thomas Street. But no action was taken by the Council as Saunders stated that the passengers had previously booked the journey! The ever vigilant National again complained that Hoare was picking up passengers within the Borough in May 1929 with his brand new 14-seat Chevrolet.

Even with the passing of the Road Traffic Act in 1930 and the creation of the Traffic Commissioners who took over the responsibility of granting licences, Weymouth Council usually objected to any application from outsiders, and the Southern Railway often backed Southern National in objections to other operator's licensing applications.

Where Weymouth had seasonal traffic created by the holiday trade, Portland had the added dimension of the Royal Navy, and during the 1920s and 1930s when the British Navy was still a force to be reckoned with, warships carried large crews, the arrival of just a few ships vastly increasing traffic potential. If the Home Fleet arrived literally thousands of men came ashore, and when the fleet sailed all was quiet again. It was against this background that the Portland branch railway and the buses operated.

In October 1921 the first regular bus service commenced between Weymouth and Portland Victoria Square, operated by Messrs Road Motors of Luton. In 1924 Richard Smith decided to operate a fare stage service between Victoria Square and Portland Bill. A year later the National Omnibus & Transport Company, having acquired Messrs Road Motors, started to look towards expanding their business, and in February 1927 bought out the local service operated by Smith, from that date becoming the principal operators of fare stage services on Portland and in the Weymouth area.

The other operators on the Island were T.H. Gear, E.S. Way. F. Saunders. L. Saunders, C.B. Tolman, L.A.S. Tolman, R.J. Fancy, and F.C. Hoare. With the exception of Gear, they had all prior to 1931 undertaken tours, private hire work, and operated a service from both Portland and Easton stations to Portland Bill during the Summer months on a 'go when loaded' principle. There was also contract work for various organisations, such as the movement of troops from the Verne Citadel, the transportation of coaling gangs for the harbour coal hulks, and other various odd jobs.

The passing of the Road Traffic Act in 1930, and the need for all operators to apply for licences for their services by 31st March, 1931, was to change previous customs and practices for ever. Although the Act become law in April 1931, its full implementation took a considerable time. The first local meeting of the Traffic Commissioners for the Southern Area took place at Dorchester on Monday 20th July, 1931, when many of Dorset's operators, ranging from country carriers and small operators to the large companies such as Southern National and Hants & Dorset applied for licences for their various routes. No opposition was forthcoming to many applications, but others were opposed where there was a conflict of interest. Some of the Portland applications were opposed by Weymouth Town Council, the Southern National Omnibus Company, and the Southern Railway. Counsel for Southern National said that there was no desire to stop the applicants having licences, and outlined suggestions for regulating the matter.

Amongst the applicants were Mr T. Gear of Southwell to operate between Southwell and Portland Bill, Mr C.B. Tolman to ply to Portland Bill and Weymouth, and Mr R.J. Fancy to operate between Easton and Portland Bill and to run excursions from the Island.

The difficulty at Portland was with a timetable. When the Fleet was in large numbers of sailors (perhaps 1,000 or more) wanted to travel to Weymouth. At the sitting it was announced that a special investigation was to be made into the circumstances existing at Portland. The Chairman said that the best thing was for him or the clerk to visit Portland soon and make an enquiry on the spot.

At a resumed hearing held at Weymouth Guildhall on 7th August many points of road traffic law were discussed, and certain accusations made against Southern National. These included a suggestion that part of the difficulty experienced by the men in obtaining licences to ply for hire in Weymouth had been due to special facilities given to the Portland and Weymouth Councillors by Southern National, creating bias against the small operators. One of the applicants alleged that Weymouth and Portland Councillors had free passes to ride on the Southern National buses (*see page 11*).

Replying to these accusations, Mr Tiden-Smith the Clerk of the Commissioners, pointed out that

. . . conditions are even more difficult in the Isle of Wight than Portland, and the operators have to toe the line, although they used to be free to do as they like. I suggest that the Portland men should get down to something definite. I cannot see why the men do not get together and share the work out and make up a programme. What they must not do is try and cut each other's throats and the throat of the Southern National. Under the Act, the person who goes in for throat cutting becomes at once not a fit and proper person to hold a road service licence.

In the course of further discussion with the applicants Mr Tilden-Smith asked them to present the Commissioners with something tangible.

Mr Lock, representing the applicants, pointed out that for many years these young men had coaches in Victoria Square, and it was only recently that the companies had come in. The trade in Portland was essentially seasonal, and that at the sitting in Dorchester the Chairman had recognised that conditions were abnormal. These men to a very large extent filled the place of the carriers, although they did not carry goods. Mr Lock suggested that this was a case where time tables were practically impossible. Mr Tilden-Smith replied that the Commissioners had discretion to deal specially with carriers and station bus operators, whereupon Mr Lock said that the case of the Portland men was parallel to that of station bus operators.

Taking the advice of the Commissioners the operators applied for licences as groups. Fancy, Hoare, and L.A.C. Tolman applied for licences to operate a stage service between Portland Bill and Weymouth, whilst L.J. Saunders, F. Saunders, E.S. Way, and C.B. Tolman all applied for station buses from Victoria Square to anywhere within five miles, and for services from Portland Victoria Square to Easton and to Weymouth. These applications were heard at Reading in December 1931 and to save an over-complicated account we will leave the details of the Fancy/Hoare/L. Tolman application at this point, this being outlined in the section dealing with 'Portland Express'.

The Portland to Easton service was mainly intended to operate in conjunction with football matches held at the Portland football ground at Grove Corner, whilst the Weymouth service was for the use of Navy men when the fleet was in. There were no objections to these services and by the end of the month the Commissioners had granted licences to Saunders, Way, and C.B.Tolman to 'run a service between Castletown and Weymouth when the ships of HM Fleet were in harbour, and between Victoria Square and Grove Corner on Wednesdays and Saturdays during the football season'.

The Commissioners reserved their decisions on the Portland Bill-Weymouth and Victoria Square-Weymouth applications until May the following year, when station bus licences were granted to the four operators. This was challenged by Southern National, Southern Railway, and Weymouth Town Council, and a hearing into the appeal was heard in August. Mr Percy Smallman, Town Clerk of Weymouth, criticised the granting of 'Station Bus' licences to the four operators with stage carriage fares and no timetable, on the basis that:

Under these licences buses could stand for several hours at the King's Statue, which was the worst possible point for traffic in the Borough. The licences issued are inconsistent in terms, and by giving them stage carriage licences as station buses, the Commissioners have given the applicants more than they expected to get. The applicants thought they were applying to bring people from Victoria Square to places within five miles, but without permission to take anybody back. That does rather coincide with the proper description of a station bus. The licences granted give that permission, and allow them to take up passengers for return journeys. The Commissioners themselves have turned the licence into a hybrid, and I submit that for them to issue such a licence is *ultra vires*. The Act does not give them power to issue such a licence.

Mr G. Woodward representing the Southern National said of the station bus service:

It has no connection with the station. It is a special type of licence, and in my submission for the Traffic Commissioners to invent a new brand and then grant them the licence apparently to fill up is quite improper. What I would call a station bus is a bus from the Gloucester Hotel to the station and from the station to the Gloucester Hotel.

For the Portland operators Mr Savage pointed out that with regard to the Station Bus licences, they had applied to take single fares only, and that was why the Portland operators found it hard to understand the attitude of Weymouth Corporation. They appeared to be labouring under a misapprehension. These men did not ply for hire in Weymouth, but merely took people into Weymouth and returned to Portland empty.

The Weymouth Town Clerk questioned the actual operations carried out by the Portland Operators and what was set out in the licence. In reply, Mr Savage said:

I think there was a clerical error on the part of the Commissioners, and I fail to see why Weymouth Town Council should object to them coming in and going back empty. They have offered to enter the Town via Westwey Road in order to avoid congestion, but Weymouth Town Council have said you are not wanted. The Portland Urban District Council have supported these operators, and at the public hearing at Portsmouth a letter was put in by the Urban District Council but not accepted at the inquiry. The present licence only allows four vehicles to stand on the rank at Victoria Square. Whether the operators were able to make a living will come up at the application for the renewal of licences, and my clients think they are justified in being granted these licences, and that the Traffic Commissioners have only granted these licences provisionally and they will be going into them again after they have an opportunity to inspect the figures and see whether the service is necessary.

There had clearly been a clerical error on the part of the Traffic Commissioners. When the results of the inquiry were later known, the Minister of Transport had observed that in his view the term 'Station Bus' was a misnomer for services of the character proposed and was liable to lead to some confusion. In the case of these services he had decided to make an order providing that the Commissioners shall attach a condition to the licences that on southbound journeys no passenger shall be picked up at any point north of Clearmount. In making this order the problem of the operators being able to pick up in Weymouth was eliminated, whilst still allowing a service from Portland to operate. The Portland operators also continued to operate contracts and private hire and they were well pleased with the outcome.

The Saunders brothers and C.B. Tolman later held tours licences from Castletown to the Borstal, via Fortuneswell and Grove Corner, to be operated between Whitsun and 30th September at a fare of 1s. An interesting clause stated that 'Only passengers who have actually landed from a steamer or motor boat shall be conveyed on this service'. As there were no through booking facilities with the steamer and motor boat owners, the drivers would have had great difficulty in knowing the source of their passengers!

The following year Victory Tours of Weymouth applied to operate a Friday-only service from the Dockyard to Weymouth station for sailors to catch the 4.45 pm Bristol train. Objections were made by Southern National, Portland Express and the other Portland operators. The application was refused by the Commissioners who were of the opinion that the work of getting the naval ratings from the Dockyard to catch a particular train was rightly and fairly that of the existing Portland operators, and the Commissioners were of the opinion that the services these people were already entitled to run were adequate for the requirements of the Navy. In this instance the powers of the Traffic Commissioners protected the small operators on the Island!

Portland Express Service

Following the problems of the July and September 1931 inquiry, three of the Portland operators decided to join forces and operate a joint service to Weymouth. Thus R.J. Fancy, F.C. Hoare, and L.A.S. Tolman each made applications to the Traffic Commissioners to operate a service between Portland Bill and Weymouth as a joint concern.

The hearing was held at Portsmouth on 17th November, 1931. Opposing the application were Southern National, the Southern Railway, and Weymouth Town Council, and the objections of both the Southern National and the railway company can be readily understood as both had a vested interest. Stating the case for the Portland operators, Mr S. Atkins said that the applicants had previously carried on what could only be described as a 'Go as you please' service, and they were asking to improve the service from being irregular and indefinite to regular and definite, and to allow three vehicles to pick up in Weymouth passengers for Portland only. He submitted that the application for the bus service was for the convenience of Portland people in particular, who wanted an improved service to Weymouth.

The objections from Southern National and the Weymouth Council embraced one another. He drew attention to the discussion with regard to the objection at the last meeting of Weymouth Town Council, remarking that

. . . almost anyone reading the report of that meeting will be impressed by the unfriendly attitude and tone towards near neighbours.

In view of the zeal and enthusiasm evinced to safeguard the interests, not so much of the public, but of the Southern National Bus Company, it left one in a dilemma, wondering whether Southern National belonged to Weymouth Corporation or if Weymouth Corporation belonged to Southern National.

Mr A.C. Savage produced a petition signed by 2,261 Portland people, together with letters of support from various local people, adding that the entire Portland Urban District Council had signed the petition. Mr B.S. Fancy told the Commissioners that the Portland operators proposed to run to Portland Bill both in Summer and Winter. Mr Savage said that Southern National took a hour and a quarter to run to Southwell, but the Portland operators proposed to do it in 35 minutes.

The result of the inquiry was not announced until May 1932 when the Commissioners granted a licence for the operation of nine journeys each way daily, the new 'Limited Stop' service to stop only at Southwell, Weston, Easton, Fortuneswell and Victoria Square.

Commenting on the result, the 'Portland Breezes' column of the *Dorset Daily Echo* for 16th May said:

Victory! If it were not for the fact the name is already well known as a motor coach service, I would suggest that Messrs Fancy, Hoare, and Tolman adopt the name of 'Victory' for their new bus service between the Bill and Weymouth Statue. Their application to run a much needed service to and from the Bill has been a long time on the stocks, but last week the Traffic Commissioners gave a much belated verdict in favour of the local men.

There has been keen opposition from the railway, the National buses, and even the Town Council of Weymouth, but the steady backing of local people must have weighed with the Commissioners. The effect is that we get nine more buses each day between Southwell and Weymouth and there will be very few long waits. I wonder what Messrs R.J. Smith and R. Hoare, the two men who had the forethought to start a regular bus service on Portland, think of the number of people who bus it nowadays?

A Portland Express Service awaits to depart from the King's Statue, Weymouth, the vehicle is Fancy's Commer Invader TK 4684. Behind stands the new bus shelter, the photograph was taken before May 1935 when the one-way system was introduced around the King's Statue and St Mary's Street.   *Omnibus Society*

AEC Regal MV 2675 outside Fancy's garage at Reforne, the AEC stickers can still be seen on the windows. When new this Brush B32R-bodied bus must have been looked very smart in the blue and orange livery of Portland Express. Becoming Southern National No. 3667 in 1936, this reliable machine ended its days on the fairground as transport for 'Dare Devil Curley' who actually was a bald-headed gentleman who dived into a tank of water from a platform.

Author's Collection

Operating under the name 'Portland Express Services', the new venture commenced on 24th May, 1932. Within weeks the Southern National applied to increase its present Summer service of 33 buses from Portland Bill to 61, and to 76 buses from Victoria Square to Weymouth compared with the 59 operated during the previous Summer. Objections were raised by Portland Express, who stated that the Southern National service from the Bill was purely seasonal and that if any extra services were granted, priority should be given to the Portland operators who ran a service from the Bill all the year.

It was the start of a 'Bus War' as accusations were made by both operators. These were heard by the Southern Area Traffic Commissioners at Weymouth in August 1932, when Southern National accused the Portland operators of running late or running ahead of schedule, running additional buses, not running or completing services, amending services, and running services not included in the schedule allowed by their licence.

Evidence given by a Southern National inspector who had been watching the Portland Express operation, spoke of three vehicles operating on one service, whilst the licence allowed for only one duplicate bus on each service. Police Sergeant Brown of Portland was asked by the Commissioner to give his own independent views. He said that he knew that the Express services had on occasions not run to time, but he could say the same thing about Southern National. He gave an instance of the Southern National's irregularity that morning. He had noticed that the Express Service had three buses arriving at the same time, but he also gave an instance of the Southern National having as many as six buses arriving at the same time at night. He said there was a duplicating of services like this when the fleet was in, in fact the only complaints that he had heard concerned the 'Express' not running enough buses!

In reply to these allegations the 'Express' operators said that they took their time from St Mary's Church clock in Weymouth, and the Portland clock could well be several minutes different. As to the operation of duplicates, Mr B. Fancy said that the service was divided between three operators. Two carried on the service in the day, and the third was a spare time man with a duplicate if required. They ran more than one duplicate bus particularly on Saturday and Sunday nights, as they had to use the extra buses to take back people who held return tickets.

Mr L. Tolman, the third operator, agreed with this view. He said he understood the licence to mean that each of the three operators was entitled to run a duplicate bus. The Commissioner Sir Reginald Ford, speaking of the duplication, explained that the operators had a timetable which had to be jointly carried out by them, and they were allowed to run only one duplicate on a service. If they wished to run two vehicles in addition to a service bus they must ask the Commissioners. Sir Reginald cautioned all operators that the timetables must be kept rigidly as regards times, fares, routes, and duplication. There was no excuse for any operator who did not know. He concluded by expressing a hope that matters in the district would run more smoothly than they had in the past.

In November 1932 the 'Express' operators applied for a modified Road Service Licence containing a revised timetable, one duplicate vehicle to be operated on each journey, except Saturdays, Sundays and Bank Holidays, when the number of duplicate vehicles should be unlimited, and a route alteration allowing the service to operate into Weymouth via the recently opened Westwey Road. Weymouth Council had recommended this to avoid St Thomas Street, which they described as narrow and congested, the route alteration taking place early in 1933.

In September 1933 Portland Express successfully applied to run an additional bus from Weymouth to Portland on Saturday and Sunday evenings and Bank Holidays. This time the objection came from the Great Western Railway, who considered that the railway facilities offered were, with the existing bus services, quite adequate. In granting the application the Chairman of the Commissioners, Sir Reginald Ford, said it was only fair to assume that no operator was going to put a vehicle on the road unless there was a need!

With the demise of the Great Western Railway buses at the end of December 1933 their timetable board at the King's Statue became disused, and in June 1934 Weymouth Council gave Portland Express permission to use this facility. In fact here was a change of policy! Weymouth Council were giving up their persistent objections to every move made by Portland operators. At the next Traffic Commissioners' inquiry, which was to be the final move for expansion by Portland Express, there was no objection from Weymouth Council, the sole objectors being Southern National and the railway companies.

An application was made for four additional journeys to be added to their service, a fare stage to be allowed from Wyke Hotel to the King's Statue, and an extension of the service through to Upwey during July and August. Traffic was on the increase during that Summer, and over 150 warships were to assemble at Portland prior to the Silver Jubilee Review. Wyke Regis was also a fast developing area, with much house building taking place. Passenger figures were rising. Portland Express carried 11,300 passengers in the first three months of 1933. For the same period in 1935 this figure had risen to 13,467, and between 1st July-30th September, 1934, 20,455 passengers used the Portland Express service.

Whilst objecting to the proposals, Southern National had to agree that there was a need for extra buses between Wyke Hotel and Weymouth during the Summer months, and at the same inquiry that company applied to increase its daily service from 74 to 123 journeys. It objected to the suggested 3d. fare from Wyke Hotel to the King's Statue, as its fare was 4d. and it would have an adverse affect on its traffic.

The extension of services to Upwey was bitterly opposed by Southern National although Portland Express only requested one stop at Radipole. After five hours of discussions the Commissioners allowed the application for four extra journeys with a fare stage at Wyke Hotel, but the fare being fixed at 4d. to balance with Southern National. The Upwey extension was refused, and Southern National was granted modifications to its Weymouth-Portland service.

Although Portland Express had gained by being able to pick up passengers at Wyke Hotel and had increased their service, they were up against the full force of a powerful company who could also rely on the backing of the railways, and it was clear to see that any future developments were going to be very hard to win - a point well expressed in the *Southern Times* of 15th June, 1935, lamenting the loss of the local bus service from Wyke Hotel.

Summer conditions demand something like a five minute bus service, and there will be obvious advantages to the public if the Portland operators were able to run a service over the Southern National route and pick up passengers at points where today crowded buses rush past waiting would-be passengers, particularly in the Clearmount and Lansdowne districts of Rodwell. The old GWR buses which ran from Radipole to Wyke Regis served the public very well as a useful connecting link, and in the larger area of operations now covered by the Southern National Company and with the economy in rolling stock the advantage may be said to be with the company and not with the general public. It is true there is a very restricted service run between Portland

and Weymouth by a number of Portland operators, but the latter find themselves up against big interest when they go before the Traffic Commissioners.

From Southern National's point of view, Portland Express was a great threat; being an express service, they had the edge for the patronage of through passengers, and the fare stage at Wyke Hotel strengthened that position by giving them a portion of the local Weymouth traffic. Apart from the other local Portland independents, whose limited licences were not a great problem, Portland Express were the only other fare stage operator in the area, and their acquisition would give Southern National a monopoly situation. Together with the Southern and Great Western railway companies, it was agreed that the purchase of the Portland Express business was desirable, and in the Spring of 1936 agreement was reached with the three operators, Portland Express being purchased for £16,851, of which just over 11 per cent was contributed by the railway companies. Of the purchase price, £11,459 was considered to be goodwill. Six vehicles from the fleets of the three owners were transferred to Southern National stock.

Southern National took over with the introduction of the Summer service in July 1936 as service No. 22E, and later the express service was integrated into the main timetable. The *Dorset Daily Echo* for the 8th July reported that 'Southern National are running three buses per hour to Portland Bill during peak times'. However, within days they had applied to the Traffic Commissioners to increase fares, although reductions were to be offered on return tickets. Part of the argument for the increase was that the opening of a cinema on the island had caused a loss of trade. A fact not mentioned at the inquiry was that the Regal Cinema had opened shortly after the introduction of the Portland Express service!

Bluebird Dennis Lancet I, TK 8937 fitted with a Dennis C32R body, awaits delivery from the builders lettered out ready to work Portland Express Services. Becoming Southern National No. 2668 in 1936, when sold for scrap in 1947 she raised £250. *Bluebird Coaches*

Richard Smith seated in his original motor vehicle a Ford 'T' with a wagonette body. The vehicle is left-hand-drive, and offers the minimum of comfort to either passengers or driver. However these Portlanders who have just boarded in Wakeham are prepared to take the chance on a dry day. *D. Smith Collection*

Richard Smith, foot on running board, with his Ford 'T', the canvas roof and sides are up, a sign of bad weather, so the unfortunate passengers will see little of the view as they travel along in what has become a motorised tent! *D. Smith Collection*

Smith & Hoare, Isle of Portland Motor Bus Company

Richard Smith's father had commenced operations in the days of horse-drawn wagonettes, and he had also provided horse-drawn hearses and other wagons. The last wagonette body was fitted onto a Ford 'T' chassis, and Richard Smith moved into the motor era.

The failure of Messrs Road Motors to extend its service from Victoria Square to Tophill must have inspired Smith to commence a service, entering into partnership with Richard Hoare, a local taxi driver.

The first vehicle for the new venture was purchased in May 1924, a second following that October. Trading under the name of 'The Isle of Portland Bus Company' to operate a service between Victoria Square, Easton and Portland Bill, thus creating not only the first regular bus service upon the island but also competition with the Easton section of the Portland branch railway. Applications to Weymouth Town Council in June 1925 to extend the service to Weymouth were refused, as it would appear were any Portland applications at that period.

In the Summer of 1925 two char-a-bancs and a third bus were added to the fleet, which operated from premises in Easton Square. One of the char-a-bancs was named *The Royal Manor*, and another *The Rocket*. The latter came to the attention of PC Cailes on the morning of 9th January, 1927, when, standing by the Royal Hotel, he saw *The Royal Manor* bus (a 14-seater) come round the bend at the Crescent on its proper side of the road into Fortuneswell. *The Rocket* - another 14-seater bus driven by Richard Hoare - came up from behind and endeavoured to pass the other. Both buses kept abreast until they were near the top of Meissner's Knap. The road was very greasy at the time and the driver of *The Rocket* bus could not have had any view of anything coming down the road. Being a two-way street in those days, it leaves little to the imagination in the event of a descending traction engine being confronted! The local magistrates were not impressed either, fining Hoare 10s. and telling him he was very lucky to retain his licence.

Later in the same month on the 25th the *Southern Times* reported:

One of Mr Hoare's buses proceeding from Tophill had just passed the Britannia Hotel at the top of Fortuneswell when it swerved to avoid an oncoming vehicle. Owing to the greasy road the bus skidded onto the pavement and ended up through some railings with part of the vehicle overhanging the drop, causing damage to the vehicle. Fortunately no passengers or passers-by were injured!

The vehicles were painted in a blue livery with the buses having 'Portland Bus Service' in large letters on the sides. Very little is known about the history of the Ford 'T', but the next four vehicles were of GMC manufacture. Although of American origin, they had right-hand drive. The last vehicle - purchased in August 1925 - was a small Chevrolet. Having acquired Messrs Road Motors in 1925 'National' soon considered extending the service to Tophill. It is said that Smith was not happy with the partnership, and 'National' took the attitude of 'either sell your service, or be pushed out by competition'. Deciding that it was better to quit whilst still winning, the business and five vehicles were sold to 'National' for a reputed £5,000, that company taking over the service on 1st February, 1927. With the exception of the Ford 'T', which had already been disposed of, the remainder of the fleet passed to the National Omnibus & Transport Company, but all were withdrawn by late 1929.

The *Dorset Daily Echo* noted the event:

PR 3275 a 14-seat GMC bus of the Smith & Hoare fleet stands at Portland Bill. It appears a 'touch-up paint job' has been applied to the off side rear corner panel. Standing alongside is L.A.S. Tolman, the 'junior' conductor is unidentified.   *C. Tolman Collection*

PR 4884 a 14-seat Chevrolet char-a-banc in the Smith & Hoare fleet stands at Portland Bill, the canvas roof up indicating it was not a glorious Summer's day. Note the tyres are fine, there appears to be no canvas showing! Passing to NOTC as No. 2389 and later Southern National, the breaker's yard of Trent, at Parkstone was her final destination.   *Author's Collection*

Omnibus Services - Portland

WE beg to advise the inhabitants of Portland and district that we have **disposed of the Omnibus and Chars-a-banc section** of our business to the National Omnibus and Transport Co., Ltd., who will take over on the 1st February, 1927.

We take this opportunity of thanking our patrons for their support during the past 3½ years and trust they will continue to give their support to the National Omnibus Company, who intend to extend and develop these services so as to give the public all the facilities possible in connection with road travel, including a through service to Weymouth.

R. J. SMITH
PORTLAND, R. R. HOARE
24th JANUARY, 1927.

Notice of transfer of business published in the *Daily Echo*, 24th January, 1927.

On February 1st the National Omnibus & Transport Company will take over the bus service to the top of the hill at Portland.

The present Portland service which was started by Mr R.J. Smith and R.R. Hoare has been in existence for 3½ years, and its value has been fully appreciated by the people living in the Tophill district. During the whole of that period not one journey was missed whatever the weather conditions. It is also noteworthy that despite the difficult route there has not been a mishap [sic]. During the General Strike additional services provided a great boon to people who had to make journeys to the underhill district or to Weymouth.

Richard Hoare returned to his taxi driving whilst Smith purchased a taxi and later several lorries, entering the haulage business for a short while. During 1934 part of the Easton premises was converted into a fish shop, the family business continuing as a combination of taxi work and fishmongers until after World War II, when his son Douglas restarted the coaching side of the business.

Smith & Hoare, Portland

No.	Reg No.	Chassis	No.	Body	Type	No.	Built	Acq.	Sold	Notes
	PR 2459	GMC K16 RH			B14		5/24	5/24	2/27	1
	PR 3275	GMC K16 RH			B14		9/24	9/24	2/27	2
	PR 4748	GMC K16 RH			C14		5/25	5/25	2/27	
	PR 4884	GMC K16 RH			C14		6/25	6/25	2/27	1
	PR 5388	Chevrolet			B14		8/25	8/25	2/27	1

Notes
1. Registered to R.J. Smith.
2. Registered to R. Hoare.

Disposals
PR 2459 To NOTC No. 3290, sold by 8/29. LO Morris, East Ham, London E6.
PR 3275 To NOTC No. 2391, 14/8/29 to SNOC No. 2391. LL 1932, LO Thompson, Gervis Wharf, Truro.
PR 4748 To NOTC No. 2392. 14/8/29 to SNOC No. 2392. LL 1930. LO Taunton Gas Company.
PR 4884 To NOTC No. 2389. 14/8/29 to SNOC No. 2389. LO Trent (breaker), Parkstone, Poole.
PR 5388 To NOTC No. 2388, sold by 5/29. LO W. Butts, Talbot Street, Yeovil.

Thomas Henry Gear, Southwell, Portland

Thomas Gear of Southwell was typical of many small operators. Having learned his trade as a motor mechanic with Messrs Ross & Garrett (later Craven Bros) of Victoria Square, Portland, he commenced operations with a Ford Model 'T'. In November 1930 it was replaced by a Ford 'AA' supplied by Crabb of Weymouth, the local Ford dealer. The new vehicle, TK 5508, was painted in an Oxford Blue livery with black mudguards and wheels, the hub caps being chrome. The mahogany body was varnished on the inside, and the seats upholstered in brown leather.

A typical day's work for the vehicle was to convey workmen from Southwell to Portland Dockyard, then return to Southwell to take children to St George's school in Reforne. After dropping the children off the vehicle would proceed to the Easton branch of the Weymouth & District Cooperative Society, from where it would deliver groceries until returning to St George's school in the afternoon. The school children would then be taken back to Southwell before proceeding to the Dockyard to collect workmen for the homeward journey to Southwell. In the evenings any private hire work that was available would be undertaken, such as taking people to whist drives and other social gatherings, whilst at weekends it was a regular feature to convey families on private outings.

Despite the other operators on the Island and Southern National, Gear had managed to secure a niche in the market, having regular customers and not being disturbed by other operators. However, like others in the business he had to conform to the 1930 Act. He was granted a special licence for the operation of his school service, a licence to convey people from the South of the Island to Grove Corner for football matches, and a limited Portland Bill-Portland Victoria Square fare stage licence, although it appears the latter had ceased by the end of 1935.

Gear continued with his service well into the war, but in 1944 the bus was laid up and Mr Gear went to work in the Dockyard. There was to be no return to pre-war activities for him, the need for his type of service having ceased to exist. The bus remained in its garage, Gear regularly starting the engine and kept the vehicle in running order. During the early 1950s it was taxed during the Summer months, and he would use it to take his family for outings around the local area. Eventually the bus was exchanged for a pre-war Ford Eight at a Weymouth car dealer's, resulting in this most interesting vehicle being broken up at Flood's scrap yard, Chickerell.

The only known picture of the Ford AA, TK 5508 owned by Tom Gear. Seen loading school children at the Eight Kings, Southwell in this pre-war view.   *Author's Collection*

Thomas Henry Gear, Southwell, Portland

No.	Reg No.	Chassis	No.	Body	Type	No.	Built	Acq.	Sold	Notes
	PR 6848	Ford T					5/26	5/26	11/30	
	TK 5508	Ford AA					11/30	11/30	12/56	1

Notes
1. LL 31/12/56.

Disposals
PR 6848 To Crabb (dealer) LO.
TK 5508 To Bournemouth Autos (Weymouth) Ltd (dealer). To Flood, Chickerell (breaker).

Eric Samuel Way

The operations of E.S. Way were, by the standards of other Portland operators, both minor and short-lived. Way's principal business was that of a coal merchant, the coach appearing to be a side-line, and only one vehicle is recorded licensed as a PSV to E.S. Way. There is little doubt that, prior to the 1930 Act, Way had been able to fit his coach activities in with the coal round! However, when affairs had to be put on a more formal footing his interest waned. As with the other operators, Way held licences for a Portland Bill-Weymouth service, Victoria Square to Grove Corner for football matches, and a Castletown-Weymouth Service for Naval ratings.

It does not appear that Way made a great success of this work, as the licences were surrendered in December 1936. His sole vehicle - a 14-seat Dennis - is reported as being in an orange livery, and remained at his premises in Chiswell until after World War II when it was towed away for scrap. However, Way remained in the coal business for many years.

Eric Samuel Way

No.	Reg No.	Chassis	No.	Body	Type	No.	Built	Acq.	Sold	Notes
	PR 9062	Dennis			C14F		5/27	5/27		1

Notes
1. Last licensed 1935. LO E.S. Way.

Eric Way stands alongside his 14-seat Dennis coach PR 9062. Acquired new in May 1927, Way did not renew his licence after 1935.
John Way

Eric Way stands in his 14-seat Dennis coach PR 9062 in Victoria Square. Behind can be seen part of the original 1865 Portland station. Way and several other coach owners are no doubt waiting for passengers off a train in the hope they will require a tour to Portland Bill.   *Author's Collection*

Frank Saunders & Leonard Saunders

The Saunders family of Chiswell, Portland, illustrate the difficulties encountered by 'outsiders' where local nick-names are used because so many people had the same surname. Alfred Saunders who was a haulage contractor, coal merchant, and also ran a tiny smallholding with a few pigs and hens, was known as 'Pump' Saunders. His two sons, Frank and Leonard, were known as 'Big Pump' and 'Little Pump'.

Both brothers commenced on their own accounts as bus operators, although the early details are vague, and a taxi service was also operated. It is almost certain that the brothers operated Ford Model 'T' or similar vehicles at the beginning, although no records to verify this remain, but there was a second-hand Crossley 14-seat char-a-banc, TA 2267, on record as being owned by one of the brothers.

However, L.J. Saunders was the driver of a 14-seat motor coach that caused an obstruction on the Weymouth Harbour Tramway on 26th July, 1928, the result being a 10s. fine.

In April 1928 A. Saunders & Sons applied to Weymouth Town Council for licences to ply for hire within the Borough, with Frank and Leonard Saunders as named drivers, but the application was refused. As with the other Portland independents, the brothers had worked as they pleased, with a combination of private hire and bus work as it suited. Following the introduction of the 1930 Act and the inquiry outlined on page 91 , both brothers held licences for a Portland Bill-Weymouth stage carriage service, Victoria Square to Grove Corner for football supporters, Castletown-Weymouth for Naval ratings, and a tour licence between Castletown and the Borstal. Frank Saunders also held a licence to operate between Chickerell and Castletown throughout the year to convey men employed on the coal hulks in Portland Harbour, this licence being discontinued in 1939.

The outbreak of war caused curtailment of both Frank and Leonard's activities, Frank joining the services and later emigrating to Canada. It appears that his bus remained in store during the war years. Leonard also had to take his bus off the road owing to the war situation, and went to work at Whitehead's torpedo factory. However, an RAF radar station was constructed at Ringstead, east of Weymouth, work commencing in January 1941, and Leonard's bus was used to convey workmen to the site, and Leonard was himself employed on the construction work. When the work was completed in May 1941 the bus was again taken off the road, and Leonard returned to Whitehead's.

In 1945 Leonard's wife, Ethel, took over Mitchell's cafe in Victoria Square and Leonard returned to his bus work. As steamers had ceased to call at Castletown pier the Borstal tour was never re-introduced, but the other licences remained the same. By the late 1940s his pre-war Albion was near the end of its working life, so JT 4425 - a 1936 Bedford WTB - was purchased from Bluebird of Chickerell, thus bringing a former Portland vehicle back to the island! The Bedford was also well past its prime and was replaced by HAA 558, a Bedford OB that had been new in the fleet of Messrs Hants & Sussex.

Following the withdrawal of Clarence Tolman in 1951, Leonard Saunders (or 'Pump Saunders' as he was then widely known) was the sole remaining pre-war Island operator still in service. Although working in an urban environment, 'Pump' had all the characteristics of a country carrier! No tickets were issued, and his young son acted as conductor until daughter Elsie was old enough to take over, and she remained working with her father until the business was sold.

During the National Bus Strike of July 1957 'Pump' became a local hero when he ran a service to convey girls from Portland who worked for F.W. Woolworth in Weymouth. Following an earlier incident at Weymouth railway station, he was stopped by pickets at both Victoria Square and on Weymouth seafront whilst conveying the Woolworth's girls. After the third day the service ceased running when it was discovered the girls were paying their own fares as a 'private hire'. The hire charge should have been paid after the event on a bill supplied by the operator. Two days later Saunders complained to the local press that sugar had been put into the petrol tank of his coach, and the engine was not running very sweetly!

In February 1962 the business and vehicle were sold to Douglas Smith, 'Pump' then returning to taxi driving until ill health overtook him, and he passed away in 1977 aged 70. His wife closed the cafe in 1984, thus bringing to a close a chapter in Portland's history. No more would that familiar whine of a Bedford gearbox be heard as 'Pump' brought sailors into Weymouth for an evening's enjoyment!

Frank Saunders, Portland

No.	Reg No.	Chassis	No.	Body	Type	No.	Built	Acq.	Sold	Notes
	TA 2267	Crossley			CB14		1921			1
	TK 2719	Willys O/Land			C19		5/29	5/29		
	RU 6875	Dennis	70103		C20		1928	6/39		

Notes
1. Which brother actually owned TA 2267 is not recorded.

Previous Owners
TA 2267 First registered to Rowse, Miller, Okehampton, as goods lorry, 9/21. To Somerset owner 10/21.
RU 6875 New to 'Charlies Cars', Bournemouth, No. 14.

Disposals
TA 2267 LL Saunders, 12/28. LO Saunders.
TK 2719 LO W.E. Masters, haulage contractor, Lychett Matravers.
RU 6875 Scrapped 6/45.

L.J. Saunders, Portland

No.	Reg No.	Chassis	No.	Body	Type	No.	Built	Acq.	Sold	Notes
	LJ 1991	Dennis					6/30	6/30		
	LJ 3895	Albion PH49	15001C		C20		5/31	1937	4/51	
	JT 4425	Bedford WTB	110365	Duple	C26R	6661	3/36	2/49	3/54	
	HAA 558	Bedford OB	93639	Duple	C29F	46614	3/49	3/54	1/62	

Previous Owners
LJ 3895   New to 'Charlies Cars', Bournemouth, No. 21.
JT 4425   New to 'Bluebird', Portland.
HAA 558   New to Hants & Sussex. To Fullbrook, Yateley, 6/50. To Shamrock & Rambler, Bournemouth 6/53. To Haynes (Ambassador) Christchurch 10/53.

Disposals
LJ 1991   Not known.
LJ 3865   Scrapped 4/51.
JT 4425   Scrapped. LL 4/54.
HAA 558   To Smith, Portland.

Clarence Bernard Tolman

C. B. Tolman had set himself up in the transport industry by 1934. Prior to this he had been employed as a driver by 'National', and was in fact the driver who had a vehicle run back on Longhill, Weymouth, on 28th August, 1928.

Any operations before the 1930 Act are not recorded, but following the Act he held three licences covering a daily fare stage service between Portland Bill and Weymouth, specials from Victoria Square to Grove Corner for football matches, and Castletown-Weymouth Lower Bond Street as an irregular service for Naval ratings when the fleet was in. To these was later added a Borstal tour licence.

World War II brought restrictions, and his vehicle was out of service between June 1942 and June 1946, whilst Tolman was engaged on Government work in the Dockyard.

The only recorded vehicles owned by C.B. Tolman were a second-hand Crossley which he replaced by a second-hand Bedford WLB from a Bristol coach company.

There was little trade post-war, and Tolman ceased operating in 1951, after which he took up taxi driving.

Clarence Bernard Tolman, Portland

No.	Reg No.	Chassis	No.	Body	Type	No.	Built	Acq.	Sold	Notes
	AF 2282	Crossley			CB		1919	b/34	1937	1
	AHW 989	Bedford WLB	109823	Duple	C20F	4347	8/34	1/37	11/51	2

Notes
1. Ex-RAF vehicle.
2. Out of service June 1942-June 1946.

Previous Owners
AF 2282   Dowman, Mevagissey.
AHW 989   G.A. Gough 'Queen of the Road', Bristol.

Disposals
AF 2282   Not known.
AHW 989   Elliott Chickerell, Weymouth (haulier), engine removed, vehicle scrapped.

Leslie Alfred Samuel Tolman

As with several other Portland operators the exact point at which Leslie Tolman (also known as 'Gunner Tolman') commenced as a bus operator is lost in the passage of time. Several early photographs show him standing beside a bus belonging to Smith & Hoare, which would suggest that he was originally one of their drivers, although it was not unknown for the Portland owners to drive each other's vehicles if the need arose! He was also photographed driving what appears to be a Ford Model 'T' with a wagonette body.

By 1927 Tolman had become established to the extent of purchasing a Reo coach, and it would appear that this was used until the arrival of the Morris Bus in May 1932. With Tolman's involvement in Portland Express and its limited seating, to conform with the other two partners an AEC 32-seat bus was acquired in April 1935.

Prior to the 1930 Act Tolman had conducted the 'go as you please' type of operation that had suited the Portland operators. However, after the formation of Portland Express he held only one licence to operate the Portland Bill-Weymouth service jointly with Fancy and Hoare.

As with the majority of Portland operators the buses were in a blue livery. Early vehicles are difficult to trace, but there is the photograph of DL 209, and in the Dorset County taxation records a 20 hp Ford van, FX 4608, registered in May 1919, is shown as last owner L.A.S. Tolman, and this chassis could well have been converted into a char-a-banc. Also registered in Tolman's name in June 1921 was a five-seat Ford saloon, Hackney, which indicates that like others he was also involved in taxi work. The taxi was last licensed in June 1927, by which time the Reo coach had been acquired.

The Reo, named after the company founder Ransom Eli Olds, was of American descent although built in Britain. The *Commercial Motor* described it as 'A Coach Chassis on Car Lines', and it certainly had a reputation for speed! The six-cylinder 24.3 hp petrol engine, multi-disc clutch, and three-speed gear box were well advanced for the time, as was the use of Lockheed hydraulic brakes on all four wheels. The body on Tolman's Reo was fitted with celluloid side windows, and a pull-over hood type of roof, which was to become dated within a few years. On each side of the body two winged crests proclaiming 'The Reo Vulture' were displayed. Sold in 1934, the Reo had a long career. Despite having become so quickly dated, it survived with various Hampshire operators until 1948!

The Morris 'Viceroy' (or 'Y' type) purchased in May 1932 was one of two types of purpose-built single-deck bus chassis produced by Morris Commercial Motors. The Viceroy was powered by a six-cylinder side-valve engine with a cylinder bore of 85 mm and a stroke of 125 mm, delivering 74 bhp. The transmission was via a single plate clutch, four-speed sliding mesh gearbox and spiral bevel back axle, servo-assisted brakes being fitted to all wheels. It was reputed that speeds of 60 mph could be obtained on a good road! The complete 14 ft wheelbase chassis cost £595.

In April 1935 an AEC Regal '4' was purchased, the same model as MV 2675 owned by Fancy, the main difference being that the 32-seat body was constructed by Lee Motors Ltd of Bournemouth. Following the takeover by Southern National this vehicle gave many years of service, latterly at Bridport. Interestingly, almost at the end of its life the Lee Motors body was replaced at Bideford works during 1949 by an unidentified 'Eastern Counties' body from a Southern National Bristol 'J' type, after which little mileage was run, the vehicle being stored at Yeovil during 1950 until disposal.

DL 2009 appears to be a Ford model 'T' fitted with a wagonette body. Leslie Tolman is the driver, it is uncertain if he was the owner or just driving for someone else. All we can be certain of is the vehicle was originally registered in the Isle of Wight.   *C. Tolman*

Leslie Tolman at the wheel of his Reo coach PR 8628, faintly on the side of the vehicle two badges proclaiming 'Reo Vulture' can be seen. A rather reckless young lady, second from left, is not wearing a hat!   *C. Tolman*

With the sale of Portland Express to Southern National, Tolman received £3,800 for goodwill and £993 for the AEC bus. Retiring from the bus business, he took over the Mermaid Inn, Wakeham. He later purchased the house next door and converted it into a garage. Installed outside was a pump selling 'Blue Star' petrol at 1s. 5d. a gallon. In 1938 he added the Pennsylvania Tea Gardens to his interests. Unfortunately the outbreak of war curtailed this activity, his involvement in war work and the decline in the licensed trade caused him to leave the Mermaid Inn several years later.

Leslie Alfred Samuel Tolman, Portland

No.	Reg No.	Chassis	No.	Body	Type	No.	Built	Acq.	Sold	Notes
	DL 2009	Ford T?								3
	PR 8638	Reo			C		4/27	4/27		
	TK 7914	Morris Vic	RP071	London Lor.	B20 F		5/32	5/32	1936	
	ARU 673	AEC Regal	642153	Lee	B32R		4/35	4/35	5/36	1, 2

Notes
1. Sold to SNOC as part of the Portland Express operation.
2. Fitted with unidentified Eastern Counties body from SNOC Bristol 'J' type in 1949.
3. Fitted with wagonette type body, ownership by Tolman unsubstantiated.
FX 4608   Ford 20 hp van registered 5/19. W. Bedford, Bere Regis. LO L. Tolman.
FX 5246   Crossley 25 hp van registered 1/20 to R.O. Roberts, St Mary Street, Weymouth. LO L.A.S. Tolman. This vehicle and FX 4508 could well have been converted into a char-a-banc.

Disposals
PR 8638   LO F.R. Purchase, Taunton, as a Reo lorry. LL 1935.
TK 7914   To Ewen, Pioneer Coaches, Petersfield. 8/42 to Odiham Motor Services. To Creamline, Bordon. LO Graceline Coaches, Alresford, Hants. LL 12/48.
ARU 673   SNOC No. 3671 in 1936 sold 1950.

Robert John Fancy

Robert Fancy commenced operating a taxi from premises in Reforne following World War I. Shortly after this he was joined by brothers Walter and William, and two Crossley char-a-bancs were acquired.

The usual range of excursions were operated, one of the most popular destinations being Cheddar Caves, and added to these outings various private hire work was carried out. It was whilst undertaking a private hire contract that a fatal accident occurred on Ridgeway Hill on Saturday 5th August, 1922.

Two char-a-bancs had conveyed a party of workmen from Portland Urban District Council on a day's outing to Bridgwater. Returning at 11.45 pm the leading vehicle - a Crossley FX 8740 - driven by Robert Fancy was descending Ridgeway and just after crossing over the railway bridge the foot brake failed. Fancy applied the handbrake and changed down into third gear, but this failed to slow the vehicle sufficiently as it headed towards the hairpin bend. Fancy attempted to steer the vehicle around the bend. This he managed, but as he came out of it he swerved into a wall, the char-a-banc overturning, all but one of the 14 occupants being trapped under the vehicle.

Many of the passengers had serious injuries, there being great difficulties in removing the injured to hospitals owing to the lack of ambulances and other facilities that we take for granted today. One of the seriously injured, William Collins Way, later died. Way was 82 years of age and it was his first ever char-a-banc trip! Many of the injured were unable to return to work for many weeks, a situation which caused great

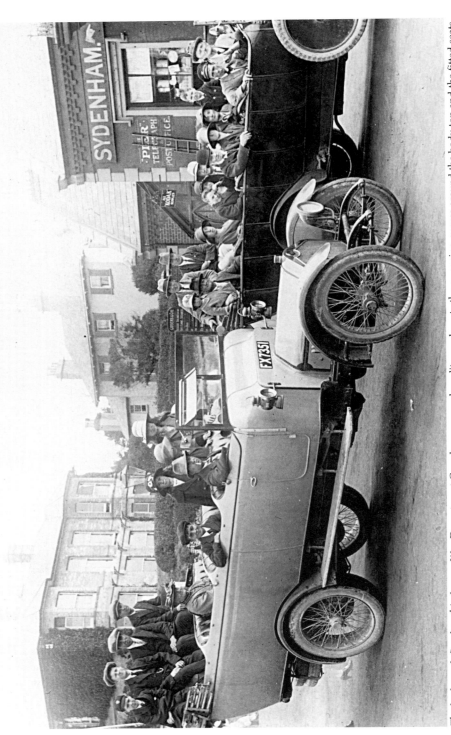

The bodywork fitted to this former War Department Crossley was good quality work, note the sweeping curves around the body top and the fitted seats. Only the small bonnet betrays the fact a small 20/25 hp engine was fitted. FX 7351 on an outing from Portland to Bournemouth stands near Bournemouth

hardship in those days. However, the people of both Weymouth and Portland set about with fund raising events, and £493 12s. 8d. - a considerable sum - was raised.

The subsequent inquest revealed the lack of rules governing the operation of passenger carrying vehicles at that time. The Coroner said: 'I think it is quite time that the provisions of the Railways Regulation Act should apply to any accidents that come from motor coaches or motor traffic on the roads, and that an Inspector from the Board of Trade especially versed in these matters, [be appointed] to deal with every accident'. In the Coroner's jury of seven men were Percy A'Court, foreman, and Mr Bell - both being involved with the Weymouth Motor Company Ltd - who asked searching questions into the accident.

Fancy told the inquest that a new handbrake and foot brake had been fitted earlier in the Summer, and both had been checked the previous evening. He descended Ridgeway hill steadily in top gear, but as he crossed the tunnel over the railway he felt the foot brake give way altogether. Travelling at about 10 miles per hour, he changed down into third gear and applied the hand brake, but it did not grip as it usually did and only steadied the vehicle. He chanced getting around the corner, but the vehicle turned over. There followed much discussion between A'Court, Bell and Fancy over the use of the handbrake and the gears, the driver explaining that he had descended Portland hundreds of times using the foot brake only.

The braking system on the vehicle consisted of a foot brake that acted as a transmission brake on the propeller shaft, and a handbrake that acted on rear wheel drums. Following the accident the vehicle was examined by Mr Shepstone, an Upwey garage proprietor, who found that the foot brake had failed owing to the adjustment nut having worked back, there being no split-pin hole to secure the castellated nut.

The jury exonerated the driver of all blame, and summing up, the Coroner said that somebody should be answerable for testing cars before they were licensed, and a driving test should be taken by prospective drivers. There was much criticism of the fact that Weymouth did not possess a motor ambulance, a matter taken up by the local press. Before the end of the month a meeting had been called, and with much help from Mr H.G. Day, the Rodwell station master (himself a railway first aider), the Weymouth St John's Ambulance Brigade was formed. Early in 1923 Weymouth Town Council purchased a motor ambulance. William Collins Way did not die in vain.

Despite the setback of the Ridgeway Hill accident Fancy's business prospered, although brothers William and Walter returned to quarry work. Other char-a-bancs were added to the fleet, followed by a Commer coach. The 1930 Act caused Fancy to join forces with Hoare and Tolman for his fare stage service licence as described in the Portland Express section. However, he held his own Tours & Excursion licences, and in March 1933 licences were granted for an express service between Portland Dockyard and Plymouth and Portland Dockyard and Portsmouth, exclusively for Naval Ratings stationed at Portland. The Plymouth service was extended to Devonport after February 1935.

The fleet was painted in a livery of mid blue, and at least one of the char-a-bancs carried a crest on its side, whilst vehicles used on the Portland Express service had an orange band at waist rail level with the words 'Portland Express Services' painted thereon.

Fancy chose the Crossley chassis for his first char-a-bancs, many of which were Government surplus, having been constructed for the Royal Flying Corps. It was a well constructed chassis which was in reality a large car, most having served as staff cars, ambulances and tenders during World War I and had proved very reliable machines. The smaller version was powered by a four-cylinder 20/25 hp engine and the larger version fitted with a 25/30 hp 4½ litre side valve engine. Well suited for a

Crossley FX 8740 stands outside Fancy's garage in Reforne, a useful lightweight machine with a good performance record during World War I with the Royal Flying Corps. The Crossley like the Ford 'T' was an exceptional vehicle and the backbone of many small businesses in the 1920s.
Dennis Fancy

The fatal char-a-banc accident on Ridgeway Hill on 5th August, 1922, detailed on page 109. The hairpin bend is away to the left. It is unfortunate incidents like this that give transport historians the rare view of the underside of a vehicle, in this case FX 8740. *Dennis Fancy*

GH 1758 waits at Portland Bill for the return of the passengers, this a slightly larger Crossley with fixed side windows. Above the rear wheels note the garter crest with 'Fancy Bros Portland' inscribed on the inside. *Dennis Fancy*

char-a-banc or small bus, many were converted. Details of the brake system having already been described, there is little else to note except the unusual wire-spoked wheels which were held on the axles by 'spinner nuts', racing car style! The rear wheels also often had two pneumatic tyres fitted to each rim.

Although the Crossley char-a-bancs had served well, changing times demanded newer vehicles. Crossley FX 7351 was taken in part exchange by Tilley's garage of Weymouth, for a new Commer Invader 6TK coach at the end of April 1930. Fitted with a front entrance Willowbrook body, complete with sliding roof, and powered by a six-cylinder Humber petrol engine, for a short while it was the most modern coach on the island. Although a coach and not a bus, it was in the early days of Portland Express Fancy's principal vehicle in the combine.

Although this was not one of the vehicles acquired by Southern National with the Portland Express takeover, it later became Western National No. 3791 upon the takeover of Martin Bros of Ponsanooth, Cornwall, in January 1947. Then reported as being in almost scrap condition, it never entered service in the Western National fleet.

In January 1933 Fancy purchased an AEC Regal '4' fitted with a Brush 32-seat bus body. Most AEC Regals, particularly coaches, were fitted with a six-cylinder engine, but despite the steep climb on Portland the four-cylinder AEC A139 type OHV petrol engine was chosen, with a bore of 112 mm and stroke of 130 mm, developing 80 bhp at 2,400 revs. Transmission was via a single-plate clutch and four-speed gear box, and triple Servo brakes were fitted.

MV 2675 was an interesting vehicle, and like several other Regal '4' chassis of the period, it had been destined to become a six-cylinder model with chassis No. 6621258, but when fitted with a four-cylinder engine it was designated No. 642020. New in June 1932 it was first employed by AEC as a demonstrator, hence the Middlesex registration. The story goes that when Robert Fancy had the vehicle for a trial period, he was so impressed by its pulling power that he told the AEC salesman 'that's the vehicle I want!' When the salesman told him he would arrange for a new vehicle to be delivered, Fancy replied, 'No! This one or nothing!' As a new AEC chassis cost almost £1,000, the demonstrator, which was disposed of in time, was sold to complete the deal.

This purchase was a good decision, MV 2675 serving both Fancy and Southern National well. She was delicensed at Bideford in late 1945 and for most of 1946, but by

April 1949 she was operating from Bridport garage. In the July, the wooden seats that had replaced the original red leather ones had again been replaced by upholstered ones. Delicensed again at the end of September 1950, the vehicle returned to Weymouth where it remained until sold in September 1952 for £40 to 'Dare Devil Curley', a fairground performer, whose act was to dive from a tower into a tank of water!

In May 1935 and January 1936 two Bedfords were added to the fleet, JT 2855 being a WTL chassis whilst JT 4140 was a WTB model, the Duple body having a sliding door at the rear. JT 4140 was also the third production WTB built. Both vehicles passed into Southern National ownership, JT 2855 becoming No. 3669 and JT 4140 No. 3670, both vehicles staying in the Weymouth area.

No. 3670 was commandeered by the Army from Weymouth depot on 13th July, 1940, and not returned to the company. She was disposed of at an auction at Weyhill, Hampshire, during 1944 being purchased by a small Gloucestershire operator, Russell, of Wormington. The original registration documents had been lost, so the vehicle was re-registered as FAD 827, and continued in service with Russell until 1951 when it was purchased by a Cheltenham contractor, Costelloe & Kemple, who used it for staff transport for a further year.

The sale of Portland Express was a turning point for Robert Fancy. Taking his share of the proceeds, £1,721 for the three vehicles transferred and £5,409 for goodwill, he withdrew completely from the motor coach business, and concentrated his efforts in taxi work and the motor repair trade for both cars and commercial vehicles, the business at its peak employing 20 staff.

Handing the business over to son Dennis in the late 1960s, Bert Fancy never in reality retired, visiting the garage every day until his later years. In 1985 the business was sold to Mr Geoff Smith, but unfortunately declining trade caused it to close in late 1989, and the site was later cleared for future development. Robert John Fancy died on 28th March, 1987 at the age of 89, the last survivor of the original independent Portland operators.

Robert John Fancy

No.	Reg No.	Chassis	No.	Body	Type	No.	Built	Acq.	Sold	Notes
	FX 7351	Crossley 8J	10169		CH		6/21	6/21	4/30	
	FX 8740	Crossley			CH		1922	1922		2
	GH 1758	Crossley			CH					
	TK 4684	Commer Inv	28036	Willowbrook	C20F	2391	5/30	5/30	5/36	
	MV 2675	AEC Regal 4	642020	Brush	B32R		6/32	1/33	5/36	1, 3
	JT 2855	Bedford WTL	875105	Wilmott	C26F		5/35	5/35	5/36	1
	JT 4140	Bedford WTB	110205	Duple	C26F	6660	1/36	1/36	5/36	

Notes
1. Sold to SNOC as part of the Portland Express operation.
2. Vehicle involved in the fatal crash on Ridgeway Hill 22/8/22.
3. Had been an AEC demonstrator.

Disposals
FX 3651 LL 4/30 to Tilleys (motor dealers), Weymouth. LO.
FX 8740 Not known. LO Fancy Bros.
GH 1758 Not known.
TK 4684 1936, Julian, Grampound Road by 8/39 with Rogers, Penryn. 11/45 to Martin, Ponsanooth. 1/47 to WNOC No. 3791. Licence records show LO WNOC. LL 12/46. Scrapped 7/47.
MV 2675 SNOC No. 3667. 5/36. Sold 10/52 for £40 to 'Dare Devil Curley' renowned for his Dive of Death.
JT 2855 SNOC No. 3669 5/36. Sold 23/1/47. LO J.D. Williams, Oxford. LL 12/49.
JT 4140 SNOC No. 3670 5/36. Commandeered by the Army 13/7/40. Purchased from Government auction in Hampshire 1944 by Russell of Wormington, Glos. Re-registered FAD 827. 1951 to Costelloe & Kemple, contractors, Cheltenham. Disposed of 1952.

F.C. Hoare, Bluebird Coaches, Portland

Frederick Cecil Hoare commenced operations in 1924, and by 1927 the first of two Chevrolets had joined the fleet. The main trade at the time was private hire, short tours, and running from both Portland and Easton stations to Portland Bill during the Summer months. The operation was run from the owner's house in High Street, Fortuneswell, whilst the vehicles were garaged in Brandy Row.

As fully described on page 93, Hoare became a member of the Portland Express syndicate in 1932. Following the 1930 Act, Hoare held a fare stage licence Portland Bill-Weymouth, worked jointly with Fancy and Tolman as 'Portland Express'. On his own account from July 1933 he held Express Service licences, Portland Dockyard-Portsmouth, exclusively for officers and men of HM Fleet, and Portland Dockyard-Devonport exclusively for Naval ratings.

With the sale of Portland Express to Southern National, Hoare received £3,963 for goodwill and £1,061 for the two vehicles taken over, a Dennis Lancet bus and a Bedford coach. Whereas his partners retired from the bus business, Hoare had kept one Bedford coach that had not been included in the takeover, and immediately he purchased a Dennis Lancet coach, and the following year a second Bedford. He thus continued to operate private hire, tours and Naval leave services.

The Portsmouth service was to cause controversy with both Southern National and the Southern Railway. Having purchased the Portland Express undertaking at great expense to remove competition, they were again faced with it - a clear case of *deja vu*!

Although the service had been licensed since 1933, and had been run in its previous unlicensed form from the late 1920s, when the licence came up for renewal in 1937 it required the authority of both the Western and South Eastern Traffic Commissioners. The latter objections from Southern National which having bought out Hoare's Fare stage service without taking the precaution of also acquiring his Express Service licence, now found itself in competition for the Naval leave services it had acquired with Greyhound!

Counsel for Southern National used various arguements concerning odd irregularities by Hoare, and stated that his licence as issued by the late Southern Area Commissioners, although not precisely restricted, was 'understood' by all concerned to confine him to leave traffic from visiting ships. However, the wording of the licence simply said 'Exclusively for officers and men of HM fleet', making no mention or distinction of Depot ships, etc.

After hearing the evidence, the Commissioners decided that the service could be operated throughout the year when leave was granted to 'Naval ratings at Portland or Weymouth, other than ratings from Depot ships and establishments' and issued the necessary licence. Two weeks later the South Eastern Commissioners amended the licence without approaching the parties concerned, this action later causing them embarrassment, as the Western Traffic Commissioners thought otherwise of the 'depot ships and establishments' clause, resulting in appeals by Hoare against the South Eastern decision, and Southern National against the Western area decision!

Several points of interest were raised. Most express services operations ran regularly, whereas these ran when required. There was difficulty in defining exactly what the words 'Depot Ship and Establishment' meant! It was stated that many ranks wore no distinguishing hat band, and Portland Depot had a large floating population whose hat bands (if any) carried the names of seagoing ships! There was also the difficulty of a coach driver questioning his passengers about their ships.

The Bluebird fleet lined up outside the Pennsylvania Castle, Portland in 1937. To the left Dennis Lancet II, C32F, JT 5828, Bedford WTB C26R, JT 4425 and JT 7273. The Dennis cost £1,200 complete, fitted with a Duple body, as were the Bedfords. JT 5828 was requisitioned by the Army in 1940. The two Bedfords

Owner of Bluebird Mr Frederick Cecil Hoare sits at the wheel of one of his Chevrolet coaches, probably PR 8969. Although visiting Cheddar, some of the ladies could well be going to a millinery contest.
Harold Cailes Collection

The Appeal was heard at the Ministry of Transport offices, London, during 1938 by Mr Willoughby Bullock, who was of the opinion that the second revised condition imposed by the South Eastern Commissioners was *'ultra vires'*. It was not competent for them to amend their decision without carrying out the formalities which would enable the parties to object to the amendment - the Treasury Solicitor took the same view. Mr Bullock found that the Western Commissioners were right, and recommended that an order be made on the South Eastern Commissioners allowing the appeal of Hoare against the first revised condition. It was agreed that Hoare's licence since 1933 had permitted him to pick up ratings from depots, and in 1936 he commenced to convey depot ship men who had previously travelled by the predecessors of Southern National. Southern National alleged that the traffic had been won by offering irregular facilities, but Hoare countered that the men were dissatisfied with the service provided by Southern National although neither party proved their allegations. The Minister of Transport accepted that the Commissioners had no power to amend their decision, and therefore it was invalid.

However, some interesting statistics were produced at the hearing. The fare was 10s. 6d. return, 8s. 6d. day return, and between 11th July, 1936 and 19th June, 1937, 903 passengers were carried on 54 journeys covering 10,492 miles raising a revenue of £461 16s. 6d. During that period seven vehicles had been run as duplicates to carry another 113 passengers, raising £52 10s. 6d.

The Bluebird fleet commenced with the usual small Ford and Crossley chassis of the period, these being later joined by Chevrolets. With the commencement of the Portland Express operation in May 1932 a Morris 'Viceroy' was purchased, a sister vehicle to that owned by L.A.S. Tolman, the mechanical details of which are described in that section. With the success of Portland Express a larger vehicle was required, and in March 1933 Hoare purchased a Dennis Lancet I. Although the Lancet chassis cost only £650 (the AEC Regal being over £1,000) it was a solid, reliable chassis with up to date features including braking on all four wheels on the Dewandre-Lockheed system. The D3 type four-cylinder side valve petrol engine with 110 mm bore and 150 mm stroke developed 85 bhp, a double-plate clutch and four-speed 'crash' gearbox forming the transmission system, the 'back to front' gear selection - a Dennis feature - catching out some drivers! Complete with a Dennis-built body, the entire vehicle cost about £1,100 and was thoroughly reliable.

A 26-seat Bedford WTL coach was added to the fleet in April 1936. The WTL was a modified 'goods' chassis but was well suited as a PSV, although it was replaced by the WTB - a purpose built PSV chassis - a year later. In 1936 Hoare purchased a WTB chassis, and a second the following year, all three vehicles having been fitted with Duple coach bodies of which nine variations were offered by the builders. The WTL had a front entrance, whilst the two WTB coaches had rear entrances. So popular was the Bedford coach that by 1939 it was claimed that 70 per cent of coaches being sold for the lightweight end of the market were Bedfords. It is said that Hoare had another Bedford on order at the outbreak of war. Needless to say, it never arrived!

When a heavy weight vehicle was required towards the end of 1936 Hoare had no hesitation in purchasing a second Dennis, this time a Lancet II, a redesigned chassis of the previous model with an improved engine with overhead valves known as the 'Big Four'. It developed 100 bhp at 2,500 rpm, and the complete chassis cost just over £700. The 32-seat Dennis body gave ample leg room.

The outbreak of war in September 1939 could well have brought operations to an end, but local press adverts stated that Bluebird coaches were still available for private hire and Naval leave services. During the Summer of 1940 Hoare purchased the established business of C. Dean & Son (Monarch Coaches) of Chickerell, Weymouth. The combined fleet was operated from the Chickerell premises, the Portland chapter in the Bluebird story coming to a close.

Bluebird, Portland

No.	Reg No.	Chassis	No.	Body	Type	No.	Built	Acq.	Sold	Notes
	FX 9341	Crossley			CH					
	PR 3265	Fiat			CH		9/24	9/24		
	PR 8969	Chevrolet					5/27	5/27		
	TK 2658	Chevrolet	52175		C14		5/29	5/29		
	TK 7913	Morris Viceroy		London Lorry	C20F		5/32	5/32		
	TK 8937	Dennis Lct I	170265	Dennis	C32F		3/33	3/33	5/36	1
	JT 2698	Bedford WTL	876081	Duple	C26F	5396	4/35	4/35	5/36	1
	JT 4425	Bedford WTB	110365	Duple	C26R	6661	3/36	3/36	2/49	2
	JT 5828	Dennis Lct II	175100	Duple	C32F	7648	10/36	10/36	6/40	2
	JT 7273	Bedford WTB	11388	Duple	C26R	8989	5/37	5/37	6/52	2

Notes
1. Sold to SNOC as part of the Portland Express operation.
2. To Chickerell with the purchase of Dean (Monarch Coaches) 1940.

Disposals
FX 9341 LO Hoare.
PR 3265 LO A. Oly Ltd (builders merchants), Ramsgate. LL 1933.
PR 8969 LO Smith, Sandford Poultry Farm, Wareham. As truck LL 1933.
TK 2658 To P.G. Webb 'Dorset Queen', East Chaldon. LL 6/5/40 as 14-seat Hackney/goods.
TK 7913 To Yearsley, Cerne Abbas. To F. Whitty, Dorchester. LO W.J. Macpherson, South Newton, Salisbury.
TK 8937 SNOC No. 3668. 1/47 to Beale (dealer), Exeter, scrapped.
JT 2698 SNOC No. 3672. To N. Born, North Lew, Okehampton. LL 6/52.
JT 4425 To L. Saunders, Portland. LL 3/54. Scrapped c. 1957.
JT 5828 Requisitioned by Army 6/40. By 5/46 with Mid Wales Motorways. LO Aberystwyth Tractor Co.
JT 7273 To Smiths, Portland. LL 6/57. Scrapped 1961 by Smith.

Chapter Six

Weymouth Independent Operators 1919-1939

The Weymouth Motor Company Ltd

The Weymouth Motor Company Ltd (WMC) was formed on the 19th May, 1919, the original shareholders and Directors all being involved in the motor trade. They were Ernest William Tilley, automobile engineer, of 45 South Street, Dorchester, Percy John A'Court, Royal Garage, Gloucester Mews, Weymouth, George Francis Bugler, Rodwell Garage, Weymouth, and Henry Arthur Bell, automobile engineer, Franchise Street, Weymouth. The first two held 150 shares and the others 50 shares each. The capital of the company was £20,000 divided into 2,000 shares of £10 each. Other shareholders were three local farmers, Edward Angus Scutt of Preston, John Edward Baunton of Broadwey, and John James Wyatt of Dorchester, and Reginald Tilley, automobile engineer of Weymouth, Francis A'Court, motor car proprietor of Gloucester Row Weymouth, and Edwin John Stevens, (Secretary) of Dorchester.

Although there was this strong involvement with the existing motor trade, the WMC was established as an entirely new company, and no part of the Directors' existing companies were acquired. The company Secretary was Edwin J. Stevens, and the registered office was 6 South Street, Dorchester. Sidney Spark Milledge, of St Thomas Street, Weymouth, was appointed Auditor.

The main purpose of the company, as set out in the memorandum of association, was to 'carry on the business of the letting of hire cars, motor boats, char-a-bancs, taxi cabs, motor lorries and other mechanically propelled vehicles and engines, and the business of general carriers and forwarding agents'. Initially premises situated in Edward Street were purchased, these consisting of stables, garage, store house, and blacksmith's shop, from Mrs Alicia Kate Passmore for the sum of £1,350.

The business was in operation by September 1919, adverts in the local press announcing 'The Weymouth Express Delivery Service' with light vans running daily between Weymouth, Portland, Easton, Osmington, Upwey, and Langton Herring. Parcel agents were established at Fortuneswell, Easton, and Upwey. Heavy lorries for furniture removals and haulage work were also available.

However, the three second-hand Ford 20 hp vans purchased from the Government's Food Production Department were quickly disposed of!

It would also appear that the company was a little quick off the mark with the char-a-banc operation, an entry in the Watch Committee minutes for 22nd October, 1919 reading that:

> The Weymouth Motor Company be informed in their reply to their application for taxi and char-a-banc licences that the committee would be prepared to favourably consider same after an inspection of the vehicles. At the same time to inform the company that it has never been the practice of the Council to issue any licences without first inspecting the vehicles.

By the middle of January 1920 additional shareholders had joined the company, including Mr Ship, the landlord of the Weymouth Hotel, Charles Foot, farmer of Bincombe, William Cosens, surgeon, and Edgar Mitchell, the company manager who held a modest five shares. The first char-a-banc, FX 5042 - a Daimler CK - was acquired in November 1919, followed by three Oldsmobiles in February 1920, and

Weymouth Motor Company Daimler CK, FX 7322, showing a good set of pneumatic tyres. The set of steps on the running board was to assist boarding and alighting from the high chassis, the entrance doors being on the near side. The driver is Bert Baker, standing alongside looking disinterested is conductor Arthur Balch who later became an inspector with Southern National.

Author's Collection

FX 4525 - an Albion from A'Court - the following month. Hackney licences for the drivers were granted by Weymouth Town Council that March. Although all seemed to be going well, Bugler resigned from the company at the same time, selling his own business and leaving the area. The passage of time has denied us any first-hand information as to his resignation, but it has to be noted that a char-a-banc owned by A'Court was taken into the WMC fleet whereas the one owned by Bugler was not! Bugler's place as a Director taken by Arthur Sylvester Hodder, a motor car proprietor of Royal Crescent, who acquired 150 shares.

At the first general meeting of the company, held on 2nd November, 1920 at Edward Street, it was stated that the Edward Street premises had been adapted to the company's requirements for a modest outlay, and a profit of £1,081 6s. 8d. had been made despite difficulties in obtaining taxi cabs, char-a-bancs and lorries. Three new shareholders had joined: Percy Cole, Harley St surgeon, Dennis Granville, the Chief Constable of Dorset, and Thomas Lynes, gentleman, of Dorchester, who was also a principal shareholder in the Tilley's Motor Business and a Director of Cosens & Company, the Weymouth paddle steamer proprietors and ship repairers.

During 1921 additional shares had been issued for the purpose of paying off a temporary loan from the bank for the purchase of char-a-bancs and taxi cabs. At the general meeting the Chairman reported that although the char-a-banc trade had been well maintained the other transport activities of the company had become retarded by the general depression in trade. Although a profit of £2,933 11s. 5d. had been made there would be no dividend and the Directors would forego their fees to place the company on a sound financial footing.

In total the company operated 12 char-a-bancs, seven Daimlers, three Oldsmobiles, a Dennis, and an Albion. The choice of Daimler was a wise one, the chassis having proved to be reliable over the years, and considering the rapid developments of the time served their masters very well. The CK chassis was one of those all-purpose models of the period, suitable for goods vehicles or both single- and double-deck buses. The wheelbase was 13 ft 6 in., and power was provided by a four-cylinder 22.4 hp engine with a cylinder bore of 95 mm and a stroke of 140 mm. Transmission was via a four-speed gearbox and cone clutch, and both the footbrake and handbrake acted on the rear wheels. In 1920 a complete chassis cost £950, rising to £1,050 the following year, but by 1925 it had dropped to £645. The Daimlers ran on solid tyres, at least until the end of the 1921 season, but the following year pneumatics had been fitted.

FX 5942, which eventually joined the Eastern National fleet and was later fitted with a double-deck body, whilst FX 5962 - also with Eastern National - was fitted with a 32-seat bus body. She finally became a showman's caravan and survived at least to 1939 - the last surviving WMC vehicle!

The three Oldsmobiles were of lightweight construction, and although popular at the time were short-lived, as the 'National' had no use for such lightweight machines. Except for FX 5333 which was acquired to obtain its body, the other two were sold privately. The Dennis, FX 5997, was also fitted with a double-deck body by National, and passing into the Southern National fleet it survived until 1933. FX 4525, the Albion, would appear to be the only vehicle not fitted with pneumatic tyres, and was disposed of to a Dorset coal merchant.

In May of 1921, when the coal strike was causing disruption and restrictions to railway services, a special bus was advertised to Dorchester, leaving the King's Statue at 10.45pm on Thursday nights and 10 pm on Sundays. That June a regular service to Bournemouth was established, departing from the King's Statue at 9 am, the journey via Dorchester and Bere Regis taking 2 hours 20 minutes. Returning at 5 pm the fare was 4s.

6*d*. return, by September 1922 being reduced to 4*s*. 3*d*. In the Winter of 1921 a 'special enclosed motor bus' left the Spa Hotel, Radipole, every evening at 7 pm with stops *en route* to the Pavilion Theatre, and returned at the conclusion of the performance.

In fact, although the weather was poor during the 1921 season, the coal strike prevented the local paddle steamers operating until 25th July, which should have provided the char-a-banc owners with extra trade. However, the third general meeting of the company held on 28th November, 1922 pointed to a disastrous year's trading. The Directors' report stated:

> Every effort has been made to increase trade, but the takings have dropped by no less a sum than £4,188 as compared with the 1921 accounts. This is chiefly noticeable in the takings from the taxi cab and motor lorry branches of the Company's business. The Summer season has been an exceptionally bad one, resulting in decreased takings. Although the accounts show a gross profit of £1,303 1*s*. 6*d*., the Directors, following their former principle, have written off a sum of £2,151 for depreciation, thus showing a loss of £847 18*s*. 6*d*. on the year's trading, and the Directors have also decided to forego their fees for the year.

The business continued through 1923, in which year WMC was the largest coach operator in the area. Its vehicles, in a light green livery, were well maintained and presented compared with many others of the time, and they also ran on giant pneumatic tyres which many others did not - a point emphasised in their adverts which regularly appeared in the local press and town guides, a degree of publicity not pursued by many other operators. The range of tours offered was the popular variety of the period, including Cheddar Caves, Lulworth Cove, the New Forest, Lyme Regis, Swanage, and Bournemouth, and tickets could be booked at the following establishments: A'Court's Garage, Gloucester Mews; Hodder's Garage, Crescent Street; Guy's Garage, the Esplanade; Bell's Garage, Franchise Street; Tilley's Garage, and Tilley's cycle shop, Weymouth; J.C. Talbot, Statue House; the Weymouth Hotel; the WMC garage Edward Street; and Tilley's Garage, South Street, Dorchester, from where passengers on tours passing through the town could be picked up.

Operating costs for the financial year ending 30th September, 1924 showed outgoings for the day to day operating of the business as £6,036 9*s*. 4*d*., and the 1924 general meeting reported a loss of £1,904 13*s*. compared with the previous year, (again the weather was blamed) and there was a shortfall of £169 3*s*. 7*d*. on income against operating costs for the year.

In their report the Directors stated that they 'have carefully investigated the whole financial position of the company and have reluctantly arrived at the conclusion that it will be in the best interest of the shareholders to wind up the business in a voluntary manner'. Following an extraordinary general meeting it was decided that the company be voluntarily liquidated, Mr E.W. Tilley, Thomas Lynes, and Percy A'Court being appointed liquidators.

The reasons for the failure of this venture are not clear, but the taxi cab and road haulage sides appeared to be the main stumbling blocks. Perhaps it is fortunate that the motor boat branch of the business was never proceeded with! As the main Directors were in the garage business on their own account and were the owners of taxi cabs it was a case of competing against themselves! Certainly there was a pool of experience, business connections, and finance available to this company that would have been the envy of many of the small operators starting up at that time, although in those days before the Road Traffic Act there were few rules or regulations and the small man could easily under-cut a larger operator. There is also little doubt that the

Directors, with the pressures of their own businesses, had little time for the attention needed to build up a coach company in the highly competitive days of the 1920s.

The Austin taxi cabs and three Leyland lorries were disposed of and, following discussions with the National Omnibus & Transport Company, a sale was agreed. For £6,200 'National' acquired the premises at Edward Street and most of the char-a-banc fleet, together with the all-important Hackney licences, early in 1925. Edward Street in its rebuilt form is still today the Southern National's depot in the town.

The final winding up meeting of the WMC took place on 22nd October, 1925. Although poor trading and weather conditions were blamed for the failure of the venture, it has to be noted that other less organised operators survived those bad Summers which also affected the paddle steamer trade. The minute books of Messrs Cosens reported poor weather and reduced trade during the summers of 1921-1924, the latter being recorded as the worst on record. Ironically, 1925 was blessed with exceptionally good weather!

The management of WMC had a professional background, so was it badly organised or simply a case of 'too many cooks'?

The Weymouth Motor Company Ltd

No.	Reg No.	Chassis	No.	Body	Type	No.	Built	Acq.	Sold	Notes
	FX 4525	Albion 32 hp			CH28		4/19	3/20	3/25	
	FX 5042	Daimler CK			CH28		11/19	11/19	3/25	1
	FX 5333	Oldsmobile			CH15		2/20	2/20	1925	
	FX 5334	Oldsmobile			CH15		2/20	2/20	1925	
	FX 5335	Oldsmobile			CH15		2/20	2/20	1925	
	FX 5523	Daimler CK			CH22		4/20	4/20	3/25	2
	FX 5836	Daimler CK	3645		CH18		6/20	6/20	3/25	2
	FX 5962	Daimler CK	3350		CH18		7/20	7/20	3/25	2
	FX 5997	Dennis 35 hp			CH30		7/20	7/20	3/25	3
	FX 6061	Daimler CK			CH22		8/20	8/20	3/25	2
	FX 7322	Daimler CK	3961		CH28		1921	1921	3/25	4
	FX 9652	Daimler CK			CH22		1922	1922	3/25	

Notes
1. Fitted with Dodson OT30/26R body by 7/26.
2. Later fitted with Strachan & Brown B32 bodies
3. Fitted with Hickman DD body 6/26.
4. Original lorry body replaced by WMC with CH30 body off FX 2410 ex-A'Court, Weymouth.

Previous Owners
FX 4525 P. A'Court, Weymouth.
FX 5997 New to G. Ford, Maumbury Garage, Dorchester 7/20 as CH20. Wine colour, to Hyde, Orchard Street, Dorchester 10/20, registered as lorry. To WMC by 3/21.

Disposals
FX 4525 To NOTC 2231, sold by 12/28. LO Pearce (coal merchant), Cattistock, Dorset.
FX 5042 To NOTC 2230, to ENOC 12/29. LO Dawson (dealer), Clapham, London.
FX 5333 To NOTC, body only required, chassis sold 31/1/26.
FX 5334 LO Grange Over Sands Motor Coach Co.
FX 5335 To P.J. Jeanes, Weymouth. Rebodied as covered bus. LO Jeanes
FX 5523 To NOTC 2228. To ENOC 12/29. LO Morris (dealer), London, E6.
FX 5836 To NOTC 2200. To ENOC 10/30 at Grays Depot. To Banfield (showman), Skegness, as goods vehicle LL 6/35.
FX 5962 To NOTC 2201. To ENOC 12/29. To Webber (showman), Streetley, Staffs, as caravan. LL 12/38.
FX 5997 To NOTC 2227. To SNOC 3/29. To Talbot (dealer), Taunton 10/33.
FX 6061 To NOTC 2229. To ENOC 12/29. LL 12/32. LO ENOC.
FX 7322 To NOTC 2223. To ENOC 12/29. LL 31/12/23. LO ENOC.
FX 9652 LO P. Hyball, Shute, Kilmington, Devon.

Daimler 'Y' type, BK 2677 belonging to George Spivey of Rambler Coaches, the photograph belies the fact this vehicle was painted in a primrose livery. Everybody appears happy despite the fact that they are riding on solid tyres, standing in front is driver Trowbridge.

Author's Collection

Rambler Crossleys stand alongside Radipole Lake, seated in EL 5754 is Harold Cailes, in KK 3564 Bill Shaves, both employed as fitters with the company, standing between the vehicles is Miss Edith Crabb, company Secretary.

H. Cailes Collection

George Spivey, Rambler Coaches

The coaching operations of George Henry Spivey are typical of the many who commenced operations in the years following World War I. It is recorded that Spivey started in the road transport business in 1908, when he inaugurated a road haulage service between Leeds and Sheffield. During the war he was employed at the Whitehead torpedo factory. In March 1919 he applied to Weymouth Council for a stand licence for one motor cab. Spivey then took premises in Gloucester Mews and formed 'The Weymouth Motor Company' (not limited). It is questionable if this was a deliberate ploy to take advantage of the name of Weymouth Motor Company Limited, (see page 119). In November 1921 Spivey applied to Weymouth Council to erect a garage of a temporary nature on reclaimed land on the Westham side of the backwater, to the north of the Portland railway bridge.

A variety of excursions, tours and private hire work was carried out. In April 1926 Spivey applied to Weymouth Council for a licence to operate six motor buses between Weymouth and Portland Victoria Square, but this was refused. At the same meeting the Watch Committee stated that they would not renew licences for his two taxis DL 909 and PR 456, for the following year, it being noted that fare charts were not exhibited in these vehicles!

In April 1927 Spivey made an application to operate a service with what he described as 'Beach Cars' along Radipole Park Drive from Westham bridge to Radipole, terminating at the junction of Milnthorpe Avenue (now the top end of Radipole Park Drive) and Spa Road. Owing to Radipole Park Drive being narrow, the Council requested specification of the vehicles to be used. By that September no such service was running, Spivey telling the Council that owing to difficulty in obtaining vehicles of the type required he was considering building them himself! By the end of June 1928 the service still had not started, and the Town Clerk was instructed to inform Spivey that unless the service commenced within seven days, the committee would grant permission to another company. The service was started at the end of July and Spivey applied to extend it along Spa Road to Dorchester Road, this request being refused. However, by that September the service had been extended to the Post Office in Spa Road without permission, Spivey's excuse to the Watch Committee being that he had done so in response to requests from local residents!

This one venture into fare stage work was operated by a small Vulcan bus which consisted of a lorry chassis with a wooden open-sided body of the 'toastrack' type constructed by Spivey himself. Tickets of the bell punch variety were issued for this journey (which cost 2*d*.), printed 'Weymouth Motor Company, Rambler Coaches. RADIPOLE LAKE DRIVE'. However, it was short-lived. In October 1930 it was pointed out to the Watch Committee that the service had not operated for nearly a year, and it was recommended that the Southern National be granted permission to operate the route.

Spivey had already incurred the displeasure of the Watch Committee; by 25th June, 1930 the Hackney Inspector had observed 29 breaches of the touting regulations that season alone. Whilst other operators were by no means perfect, their indiscretions reached only single figures! Two years earlier there had been several complaints about the methods adopted by the employees of Spivey in obtaining passengers for coach trips!

The fleet was painted in an attractive livery of dark cream, with the chassis and wheels painted in primrose, the fleet name 'Rambler' was added to the vehicles in gold block. The exact order in which the early vehicles arrived is unclear, a report in *Motor Transport* during September 1923 stating that Spivey had two Fords and a Daimler in service.

There were two Daimlers in the fleet. BK 2677 was a second-hand 'Y' type of which the origins are unknown, except it was originally registered in Portsmouth. The chassis was probably ex-War Department. PR 2650 (a 'CK' model) had been purchased new in June

The Rambler fleet line up in Hope Square before departing with a brewery staff outing. From the left Daimlers BK 2877 and PR 2650; Crossleys EL 5754 and KK 3564, Ford 'T' FX 7675 and FX 9136, the latter owned by J.O. Moore. *Weymouth Museum*

1924 and in 1929 this vehicle was rebodied with a fixed back, and side windows, the folding canvas roof sliding forward on runners. BK 2871 was a Dennis, and again this chassis was probably ex-War Department. It also had a Portsmouth registration, and again its stay with Spivey was short, the vehicle being sold to the London area in September 1925.

Two Crossleys were also purchased second-hand, but little is known about the Vulcan except that Spivey built the toastrack-type body himself. Although it was said that Spivey maintained his vehicles in good mechanical condition, they were mostly dated, and with the pending introduction of the 1930 Act, few had a future!

The operation of the Swannery garage had not been without difficulty, as there was no gas, water, or electricity laid on at the premises which was a corrugated iron structure. Originally there was no facility to refuel his vehicles either, petrol being stored at the Gloucester Mews premises in sealed two-gallon cans, his petroleum licence allowing 200 gallons to be stored. In 1925 permission was granted for the installation of a 500 gallon underground tank at the Swannery garage.

Early in 1927 Spivey vacated the Gloucester Mews garage, which was taken over by Messrs Channon & Sons, Motor Engineers. In the 1926/7 town guide the business was entered as 'Weymouth Motor Company, George Spivey engineer and motor coach proprietor, Swannery Garage, and 1 & 3 Abbotsbury Road, tele. 360'. He also had letters behind his name, AMIAE (Associate Member of the Institution of Automobile Engineers), and FIMT (Fellow of the Institute of the Motor Industry). Despite the grand sounding entry in the guide, '1 & 3 Abbotsbury Road' was just a small plot of unused land near Westham Halt.

The sands of time were running out for the Swannery garage in January 1928 as the Council was giving consideration to use the area for a coach park, and in May Spivey was given notice to quit. In January 1929 a plan was submitted by Spivey to erect petrol pumps and construct a run-in for motor cars on the Abbotsbury Road site, this idea bringing immediate protests from nearby residents. Spivey applied to extend the tenancy of the garage in January 1930, informing the Council that he had endeavoured to obtain another site but was unsuccessful, and could therefore not take down the buildings or remove the plant contained therein. A sub-committee was appointed to negotiate with Spivey with a view to ascertaining the lowest price which he would accept for some or all of the buildings.

There the matter rested until the night of 5th August, 1930, when just before 11 pm the garage caught fire. The fire spread rapidly and within a short time was an inferno. Despite the efforts of the Weymouth Fire Brigade, within two hours the building was just a mass of twisted iron. Ten coaches, the Vulcan bus and five cars were lost. Of the vehicles saved, one was a Bentley belonging to the manager of the local Midland Bank. Three employees managed to rescue the safe containing the day's takings!

As Spivey did not have 10 operational coaches in his fleet, some of those lost were what could be described as 'scrappers', being used for spares to keep others in service. The one vehicle to survive the fire was Spivey's lorry, a Ford model 'T' with left-hand drive that had been converted from a char-a-banc, which was not parked in the garage that night. Later it was used to assist in the conversion of new premises Spivey acquired, formerly stables on the corner of Gloucester Street and Gloucester Mews, the intention being to convert them into a motor coach station. Little was done in that direction. In March 1931 a new 14-seat Willeys coach was purchased. Reputed to have many chrome fittings, it would often be employed to take the young men of Weymouth to dances at Bridport on Saturday evenings for a fare of 3s.

In May 1932 a decision was made to build a cinema on the site. A private company, Picture House (Weymouth) Ltd, was formed, the Directors being Mr Oscar Deutch of Birmingham and George Spivey of Weymouth. A Dennis Dart

The morning after the night before, Monday 6th August, 1930, onlookers survey the remains of the Rambler premises following the fire. In the foreground the remains of Daimler CK PR 2650, in the background the railway arch of the Portland branch. *H. Cailes Collection*

coach with a Duple C20 body was on order, but in the meantime Spivey sold his licences and goodwill for £100 to Southern National plus £850 for the Dennis which was delivered to them as fleet No. 3393, YD 4906. The Odeon Cinema opened on Friday 2nd June, 1933, showing *Letting in the Sunshine*, and like the ending to all good films George Spivey lived happily ever after!

George Spivey, Rambler Coaches, Weymouth

No.	Reg No.	Chassis	No.	Body	Type	No.	Built	Acq.	Sold	Notes
		Ford T			CH14					4
	BK 2871	Dennis			CH		1919		b/25	1, 7
	FX 7675	Ford			CH		1921		6/24	
	FX 9174	Ford T	4691307		CH14		6/22	6/24	1927	5
	BK 2677	Daimler Y			CH28				8/30	1, 6
	EL 5754	Crossley			CH14				8/30	1
	KK 3564	Crossley			CH				8/30	1
	PR 2650	Daimler CK			CH28		6/24	6/24	8/30	1, 2
		Vulcan		Spivey	B?T				8/30	1
	TK 5890	Willys	14573		C14		4/31	4/31	12/31	
	YD 4906	Dennis Dart	75744	Duple	C20	2303	1931		1931	3

Notes
1. Vehicle destroyed in garage fire, 5th August, 1930.
2. Rebodied by Bournemouth coach builder in 1929.
3. Vehicle ordered by Spivey, but delivered to SNOC as No. 3393, registered YD 4906.
4. This vehicle was almost certainly converted to a lorry by Spivey.
5. LL 30/9/24.
6. On pneumatics by 1925.
7. Portsmouth LO card shows, transfered to Dorset CC 23/7/21, destroyed by fire.

Previous Owners
BK 2677 Not known
BK 2871 Not known.
KK 3564 Not known.
WR 2617 Not known.
EL 5754 New to H. Barnes, Bournemouth, registered as a convertible lorry/van.

Disposals
BK 2871 Transferred to LCC area 26/9/25 registered as a hackney.
TK 5890 Exported abroad, destination unknown.

Henry George Rugg

Henry George Rugg first appeared on the local transport scene in January 1915 when he registered a Fiat 30 cwt lorry, FX 2674. Rugg's home address was then 'Eppingdale', Milton Road, Westham, Weymouth. In April 1916 the Fiat was transferred to the ownership of Messrs Bryer Ash of Weymouth, coal merchants. The next two known vehicles Rugg acquired were a Daimler 30 hp in July 1919, FX 4728, which was registered as a 3-ton flat lorry painted dark green, and in the following month FX 4821 was registered as a Lacre 30 hp chassis, painted green. History does not record if either of these chassis carried a bus or char-a-banc body at any time, however a Ford 'T' bus FX 7970 was acquired in 1921.

By March 1921 Rugg had moved into garage premises formerly used by Norman Wright at 114 Abbotsbury Road, Westham, from where he operated as a haulage contractor and furniture remover. At the September Council meeting Rugg was granted a Hackney licence for vehicle FX 7970 to operate an hourly bus service between Weymouth and Chickerell. There were no reports of difficulties with the service. In November 1922 the Watch Committee approved his timetable, and all went well until 14th April, 1923 when he decided to use the vehicle to operate an excursion to Dorchester for a football cup final!

Complaints were received over the depletion to his service, and the Watch Committee then granted Rugg a three month probationary licence, after which the case would be reviewed. But the events of 14th April were to pale into insignificance within weeks as Rugg became the victim of a *Femme Fatale*. On 27th June Mrs F.M. Rugg applied to run the bus service to Chickerell, Mr H.G. Rugg having left the district! In those days of stiff competition others applied for the service, including Jeanes Bros, Smith & Miller, and Road Motors, but in the event the Council decided to allow Mrs Rugg to operate from the King's Statue via Westham, and Jeanes Bros via Pye Hill. Within a month the inevitable happened, when Mrs Rugg informed the Council that she was compelled to dispose of her interest in the bus service to Chickerell. The Council decided to transfer the licence to Jeanes Bros, who also acquired the Ford bus, FX 7970.

Henry George Rugg, Weymouth

No.	Reg No.	Chassis	No.	Body	Type	No.	Built	Acq.	Sold	Notes
	FX 4728	Daimler						7/19		1
	FX 4821	Lacre 30 hp						8/19		2
	FX 7970	Ford			B		1921	7/21	7/23	3

Notes
1. Was originally registered as a flat lorry, 3 ton, painted dark green.
2. Was originally registered as Lacre chassis 2 t. 13 cwt 3q., painted green.
3. In documents of Messrs Jeanes quoted as Ford Saloon bus.

Disposals
FX 4728 Not known.
FX 4821 Tilley's Garage (motor traders), Weymouth. LO.
FX 7970 P.J. Jeanes, Weymouth. LO.

An unidentified Ford model 'T' belonging to Jeanes. Little more than a lorry, close examination of the cab reveals a destination board 'Osmington' lying on the seat giving a clue that this vehicle actually operated a bus service.   *A.G.H. Jeanes*

Jeanes' White Star bus outside the Turks Head Inn at Chickerell; note the use of a star instead of the word in the fleet name of the red and cream liveried vehicle, which could be a Dennis.   *Author's Collection*

P.J. Jeanes & Company, White Star Bus Services

The Jeanes family became involved in the omnibus and garage trade following World War I. The main driving force behind setting up the business was Percy John Jeanes. Born in 1887, he was employed as a chauffeur to various gentlemen, and in June 1915 he became chauffeur to Albany Ward, who was operating civil and military cinemas in the Southern Counties. Just over a year later Jeanes decided to commence business on his own account, but within a short while he was called to the Colours, becoming a driver in the RASC.

Returning from the Army in March 1919 Percy Jeanes took over the Military Cinema in Abbotsbury Road Weymouth, this having been run by Albany Ward for the Australian Army camp situated nearby. At this point he was joined by his brother Cyril Edward Jeanes who had previously been a taxi driver with George Bugler of Rodwell Mews garage. As Jeanes Bros they commenced a taxi business, and a bus service from Weymouth to Preston, Sutton Poyntz, and Osmington Mills. This must have been successful, for in April 1922 Weymouth Council granted permission for two additional vehicles to be added to the route.

As previously stated, the affairs of H.G. Rugg allowed Jeanes an opportunity to expand operations in the Chickerell direction, when in July 1923 he was granted a licence to operate to Chickerell and Langton Herring, the route from the King's Statue being via the Town bridge, North Quay and Chickerell Road. A month later he acquired the licences and service of Rugg, together with Ford bus FX 7970, gave Jeanes a monopoly of the Chickerell area.

The dark nights of winter were to bring forth the first problem. In October 1923 the Clerk of Chickerell Parish Council was instructed to write to the owners of the buses, asking 'that proper lighting should be maintained inside, and better headlights outside be provided on their Chickerell bus service'.

In March 1924 the fleet consisted of four Ford and two Dennis saloon omnibuses. At this stage a partnership was formed with George Davis Morrice to inject new capital into the business. Two new vehicles were purchased; a Daimler char-a-banc (PR 2220), at the end of March, and a GMC bus (PR 7548) a few weeks later in May. The trading name was also changed from Jeanes Bros. to P.J. Jeanes & Co. and it would appear that Cyril Jeanes departed from the business around this time, setting up as a carrier at Alton Pancras, and taking with him Ford saloon bus FX 6416.

By April 1924 Percy Jeanes had taken over from Mrs Florence Rugg as occupier of 114 Abbotsbury Road. In June 1924 an application was granted for the erection of 'over the pavement' petrol pumps at the premises, Lorries were also operated, mainly employed on contracts to various local businesses including the power station and the gas works, but as these organisations obtained their own vehicles the lorries were replaced by furniture vans.

The arrival of 'National' in March 1925 was to have a profound effect on future bus services, and Jeanes were the first to feel the effect of a capacious company. At a Council Meeting held on 22nd July, 1925 members were informed of a letter from the National Omnibus & Transport Company stating that they had been approached by Messrs Jeanes, and they were taking over the services operated by the latter between Weymouth and Chickerell, and proposed extending them to Abbotsbury. On 30th July, 1925 'National' accordingly commenced operating a half-hourly service to Chickerell, and four services a day through to Abbotsbury.

Jeanes had never advertised the Chickerell service in the Town Guides of the period, whereas the Preston and Osmington Mills services - which no doubt were more successful - received full page advertising in the Guides between 1923-1928. However, owing to the problems of turning what were described as 'large buses' at Osmington Mills, in the Summer of 1926 the Council licensed small Crossleys FX 5736 and CX 3681, provided they were used on that route only.

Despite having handed the Chickerell service over to National, Jeanes were looking towards expansion in other directions. In July 1926 the Weymouth Corporation Hackney Inspector reported that Messrs Jeanes had made an application for permission to operate an omnibus service between Weymouth and Dorchester, but this was later withdrawn.

Lack of staff discipline was a cause of complaints frequently brought to the attention of the Watch Committee. In October 1924 a letter complaining of excessive overloading was received. The Hackney Inspector had cautioned driver D. Buttle for carrying passengers on the platform of his bus in a manner dangerous to such passengers. But this caution being apparently ignored, in June 1926 the Town Clerk informed Messrs Jeanes that unless driver Buttle carried out the instructions of the inspector, the committee would consider the question of suspending his licence. In March 1927 the Town Clerk received a complaint that a driver had filled his petrol tank whilst smoking and whilst passengers were on the bus, and that particular vehicle had no emergency door at the back! Further complaints were made about drivers and conductors smoking whilst the vehicles were travelling with passengers, overcrowding, and the condition of the vehicles. The Town Clerk was instructed to communicate with Messrs Jeanes drawing their attention to the complaints, and requesting that P.J. Jeanes attend the next meeting of the Watch Committee!

It was only to be a matter of time before 'National' took an interest in the routes to the east of the Town. A letter to the Council in May 1928 from the National Omnibus & Transport Company stated that it had taken over the White Star Omnibus Company, and requested that licences held by P.J. Jeanes be transferred. This brought to an end the stage carriage services operated by Jeanes. Until that time the fleet had been known as 'White Star Bus Service', the fleet name on the side of the vehicles being unusual as it incorporated a star symbol instead of the word. The main colour scheme of the vehicles was red, with white relief and roofs. The Williamson, bell punch type ticket system was employed, the tickets being printed 'White Star Bus Service'. This was unusual for a small operator, as most used a standard nondescript ticket.

How long the partnership lasted, which in any case had only been intended as short term, is not recorded, neither are the details of the 'National' takeover of the Chickerell and Osmington services, although five vehicles were transferred to 'National' ownership between 1925 and 1928.

The structure of the company had changed by May 1927 when Mrs Edith May Jeanes, wife of Percy Jeanes, applied to the Council for a Hackney licence for Ford bus FX 9033. Following the disposal of the stage carriage side of the business the coaches ran under the fleetname of 'Gem Coaches' in a yellow livery.

Like many small operators of the period Jeanes ran a heterogeneous selection of vehicles, and apart from the two vehicles purchased new in 1924 the remainder had already seen service with other operators. Of the acquired vehicles, particularly interesting was IB 806 - a McCurd 40 hp - new to Wilts & Dorset Motor Services in August 1916 as their fleet No 6. It was the first vehicle in the fleet to appear in red livery.

Wilts & Dorset had collected this vehicle from the Thomas Tilling premises in London, it was fitted with a second-hand body with perimeter seating that had originated on a Southend-on-Sea Tilling-Stevens. Also of interest was the fact that the vehicle, like others of the period in the Wilts & Dorset fleet, was registered with Armagh County Council (Ireland), as that authority was the only one prepared to grant consecutive numbers entering service at widely spaced intervals. The McCurd proved to be a good work-horse covering 60,000 miles by early 1921 and being sold out of the fleet in 1926 to Jeanes. However, by then it was obsolete and its life was short. It was remembered by the late Maurice Jeanes because of its clerestory roof.

A purchase from Hants & Dorset Motor Services of a Leyland single-deck was also of interest. FX 8288 was new to G. Robertson of Longham in 1922, the vehicle passing to Hants & Dorset when the stage carriage services were acquired by them in February 1925. Although the new owners operated Leyland vehicles, for some reason FX 8288 was not retained long (it did not receive a fleet number) before passing to Jeanes.

At least three other vehicles that entered the fleet were fitted with bus bodies, it being thought that one was constructed locally by Messrs Betts Joinery Works. FX 5335 an Oldsmobile, formerly owned by the Weymouth Motor Company Ltd, received a bus body, as did FX 9033, a Ford char-a-banc acquired from Victory Tours of Weymouth, whilst PR 1557 was reconstructed from a Ford taxi.

The problems associated with the operation of both second-hand and older vehicles were highlighted on several occasions. At the 1925 annual Hackney inspection it was discovered that it was impossible to fit a rear emergency door to GMC PR 2548, and it was decided to allow Messrs Jeanes to have a large window in the rear that would move up and down. This, however, was a purely technical point compared with that of May 1930, when the Hackney Committee were of the opinion that vehicles LW 9252 and XA 1570 failed to come up to the standards required, and Messrs Jeanes was requested to supply up to date vehicles for inspection. What constituted an 'up to date vehicle' is difficult to define with so many new models coming onto the market. Even the last two vehicles to enter the fleet, a Gilford and a Leyland, were quickly dated, having previously seen service with leading companies!

In fact Jeanes did not apply for a licence with the introduction of the 1930 Act, but eventually applied for one for a group of excursions and tours in July 1932, the necessary licence being granted that October.

At this stage the operations of the company become a little unclear. At a Watch Committee meeting in May 1932 it was revealed that Jeanes had a position for two coaches allocated to him at the King's Statue for the past 11 years, but during 1931 he had only placed one coach on the stand and desired to continue doing so. It transpired that the licence issued to Jeanes by the Traffic Commissioners in respect of his vehicle was for contract carriages, which did not allow him to ply for excursions and tours.

At the October 1932 meeting P.J. Jeanes applied to place one coach on the stand at the King's Statue, but the committee were informed that at that time Mr Jeanes did not possess a coach!

The licences held by P.J. Jeanes were transferred to Mrs E.M. Jeanes on 11th January, 1937. That April Mrs Jeanes applied to the Traffic Commissioners to increase the number of vehicles licensed for tours from one to two, and provide additional excursions during the Summer months. The Commissioners granted only additional tours. With these restrictions, and the competition of Southern National, there was little scope for the small operator. In September 1937 Mr T.A. Smith of Bournemouth offered Mrs Jeanes £1,125 providing 'he was up front as General Manager and the company was renamed Jeanes (Weymouth) Ltd'. He was the T.A.

Towards the end of its life Jeanes purchased IB 806, a McCurd, from Wilts & Dorset Motor Services with whom it had given sterling service. Photographed at Salisbury, the clerestory roof was a striking feature on the second-hand 26-seat body had previously been fitted to a Southend-on-Sea Tilling Stevens. Unfortunately the camera never recorded this vehicle in action at Weymouth.

D.J.N. Pennels Collection

One of Jeanes' Crossleys rests at Hardy's Monument, whilst on a tour of the South Dorset countryside. Percy Jeanes is sitting on the radiator. Although by today's standards an excursion of such a short distance appears trivial, in the days before the common ownership of cars, any trip outside the town was viewed upon as an event to be appreciated .

A.G.H. Jeanes

Smith who had been formerly a Director of Victory Tours (Weymouth) Ltd! However, the offer was not acceptable, and following negotiations with Southern National on 9th October, the licences were transferred on 13th October, 1937, the Southern National paying £775 for the licences and goodwill of the business, thus ending the operations of yet another independent in the area.

Jeanes Garage continued to function for motor repairs, a filling station, and as furniture removers, then known as P.J. Jeanes & Sons, the three sons Maurice, Tony and Arthur assisting with the business and running various sidelines. Maurice was a dealer and repairer of wireless sets, whilst Tony was a cycle agent. During World War II part of the garage served as an Auxiliary Fire Station for the National Fire service. Returning to the motor trade following the war, a rearrangement of the business took place in 1951 when the furniture removal vans were sold to Allways of Weymouth and the lower garage at 155-159 Abbotsbury Road was disposed of. The premises at 114-116 Abbotsbury Road were altered, the small shop on the left side, formerly a gents' hairdressers and later a cobblers, was rebuilt, together with the garage entrance, the shop becoming a cycle depot.

In 1961 the two remaining brothers in the business, Arthur and Maurice dissolved the partnership, Arthur departing. Within five years the business was out of the Jeanes family, and following several changes of ownership trading ceased. Later the site was cleared, and is today occupied by a block of flats.

P.J. Jeanes, White Star Bus Service & Gem Coaches

No.	Reg No.	Chassis	No.	Body	Type	No.	Built	Acq.	Sold	Notes
	FX 5736	Crossley					5/20			2
	LW 9252									
	XA 1570							c./21		4
	NC 1843	Daimler			CH16				1928	4
	FX 9033	Ford			B		1922	4/23	10/24	
	CX 3861	Crossley	2642				c./21			
	FX 7970	Ford			B			b/21	7/23	2, 3, 5
	LU 7162	Ford			B			b3/24		5
	FX 7234	Ford						b3/24		6
	EL 4833	Dennis 40 hp			B			b3/24		5
	EL 4897	Dennis 25 hp			B			b3/24		5
	FX 8718	Ford			B			b3/24		5
	FX 6416	Ford	4123094		B14F		2/21	b3/24		5
	EL 7660	Crossley	1873		CH14		3/23		b9/29	2
	PR 2220	Daimler			CH24		3/24	3/24	6/27	
	PR 2548	GMC K16RH			B16		5/24	5/24	1928	
	PR 1557	Ford			B		11/23	10/24		3
	FX 5335	Oldsmobile			CH15		2/20	3/25		2
	IB 806	McCurd 40 hp	395		B26R		8/16	1926		1, 2
	FX 8288	Leyland			B R		1922	b12/27	5/29	2
	KP 1048	Morris	T16938				1928	1928?	11/28	
	GU 2953	Star VB	1030		C26R		2/29		7/36	
	MT 2931	G/ford 166SD	10638	Thurgood	C26D	1496	3/29	11/33	11/37	
	VX 4069	Leyland LTB1	50558	Duple	C26R		2/30	b7/36	10/37	

Notes
1. Left-hand drive.
2. No further operator after Jeanes.
3. Last owner, Jeanes.
4. Hackney licences not renewed by Weymouth Council for 1931 season.
5. Vehicles in fleet at March 1924.
6. In March 1924 listed as chassis only.

Previous Owners
FX 5736   New to Bolt Bros, Royal Mail Garage, Dorchester. Registered 21/5/20 as lorry and public
           conveyance.
LW 9252   Not known.
XA 1570   Not known.
NC 1843   Not known.
CX 3861   New to Eccles & Watson, Huddersfield.
FX 7970   New to H.G. Rugg, Weymouth.
LU 7162   Not known.
FX 7234   Not known.
EL 4833   New to A.F. Matthews, Parkstone, Poole, reg. as lorry/van 6/4/20.
EL 4897   New to H.H. Bates, Veno Garage, Christchurch Road, Boscombe, Bournemouth, as red CH
           1/7/20. To Capt. W.H. Addis, London Hotel, Poole, 1/11/20.
EL 7660   Not known.
PR 1557   New to R. Hoare, Portland 11/23. Rebuilt/rebodied as bus upon purchase by Jeanes.
FX 5333   New to Weymouth Motor Company Ltd.
IB 806   New to Wilts & Dorset as No. 6.
FX 8288   New to G. Robertson, Longham, Wimborne. 2/25 to Hants & Dorset.
KP 1048   Not known.
GU 2953   New to Fisher, Maida Vale, London.
MT 2931   New to Valiant, London, W5. To R. Armstrong 'Majestic Saloon Coaches', Ebchester. To
           Majestic Coaches, Newcastle & London Ltd. 8/32 to United Automobiles Services,
           Darlington, as No. MB 12511/33 to Dawson (dealer), Clapham, London, then to Jeanes.
VX 4069   New to W. Harris & Sons, Grays, Essex. 5/34 to London Passenger Transport Board. 4/36 to
           Cook (dealer), Battersea, London. 1936 to Horne Products (dealer), Slough, and then to Jeanes.

Disposals
FX 9033   To Victory Tours, Weymouth.
CX 3681   To NOTC. LL 6/26.
FX 6416   To C.E. Jeanes, Alton Pancras. LL 24/3/26. LO C.E. Jeanes.
GU 2953   To J.W. Tupper, 'Seaway', Leigh-on-Sea, 7/36 withdrawn 7/37.
KP 1048   To NOTC, 1928, No. 2746, as lorry. To SNOC 8/29. To F. Taylor & Son 1944.
LW 9252   Not known.
MT 2931   To A. Towler & Sons, Brandon 9/38. To Day, Bury St Edmunds, 1939 WD 9/39.
NC 1843   To NOTC 1928, No. 2744. To ENOC 6/30. WD 1934.
PR 2220   To NOTC 6/27, No. 2747. New Strachan body 1928. To Dawson (dealer), Clapham, London. LO.
PR 2548   To NOTC 1928, No. 2745. To ENOC 6/30. Dismantled for spares 5/35.
VX 4069   To B.R. Shreeve & Sons Ltd 'Belle Coaches', Lowestoft 7/38 as C32. Withdrawn 9/51 as
           store room at Oulton Broad Shipyard by 8/55.

The Wessex Tourist Company Ltd

The Wessex Tourist Company's operation in Weymouth was short-lived. The
company was incorporated on 21st May, 1920, being quoted in *The Worlds Carriers*
for 15th July as, 'Wessex Tourist Co. Ltd - Office, The Garage, Rocky Knap,
Dorchester Road, Weymouth. Private Company with a capital of £5,000. To carry on
the business of transport contractors, motor, ship, launch, boat, and aircraft
proprietors, etc. Directors; W. Rinman, C.W. Norris, W.J.H. Longman'.
    Little remains of the documentation of the company. The Managing Director and
Secretary was Wilfred John Hain Longman, of Lancaster House, Littlehampton,
West Sussex. Fellow Directors were   Charles Willian Norris, who resided at
Emsworth, and William Rinman, Fitzalan Street, London S.E. proprietor of Rinman
Commercial Motor Works. In July 1920 each Director held 350 ordinary shares, but
in October 1921 it was recorded that the authorised share capital of the company was
£5,000 in £1 shares. It is   interesting to note that all three gentlemen were also

Directors of South Coast Tourist Coaches, Littlehampton, and Southsea Tourist Coaches of Portsmouth. There are many questions unanswered. How close was the connection between the Littlehampton and Portsmouth companies and the Weymouth operation, and was there a long term plan for the South Coast or just an opportunist chance at another seaside resort? We may never know.

In January 1924 South Coast Tourist, with its fleet of 10 vehicles operating both stage carriage and tours, was acquired by Southdown Motor Services, and on 28th February, 1925 Southsea Tourist - a large concern with 30 Dennis vehicles including two double-deckers - also sold out to Southdown.

Wessex Tourist first came to the notice of Weymouth Town Council in February 1920 when Mr W.J.H. Longman applied for licences to operate motor vehicles. The application was deferred until a Watch Committee meeting of 28th April when a licence for 'char-a-bancs' was granted, subject to the vehicles being approved by the Borough Chief of Police and also that they were garaged within the Borough.

Watch Committee reports record in June 1920 that the conductors were F.W. Shorto and E.E. Washer and drivers A.S. Ray and W.J.H. Longman. The vehicles were garaged at Rocky Knap, Radipole, which was also in the early days the company's office. In fact Rocky Knap was a group of buildings which had been used by several transport concerns over the years. An advert in the *Southern Times* during January 1921 stated the company would undertake all kinds of haulage, furniture removals etc. 'Distance no object. Quotations given for contracts'.

Like many small char-a-banc proprietors, their char-a-bancs became lorries when required, but the vehicles in the fleet are not clearly recorded. As two drivers and conductors were employed there must have been two vehicles during 1920, But only one was registered locally - a Daimler CK, FX5820. A vehicle could well have been brought in from the associated companies. By the Summer of 1921 an office for booking tours had been established at 9 Royal Arcade, the Esplanade, Weymouth, this moving to No. 5 kiosk on the Esplanade the following year. In fact 1922 appears to be the last year of operation, a Fiat 13 seat char-a-banc, FX 9275, being acquired that January.

The Wessex vehicles were in the same light grey and black livery as the Southsea Tourist Company, but apart from the odd newspaper advert little was recorded. They certainly never hit the headlines or incurred the wrath of the Council Watch Committee, but just quietly disappeared, the company being dissolved in 1925.

W.J.H. Longman remained resident locally, moving from Styner House, Nottington, to the Berkeley Hotel, Weymouth Esplanade, where he and Mrs Longman remained for many years. Their son, R.I.H. Longman, became General Manager of Wilts & Dorset Motor Services Ltd.

Wessex Tourist Coaches

No.	Reg No.	Chassis	No.	Body	Type	No.	Built	Acq.	Sold	Notes
	FX 5820	Daimler CK			CH26			6/20		1
	FX 9275	Fiat C13	27528		CH13			1/22		2

Notes
1. 6/20 date registered by Wessex to Dorset CC.
2. 1/22 date registered by Wessex to Dorset CC. LL 30/9/22. LO Wessex Tourist.

Disposal
FX 5820 LO A.J. Mackay, Whetstone, Middlesex, LL 9/22.

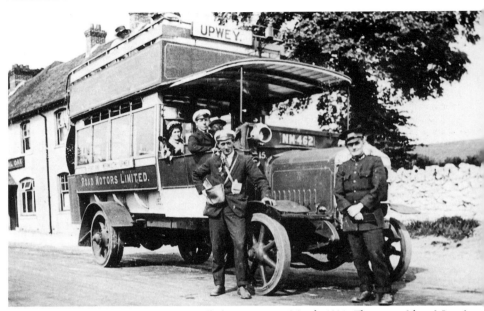

Road Motors No. 15, NM 462, a Palladium, new in March 1921. The second-hand London General Omnibus body fitted well back on the chassis allowed the 'pew' seat to be fitted between the main body and the driving position, note the lady and her dog occupying the seat. Photographed outside the Royal Oak at Upwey, the conductor is Ben Nutman, later an inspector with Southern National.   *Author's Collection*

Road Motors No. 5, BM 5697, a Palladium of 1921 with a B29R body, awaits departure from Upwey, Royal Oak. No.5 became NOTC No. 2243 in March 1925, but was withdrawn by July 1929.   *G. Bruce Collection*

Road Motors Ltd

Road Motors, a Luton-based company, opened a branch at Weymouth in 1921. The company's founder, T.J. Attree, had registered the company on 6th May, 1910 and commenced operations between Maidstone and Chatham, where he came into contact with the 'Maidstone, Chatham, and Gravesend and District Motor Omnibus Company' (later Maidstone & District) operated by that great pioneer of the motor bus, Walter Flexman French. That November Attree withdrew from the area, and during 1911 started a service between Canterbury and Margate. Unfortunately Strong's Garage and Motor Car Company of Canterbury was another of French's interests, and early the following year French took over Attree's service and renamed it 'Canterbury & District Motor Services', which later became a founder part of the East Kent Road Car Company.

Attree moved well away to Luton where in May 1912 he commenced a service to Hitchin and Letchworth. Despite the difficulties of World War I, Road Motors developed and by 1921 had become established in the Luton area.

An application to Weymouth Town Council to operate a service of buses between Weymouth and Portland and Weymouth and Dorchester was granted on 14th July, 1921, this also being placed before the Highways Committee of Portland UDC, because of the Portland element of one of the routes. It was agreed that the licence be granted subject to satisfactory arrangements being made as to a service of buses from Easton, and also the fares charged. As the company proposed to operate only as far as Victoria Square there was disagreement over the Easton proposal which was the idea of the Council. A representative of Road Motors reassured that 'there would be no difficulty in taking the buses to the top of the hill', but the timetables were now at the printers and showed a service only to Victoria Square, and he suggested that the buses be allowed to run that far for the initial month. The fares proposed were 8*d.* to Weymouth, with a probable fare from Easton of 1*s.*

Councillor Stewkesbury, who was concerned about the livelihood of the Portland taxi drivers, told the committee 'you can stop the buses from picking up passengers in the road at Victoria Square'. But just how this could be done Councillor Stewkesbury failed to explain!

The service commenced in October under the supervision of Mr Cousins, the Luton foreman. Until the opening of Radipole garage, the company's address was Commercial Road, it being most likely the vehicles were based at the Central Engineering Works, which at the time was the only suitable building available. This could also have been a reason why permission was sought in July 1921 to erect two temporary sheds on the site. Being sub-let accommodation, the Council rate books show no trace of a tenancy.

On 29th October the *Southern Times* reported: 'The buses put on the road by the Road Motors Company are now in full swing, and there are altogether no less than 18 plying between Weymouth and Wyke daily. The company also announces a Sunday service at the same times'.

In actual fact, the 18 journeys were actually eight in each direction between the King's Statue and Portland Victoria Square, as the 12.15 pm terminated at Wyke Hotel. The service between the King's Statue and Radipole Spa Hotel consisted of 10 return journeys, four being extended to Upwey Royal Oak, of which the 2 pm and 6.15 pm were further extended to Dorchester Museum. Again, as with the early days of the GWR buses, no early services were available for work people.

What was stated to be an 'improved service' commenced on 1st November, the last two Portland services being retarded by 10 minutes, whilst the Radipole service was rescheduled to allow an extra through working to Dorchester.

Between Wyke Hotel and Upwey (Royal Oak) Road Motors were in direct competition with the buses of the GWR, which had extended its service from Radipole Spa Hotel the previous year. It was also a direct challenge to the railway as the service ran parallel to both the main line between Upwey and Weymouth, and the Portland branch as far as Victoria Square. It was also the first challenge to the Portland taxi and char-a-banc owners, who signed a petition which was produced at the November Council meeting protesting at the Council allowing the buses to operate! Councillor Rendell asked why the buses were allowed at Castletown, to which the Chairman replied that 'this was arranged by Wyke Regis men working in the Dockyard'. Given this statement it is clear that, virtually from the beginning, certain services worked almost to the Dockyard gates!

A further challenge to the railways came on 20th March, 1922 when buses to and from Dorchester commenced to operate directly to Portland, thus saving passengers changing at the King's Statue. The July 1922 timetable gave 20 return journeys to Portland and Radipole, 17 being extended to Upwey Royal Oak, with five continuing to Dorchester.

The promised extension between Victoria Square and Easton failed to materialise. In January 1922, Road Motors had told Portland UDC that they did not consider it safe to run buses to Tophill, because the road was extremely steep and otherwise unsuitable and unsafe for a motor bus route. In places it was only 12 feet wide and the buses were seven feet six inches wide, and it would therefore be impossible to pass other similar vehicles. The road was heavily used by heavy traction engines dragging trailers loaded with blocks of stone from the quarries, sometimes as much as 20 tons in weight. In descending the steep hills it was naturally difficult to keep such large vehicles under complete control. In the opinion of Messrs Road Motors, this constituted a grave danger to passengers in buses, and the company would not take the risk. There was within the Council suspicions that both the company and their drivers were nervous of the hill, with which other char-a-bancs appeared to have little difficulty. Portland UDC withdrew Messrs Road Motors' licence that March, virtually out of spite, for refusing to comply with the Council's wishes over the Tophill matter. However, as it was quite legal to run a service without a licence providing no charge was made, the almost comic situation took place where fares were not collected until the bus crossed the boundary out of Portland!

At the same time Major Augustus Slater who had been Agent/Manager for Road Motors, decided to set up on his own account and applied to Portland UDC for a licence, promising to operate to Easton with a 14-seat bus if trials were successful. Portland UDC appealed to Weymouth Council for assistance in granting this licence, but the reply was in the negative as they considered the services within the Weymouth area were already suitable.

Both Messrs Road Motors and Major Slater appealed to the Ministry of Transport concerning the decisions of the respective councils, the Ministry supporting Weymouth on its refusal of Major Slater. However, Portland UDC were left in no doubt that its decision to refuse Road Motors was wrong, and if the licence was not renewed immediately, action would be taken by the Minister!

In November 1922 the Weymouth Hackney Inspector reported an irregular service by Road Motors, the margin between them and the Great Western buses being insufficient, and racing was taking place. He warned that if this close running did not cease action would be taken.

By June 1923 Road Motors' new garage at Radipole had been built, and their services were well established. Good advertising was used through the medium of roadside timetable boards, it being agreed with the Town Council that these be fixed to lamp posts at a wayleave of 1s. per post. From 7th July, 1923 the Great Western Railway buses ceased running to Upwey, reverting to their original terminus at Radipole Spa Hotel, thus giving Road Motors a monopoly situation north of Radipole. The entire route between Upwey and Portland Victoria Square was to form the backbone of Weymouth bus services for many years to come.

To begin with, the Weymouth fleet consisted mainly of assorted Palladium vehicles, later Dennis 35 hp vehicles being introduced. Most of the Dennis chassis were ex-War Department, some being fitted with former London General Omnibus Company bodies that were acquired for £1 each! No. 15 was fitted with one of these double-deck bodies, the seating capacity being increased by placing the body well back on the chassis and inserting a bench (pew) seat outside at the front. This allowed two passengers to sit alongside the driver increased the capacity by six. The total seating capacity was 16 lower deck, 18 upper deck plus six outside, the front overhanging canopy being extended to afford minimum protection.

The livery of the fleet appeared to vary. During World War I dark green had been used, this later being replaced by red, and a few vehicles appeared in chocolate. It is however noted that vehicle No. 23 was delivered in May 1922 with a green livery. Likewise lining out and relief colours varied according to the style of the bodywork, although on almost all vehicles the words 'Road Motors Limited' were displayed on the lower side panels in gold block.

It is impossible to list fully the vehicles allocated to Weymouth, as many exchanges took place with Luton when vehicles became due for overhaul and other factors. The table below gives the information available gathered from records and photographic evidence. Following the purchase of the company several Weymouth-based vehicles moved away, whilst other former Road Motors' vehicles arrived. Later there was more movement with the splitting up of the NOTC fleet as some vehicles entered the Southern National fleet.

Early in 1925 the National Omnibus & Transport Company purchased the whole Road Motors operation for £64,000, taking over Weymouth depot from 1st March, and that at Luton from 8th April, the 44 vehicles being integrated into the National fleet.

At Weymouth the acquisition of the company, and the purchase of the Weymouth Motor Company Ltd at the same time gave 'National' the foothold they needed and set the course of history for Weymouth's bus services for the next 60 years! Ironically, although the local bus service was set to improve, the conditions for the staff diminished, Road Motors' employees had received a higher rate of pay than that paid by 'National', and under the previous ownership there had never been any labour disputes.

A picture of all innocence, smiles and hats of the period. Jack Radford's Garford poses for the camera before departing from the King's Statue with what appears to be a group outing. As the Garford was American left-hand-drive was standard. Note the oil side lights and carbide-operated headlight, the gas producer for which is behind the offside front mudguard. The wooden wheels and solid tyres all added to the thrill of the ride.   *Author's Collection*

This Austin char-a-banc owned by Jack Radford ended its days as a lorry for a local coal merchant, by the look of it the transition was not that difficult. Note the aerodynamically-styled mudguards, and the windscreen fitted behind the driver only giving benefit to the passengers. A close look at the chassis will reveal separate drive shafts from an amidships gear box to each rear wheel, an idea reintroduced in 1949 with the experimental model Bristol Lodekka. This photograph taken at Radipole Spa shows railwaymen from Weymouth engine shed off on an outing in 1921. Being used to the rigours of the footplate they no doubt enjoyed the ride.   *Author's Collection*

Road Motors Ltd, known Weymouth fleet

No.	Reg No.	Chassis	No.	Body	Type	No.	Built	Acq.	Sold	Notes
4	BM 5375	Palladium	YE31657		B26R		1/17	1/17	3/25	6
5	BM 5697	Palladium	YE31690		B29R		1/17	1/17	3/25	
15	NM 462	Palladium	YE20391		22/18 RO		3/21	3/21	3/25	5
23	NM 1422	Dennis	9061		18/18 RO		12/21	12/21	3/25	1, 2
25	NM 1424	Dennis	9153		18/18 RO		12/21	12/21	3/25	7
29	NM 2613	Dennis	9103		18/18 RO		1/23	1/23	3/25	7
36	NM 4481	Dennis	8325		18/18 RO		4/24	4/24	3/25	1, 2, 8
38	NM 4568	Dennis	8935		18/18 RO		4/24	4/24	3/25	1, 3, 9
39	NM 4809	Dennis	9603		18/18 RO		5/24	5/24	3/25	1, 2, 10
46	NM 5809	Dennis	11457		B32R		1/25	1/25	3/25	4
47	NM 5810	Dennis	11698		B32R		1/25	1/25	3/25	1

Notes
1. At Weymouth depot on takeover 1/3/25.
2. Rebodied Dodson B32F 5/27 on extended chassis.
3. Rebodied Dodson B32F 4/26 on extended chassis.
4. Later fitted B33R.
5. Ex-LGOC body, extended canopy 'Pew' in front of driver.
6. Later rebodied 40 /RO.
7. Chassis ex-War Department. Rebodied 6/26 Dodson B32R on extended chassis.
8. Chassis ex-War Department. Rebodied 1927 Dodson B32R on extended chassis.
9. Chassis ex-War Department. Rebodied 4/26 Dodson B32R on extended chassis.
10. Chassis ex-War Department. Rebodied 5/27 Dodson B32R on extended chassis. Rebuilds on pneumatic tyres.

Disposal
4 To NOTC 2242, sold 1928.
5 To NOTC 2243, withdrawn by 7/29.
15 To NOTC 2251, sold 1928.
23 To NOTC 2235. To SNOC 2235. 1933 chassis to Hopwood £15, body Holland, Instone £6.
25 To NOTC 2260. To SNOC 2260, 1933 to Bebbington, Didsbury, Manchester.
29 To NOTC 2264. To SNOC 2264, 1933 to Bebbington, Didsbury, Manchester.
36 To NOTC 2236. To ENOC 12/29 2236. Withdrawn 1933.
38 To NOTC 2237. To SNOC 2237, 1933 to Bebbington, Didsbury, Manchester.
39 To NOTC 2238. To SNOC 2238, 1932 to Bird Bros, Yeovil as lorry.
46 To NOTC 2240. To SNOC 2240, 1932 to Bird Bros, Yeovil as lorry.
47 To NOTC 2239. To ENOC 2239. Withdrawn 1932.

Jack Radford, Westham Garage

Jack Radford took over Westham Garage from E.W. Puffett in March 1920, the only recorded bus included in the transaction being the Austin char-a-banc, FX 1871.

In May 1920 Radford acquired a Garford 24-seat char-a-banc. A left-hand-drive model built in 1919, there is little doubt that this was a reconditioned military chassis. Almost nothing is known of Radford or his business, his advert in the 1920 Town Guide was the same as used by Puffett in 1916, except the name was changed to 'Jack Radford, Proprietor'. The advert for the following year was an improvement, revamped and stating 'a well appointed char-a-banc will run excursions leaving the King's Statue daily during the season for all places of interest'.

One hopes that the advert referred to the Garford, which was as good - if not better - than many plying for trade at the time. The Austin was certainly not a good example of what a char-a-banc should have looked like, even in those hard pressed times! It was a standard 20 hp lorry chassis with unusual features including a coal-

A view looking towards North Square, Chickerell, and the start of an outing sometime between 1927 and 1932, two vehicles of Victory Motors are followed by two from the Greyhound fleet. Leading is Crossley, CR 5858, followed by Crossley, OH 2209. The third vehicle is Greyhound Dennis, PR 8683, and the Daimler at the rear is Greyhound, PR 2645.

D.M. Habgood Collection

The Weymouth Salvation Army Home League outing of 3rd June, 1926 photographed before departure. Mr T.A. Smith of Victory Motors stands alongside the chalk board in front of a Crossley, to the left Fiat PR 2014, to the right Ford FX 9033.   *Author's Collection*

scuttle style bonnet, the radiator being mounted behind the engine with a fan drawing air over the engine. The transmission arrangements were also unusual, the differential being fitted behind the gearbox. From this unit two propshafts, one each side of the chassis took the drive independently to the rear wheels. The char-a-banc body placed upon it was a crude affair of timber construction, a bench-type seat running down each side. The windscreen gave no protection to the driver as it was placed behind him to protect the passengers, indeed the whole thing was little more than a lorry, and it did in fact end its days with a local coal merchant.

Although Radford also provided a taxi service, there appeared to be little expansion in the business, and in November 1922 Radford sold the concern, including the two char-a-bancs, to T.A. Smith who later formed Victory Tours.

Jack Radford, Westham Garage

No.	Reg No.	Chassis	No.	Body	Type	No.	Built	Acq.	Sold	Notes
	FX 1871	Austin 20 hp			CH			3/20	11/22	
	FX 5694	Garford	MA17769		CH24			5/20	11/22	

Previous Owners
FX 1871 E.W. Puffett, Westham Garage, Weymouth.

Disposals
FX 1871 To Victory Tours, Westham Garage, Weymouth.
FX 5694 To Victory Tours, Westham Garage, Weymouth.

Victory Tours (Weymouth) Ltd

The formation of Victory Tours involved a number of parties and is therefore somewhat complex. Operations were centred around Westham Garage, Holly Road. In November 1922 the Hackney licences held by Jack Radford were transferred to Thomas Allan Smith, then in February 1923 Smith was joined by William Harris Miller, and they traded under the name 'Victory'. During March 1923 they applied to Weymouth Council for Hackney licences for two vehicles, together with a licence to operate a bus service to Chickerell. They were granted the two Hackney licences, but the Chickerell operation was refused. On 20th February, 1925 the limited liability company, 'Victory Motors (Weymouth) Ltd' was registered, headed by W.H. Miller, T.A. Smith, and J.J. Duffy.

It appears that at this point a second business was acquired, when the premises of the Central Engineering Works in Commercial Road came under the control of Victory Tours. This motor vehicle repair business had been set up by Carl Metz on the site of the former Corporation Yard. Edgar Dawe served his apprenticeship under Metz, and following service in the Royal Navy during World War I returned to the Commercial Road premises where, by 1921, he was in partnership with Metz, but shortly after this Metz left to cultivate other business interests.

In March 1925 a petroleum licence was issued to 'Victory Tours', Commercial Road, Weymouth; clearly by this time both concerns had become one! In the 1926/7 town directory, Victory Tours was listed as, 'Victory Motors (Weymouth) Ltd, Motor garage & removals, Holly Road. Engineering & repairs, Commercial Road. Booking office, Kiosk No. 5, The Esplanade'. In June 1928 Victory informed the Town Council that owing to an increase of rent it would vacate the premises in Commercial Road. Later these were converted into class rooms and an enlarged playground for Melcombe Regis school, the iron huts remaining in use until closure of the school in 1970.

By 1928 Duffy had left the business, becoming a butcher at Portland, and Norman W. Wright had joined Victory to become the Secretary. Having learned his trade in the mills at Nelson, Lancashire, he was based at Portland with the Royal Navy during World War I. Wright was both an engineer and a very astute businessman. His first venture as a motor engineer was at 114 Abbotsbury Road, Weymouth, commencing in August 1919. Before long these premises passed to Rugg, and later to Jeanes. By 1922 Wright was involved in the business of Marsh & Wright, with premises in Victoria Street, manufacturing hoods for cars, tents, shop awnings and general canvas work, and also hiring out bathing tents from a site on the beach. In 1930 the Directors of Victory Tours were listed as W.H. Miller, E.L. Dawe, T.A. Smith, and W.F. Deacon, but in 1932 both Deacon and Smith had departed, Norman Wright having become a Director. By that time the pre-booking of bathing tents for Marsh & Wright could be made at the Victory offices at 3 Royal Terrace!

Like many small operators of the period, Victory mainly relied on private hire and excursion work. For example, on Whit Monday 1926 the following tours were on offer: London (with six hours in the capital), there being a 6 am departure for this 30s. excursion, whilst for the less enthusiastic there were 8.30 am departures for either Cheddar Caves or Torquay. Although there was much competition at this period, Victory carried out no Sunday work. Smith, an active Salvationist, is said to have adopted the 'Victory' fleet name because of this, and his upholding of the Sabbath brought much private hire work from other church organisations. In fact it was only in 1921 that the local paddle steamers had started to run on Sundays, mainly due to the competition from the newly arrived char-a-banc operators.

Victory also carried out general motor repair work at the Holly Road premises, the garage being well equipped with various power tools including two lathes, and Edgar Dawe was able to carry out most repairs including the re-metalling of bearings.

During the late 1920s Victory was also acting as agents for Dennis Bros of Guildford. In July 1928 it sold a new 30 cwt chassis to R. Green a Chickerell (haulier) for £340, and took an old Maxwell lorry in part exchange for £26. Surviving receipts from 1931 showing that Green was paying instalments of £27 11s. 3d. to Victory for a Dennis lorry. There were also references in the Council minutes for 1932 to Victory being Dennis agents and carrying out repairs to the Borough fire engine, a 1923 Dennis (PR 477). Dawe was also engineer/driver of the Borough fire brigade, and the Council minutes refer to payments to E. Dawe between February and November 1934 of £311 15s. 9d., including a £5 retainer from the brigade. Dawe also had a sideline of refurbishing lawn mowers for Thurmans, the local ironmongers.

Furniture removals were also undertaken, both a small and large van being owned by the company. 'The Victory School of Motoring' was another sideline and chauffeur-driven cars were also available, the 1933 Weymouth Town Guide advertising these as being available at 50s. per day.

High standards were maintained, the coaches looking smart in two shades of blue - Cambridge Blue and Royal Blue - being washed cleaned and polished inside and out each night. On the garage wall was a chalk board on which every evening Dawe would allocate each coach its driver and work. All the later coaches had an Austrian woven blanket for passenger use on the rail at the back of each seat, and all carried a complete tool kit including a hydraulic jack.

Content with tours and private hire work until 1929, Victory then commenced a Saturdays (Summer only) express service to and from London. Departing Weymouth at 8 am, it arrived at the Central Station, Crescent Place, WC1 at 2 pm, a 2.45 pm departure returning to Weymouth at 9 .15 pm, the fares being 15s. single, 25s. return.

In April 1930 the Weymouth Council Watch Committee were informed that Victory Tours was operating a regular service between Weymouth and Bournemouth without having informed the Council of its intention of doing so. At the December meeting it was reported that an application from Victory to operate a Portland-Weymouth-Bournemouth service might be reconsidered, and Victory had also applied to operate a Easton-Weymouth-Dorchester service, and a service from Westham housing estate to the King's Statue via Kitchener Road and Cromwell Road. However, with the 1930 Road Traffic Act shortly coming into operation the committee could not see their way clear to grant permission. Clearly the company was attempting to establish services and gain a foothold before the introduction of the Act, in particular with the Westham service, which in later years became very remunerative for Southern National.

Having been unsuccessful at Weymouth, Victory commenced to operate a bus service in the neighbouring town of Dorchester on 2nd March, 1931, two buses being required to operate the 'figure of eight' route which ran from Fordington Green to the top of South Street, thence to the Great Western station and the Victoria Park district, through Gloucester Road to the Laundry, before returning to South Street, thence to Monmouth Road and down to Eddison's and Fordington Green. A fare of 1d. was charged for any distance. This service was operated mainly by two Dennis Dart 20-seat buses. To operate the service, Miller and his family moved to Dorchester, taking up residence at No. 16 Princes Street, this property having an adjoining garage in which the buses were kept.

By April 1932 Miller had brought his brother-in-law, Richard Deacon, over from Ireland to run the Dorchester operation, which was renamed 'Dorchester Motor Services'. Deacon moved into No. 29 Cromwell Road, the the garage and open space alongside this end-terrace house allowing parking of the fleet which then consisted of two Dennis 'GLs' and a Ford 'AA'. Having been a farmer before coming to Dorchester, Deacon was not happy running a bus service, and following negotiations with Southern National, Dorchester Motor Services passed into that company's ownership in January 1935, Deacon thereupon moved to the Bridport area and resumed his farming pursuits. Just how separate from the Victory concern Dorchester Motor Services really was is not known, but the Dorchester operation was Victory's only venture into stage carriage operation, and it was claimed not to have been the success it thought it would be!

Although already in operation, Naval Leave Services were put on a proper footing in November 1932 when the Traffic Commissioners granted licences for a Portland-Portsmouth service at 8s. 6d. day return, 10s. 6d. period return, Portland-London 15s. 6d. return, 17s. longer periods, and Portland-Plymouth, 15s. Friday-Monday, 16s. longer periods. However, in September 1933 the Southern Railway successfully opposed an application for a new service between Weymouth and Chatham, and likewise in December the Traffic Commissioners refused a 'Fridays only' service from the Anti-Submarine School (HMS *Osprey*) Portland at 3.45 pm direct to Weymouth station for Naval personnel, to enable them to join the 4.15 pm Great Western train which had connections to Bristol, South Wales, and the Midlands.

As with other operators of the time, the Victory fleet slowly developed during the char-a-banc era. The Austin and Garford vehicles acquired with the Radford business were quickly disposed of, being replaced by other small char-a-bancs of the period - including a Ford 'T' and a Fiat. Ex-RAF Crossley chassis in rebodied form was also acquired, with seating capacities ranging from eight to fourteen.

In April 1929 a Gilford 26-seat coach entered the fleet, without a doubt being purchased to operate the London service. However, at the time there was no other

Mr W.H. Miller, a principal shareholder in Victory Tours, poses on the running board of Crossley OH 2209. Passing into the amalgamated fleet of Greyhound (Weymouth) Ltd, this all weather Crossley went to a dealer by the end of 1934. *Mrs V. Tilley*

TK 4628, a Dennis Dart 20-seat coach with all-weather bodywork, awaits delivery to Victory Motors from the builders. The roll back canvas roof shows the advantage over the previous char-a-banc concept. *Author's Collection*

vehicle in the fleet capable of acting as a substitute in the event of the Gilford being off the road - a risky situation for any operator! The remainder of the fleet were char-a-bancs of a fast disappearing era. The Gilford 166SD was very advanced. A Lycoming six-cylinder side valve engine developing 42 bhp at 1,000 rpm drove through a four-speed gearbox, and braking on all four wheels was assisted by Dewandre Vacuum Servo, with good springing and a self-starter. The complete chassis cost £845.

The bodywork was also of a very high standard, and a roof-mounted luggage rack at the rear of the sliding roof added to the new comforts of coach travel. The Gilford could also 'move', maintaining 60 mph on a level road - and what was more important the brakes could actually stop the vehicle from that speed! Unfortunately Gilford became a victim of stronger competition and ceased trading in 1935.

The Gilford marked the introduction of modern vehicles and expansion of the company but the new regulations of the 1930 Road Traffic soon brought about the end of the old char-a-banc. In May 1929 the inspector of hackney carriages had deferred granting licences for vehicles OH 2209, XE 6383, and BO 2954, as they were not fitted with rear emergency doors, the latter vehicle and OH 2209 being eventually passed the following year. The old Ford and Crossley vehicles were gradually withdrawn, with a Dennis Dart and GL models entering the fleet. Dennis Dart TK 4628, was purchased in May 1930. She was powered by a Dennis six-cylinder overhead valve engine producing 70 bhp at 2,000 rpm, and fitted with Dewandre servo brakes. The 20-seat Dennis body was fitted with a roll-back canvas roof. In July 1930 and March 1931 four Dennis GL vehicles were purchased. As built this model had either a four- or six-cylinder overhead valve engine fitted, but in 1957 Mr Miller told a member of the Omnibus Society that 'he had small side valve engines fitted for economy, and low gear axles to give a reasonable top gear performance in the congested streets of Dorchester'.

Although the Dennis Arrow and Lancet models had been introduced in 1930 and 1932 - and given Victory Tours previous involvement with Dennis Bros - it is surprising that the choice for the next new vehicles fell to AEC, with the arrival of an AEC Regal, Harrington-bodied coach in June 1932. This vehicle, TK 7892, was also fitted with twin speakers alongside the clock on the front bulkhead, a microphone in the cab allowing the driver to give a commentary *en route* - a great novelty at the time which was reported in the local press. A second Regal was purchased the following year, but the final purchase by Victory in 1934 was a Commer Centurion, although a Harrington body was selected.

Early in 1934 the Victory fleet consisted of eight vehicles, of which the two AEC Regals and the Commer were of the latest design. Outside forces were conspiring against the small operator, Southern National gradually gaining a stronger foothold, and Victory's 'No Sunday trading' policy could have done little to help, as Sunday was always considered the best trading day in excursions and tour work. Although after the departure of Smith this could well have been relaxed, it is difficult to see how Naval leave services could be operated without Sunday working!

Victory Tours and R.G.W. Austin of Greyhound Coaches had always been on good terms so when in July 1934 both companies had their Excursions and Tours Licence suspended for seven days by the Traffic Commissioners for wilful contravention of its conditions, it was agreed to combine the two businesses, the name changing to Greyhound Coaches (Weymouth) Ltd from 29th September, 1934. The registered office was the former Victory premises at No. 3 Royal Terrace. This was the end of Victory as an independent company, the coaches being transferred

Right: Victory Motors, Ford AA TK 5901, a 20-seat bus purchased new in February 1931 to operate the Dorchester Town service. Seen here at the King's Statue, this photograph was probably taken after the vehicle had been acquired by Southern National. *Mrs V. Tilley*

Below: AEC Regals TK 9301 and TK 7892, the pride of the Victory Motors' fleet stand at the King's Statue, their two-tone blue paintwork suiting the Harrington 32-seat bodies. Chalk boards against the coach display the tours on offer. Both vehicles later survived in the Southern National fleet until the early 1950s. *Author's Collection*

to the Greyhound garage at Charlestown and the Holly Road premises disposed of. The new arrangement was short-lived, for in January 1936 Greyhound was acquired by Southern National.

Several of the principal people involved in Victory Tours continued in the business life of the area. Edgar Dawe continued with the Borough fire brigade, becoming 2nd officer. In June 1940 he became Chief Officer - which under wartime conditions became a full time occupation. With the formation of the National Fire Service he became Divisional Officer, remaining in the same capacity when the brigade became the Dorset County Fire Service. Following a period of ill health Edgar Dawe died in July 1953, aged 56, whilst still in the service of the fire brigade.

Thomas Smith had been born in Carnforth, and later lived in Carlisle, Newcastle and Bradford, before moving to Weymouth because of his health. In fact, he never drove a vehicle! For several years whilst a Director of Victory Tours he resided in Guernsey, later returning to Weymouth until relinquishing his directorship. He then moved to Southampton, where he was involved in the coal trade for a short while before moving to Bournemouth, from where in September 1937 he made an unsuccessful offer to take over P.J. Jeanes of Weymouth (*see page 133*). Despite a lifetime of indifferent health, Thomas Smith lived until 89 years of age, passing away on 18th April, 1959.

William Miller joined the Southern Counties Car Finance Corporation as a representative to cover the Wessex area, opening a branch office in Dorchester after the war. In 1966 he was appointed a local Director, and he died in December 1970 aged 70 years. One of his daughters, Vivienette, married John Tilley, son of Ernest Tilley, one of the founders of Tilley's Garages of Dorchester and Weymouth, and a partner in the former Weymouth Motor Company Ltd.

Norman Wright after 1936 became involved with W. & J. Tod Ltd, the Wyke Regis boat builders. Following war service with the Auxiliary Fire Service, he guided that firm from the construction of small wooden boats into fibreglass dinghies and motor boats. By then he was Managing Director, and expanded to build the fibreglass lifeboats for liners and specialist work for the Admiralty. Awarded the MBE in 1960 for his work with fibreglass, Wright retired from business in 1969. He passed away on 12th July, 1982, aged 83 - the last of the Victory Tours Directors, and a most successful businessman.

The Holly Road premises remained in use by the motor trade until the 1980s when the garage was demolished and flats built on the site, Overdale House survives, having passed through several owners. Today just a stone inscribed 'JHY' in the wall of Overdale Terrace is a reminder that the first omnibuses in Weymouth operated from the site!

Victory Motors (Weymouth) Ltd

No.	Reg No.	Chassis	No.	Body	Type	No.	Built	Acq.	Sold	Notes
	FX 1871	Austin 20 hp			CH		11/20	11/22	1924	
	FX 5694	G/ford 25 hp	MA17769		CH24		5/20	11/22	1924	3, 4
	FX 8273									
	CR 5858	Crossley			CH14		1/17	b/23	3/31	2
	XF 9040						1921	b/23		
	FX 9033	Ford			CH		2/22	10/24		4, 5
	PR 2014	Fiat			CH		2/24	b6/26		
	BO 2954	Crossley						12/28	b8/33	
	XE 6383						1920	b/29		
	OH 2209	Crossley			CH14			b/29	12/34	1
	TK 2584	G/ford 166SD	10613	Wycombe	C26		5/29	5/29	12/34	1
	L 6578	Crossley			CH14		b2/21	7/29	b2/31	
	TK 4628	Dennis Dart	75704	Duple	C20F	2175	5/30	5/30	12/34	1
	TK 4978	Dennis GL	70670	Dennis	B19F		7/30	7/30		
	TK 4979	Dennis GL	70662	Dennis	B20F		7/30	7/30	12/34	1
	TK 5901	Ford AA			B20F		2/31	2/31	c.1/32	
	TK 6024	Dennis GL	70714	Dennis	B20F		3/31	3/31	c.1/32	
	TK 6025	Dennis GL	70715	Dennis	B20F		3/31	3/31	c.1/32	
	TK 7892	AEC Regal	6621358	Harrington	C32R		6/32	6/32	12/34	1
	TK 9301	AEC Regal	6621505	Harrington	C32R		5/33	5/33	12/34	1
	JT 990	Commer Cent.	56040	Harrington	C20 F		5/34	5/34	12/34	1

Notes
1. Vehicles passed into reconstituted fleet of Greyhound Coaches (Weymouth) Ltd in December 1934.
2. LL 3/31. LO Victory Tours.
3. Registered 14/3/21 (1919 mod.).
4. Left-hand-drive.
5. Whilst working for Jeanes had a saloon bus body.

Previous Owners
FX 1871   Ex-J. Radford, Weymouth.
PR 2014   Registered new 2/24 to Seager Bros, Sherborne.
FX 9033   P.J. Jeanes.
FX 5694   Ex-J. Radford, Weymouth.
L 6578   New to H. Lewis, Porthcawl, 7/23 to D. Delecoy, Cross Keys, Dowlais. 5/24 to C. Davis & Sons, Dowlais. 10/25 to A. Griffith, Cardiff. 6/27 to J. Parsons (dealer), Cardiff. 7/27 to P.C. Irons, Hirwaun, then to Victory Tours.
BO 2978   New to E.E. Davis, Cardiff.
CR 5858   New to A.J. Murray, Shirley Road, Southampton.
OH 2209   Not known.

Disposals
FX 1871   T. Clarke (coal merchant), Weymouth as a lorry.
FX 5694   T. Gutteridge Victoria Garage, Station Road, Carlton, Nottingham, LL 1924.
L 6578   Rebuilt as a van by 2/31. 12/34 to W.J. Cave, Weymouth as a van, LO.
BO 2954   Registered to unidentified London operate 8/33, licence void 11/34.
FX 8273   LO Victory Tours.
PR 2014   LO Tilley's Garage, Weymouth (dealer).
TK 4978   G.C. Mosman, Luton. LL 9/48.
TK 5901   W. & R. Deacon 'Dorchester Motor Services', Dorchester c.1/32. To SNOC 10/34, as No. 3504. 1037 to W. Talbot (dealer), Taunton, scrapped.
TK 6024   W. & R. Deacon 'Dorchester Motor Services', Dorchester c.1/32. To SNOC 10/34, as No. 3503. 12/37 to A.E. Thomas, Chagford. LL 3/43. LO.
TK 6025   W. & R. Deacon 'Dorchester Motor Services', Dorchester c.1/32. To SNOC 10/34, as No. 3505. 12.37 to Jordan (dealer), Biggleswade, 9/39 to R.F. Soul 'Soul Bros', Olney. LL2/45 LO.

Greyhound Tours, R.G.W. Austin

Reginald George Watts Austin had served with the Army at Bovington Camp during World War I, after which he remained living locally and operating a taxi service from the camp. By 1922 he had moved to Weymouth and set up Greyhound Coaches, Hackney licences being granted in that June.

The backbone of Austin's work was tours and private hire, one of the features of the period being the annual pub outing where the landlord and his regular customers (plus many crates of brown ale) set off for a day's enjoyment! To supplement the private hire and tour work, Greyhound commenced a regular weekend service between Weymouth and London via Blandford, Salisbury, and Stockbridge, on Thursday 28th March, 1929. The Weymouth departure from the King's Statue was at 8 am and the London departure from Eccleston Street was 2.45 pm. The single fare was 14s. and the period return 25s. The advert appearing in the Weymouth Town guide for the new service stated 'latest type all weather coaches'. A Star Flyer with a sliding canvas top had been purchased that March, followed by a Bean - also with a sliding canvas roof, in July.

The London service was successful. When Austin applied for licences under the 1930 Act in July 1931, both the Great Western and Southern Railways and the Aldershot & District Traction Company objected, the action of the latter doubtless being prompted by their principal shareholder, the Southern Railway! However, the application was granted, it being revealed that the service had carried 3,008 passengers during 1930, of which 207 were picked up or set down at Blandford, which Mr Austin described as an important picking up point. It also emerged that between 25th March and 13th July, 1931, 1,625 single tickets had been issued.

By the Summer of 1933 the Saturday service had been doubled to give both a morning and afternoon departure from both Weymouth and London, from where the departure point had moved to Eccleston Bridge, Victoria.

Although already operating an express service between Weymouth and London, fearing the Greyhound operation might be acquired by a competitor in particular Royal Blue of Bournemouth, a separate concern at that time - Southern National entered into negotiations with Austin during 1933. An amicable agreement was reached, the licence being transferred on 4th May, 1934.

Austin retained his Naval Leave Service licences, these having been granted in 1933. On 20th January, a Portland-Portsmouth service (8s. 6d. day return, 10s. 6d. period return), and Portland-London (15s. 6d. return, 17s. longer periods) were granted. A Portland-Plymouth licence was granted on 27th July with a period return fare of 11s. 6d. Austin and Greyhound, and other operators, had run Naval Leave Services before the 1930 Act, the work being carried out as 'Private Hire' to circumvent any problems with local authorities.

The realities of the 1930 Act came to the fore in September 1933 when Austin was asked by the Commissioners why he had applied for a short period licence to cover Sherborne Fair on 16th October, proposing to charge a fare of 2s. 6d. The Chairman drew Austin's attention to the fact that all other Weymouth operators had agreed on a fare of 3s. 6d., and it appeared that he was deliberately undercutting his competitors! Austin agreed to amend his application to the 3s. 6d. fare.

However, competition was strong, Victory had acquired two AEC Regals with Harrington bodies, and a rather dashing Commer with attractive Harrington bodywork, and Southern National also had the latest products of both AEC and Leyland available for tour work, all on show to an eager public at the King's Statue starting point.

Austin's first vehicle, a Ford TT, waits to depart from the King's Statue. The little boy in cap looking out from behind the driver's seat is Clifford Austin, son of the proprietor.

Author's Collection

Austin's Fiat PR 1988 about to depart from Weymouth, for East Stoke Church on 2nd August, 1922. The occasion was the wedding of Mr Douglas Accutt, sitting at the front next to the driver. Douglas Accutt until his retirement was a well respected teacher at Melcombe Regis Boys School. He was also the author of *Brigade In Action*, a detailed history of the St John's Ambulance Brigade during World War II, Weymouth`s first official war history.

Author's Collection

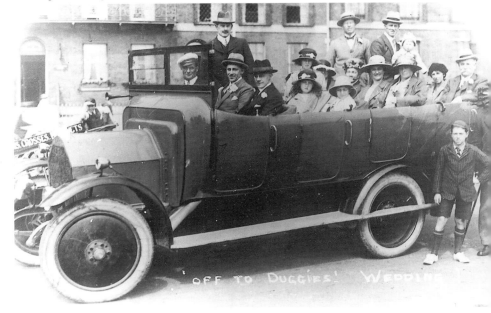

The erection of the shelter at the Statue had caused a reduction in the number of coaches each operator was allowed to park at any one time, and this in turn made touting for trade more vigorous. The strict rules governing touting which the town council insisted upon were now compounded by the regulations of the 1930 Act, strictly enforced by the Traffic Commissioners and their inspectors. It was the over zealous action of the touts employed by both Victory and Greyhound that caused a problem in July of 1934, when both companies had their Tours & Excursion Licences suspended for seven days for 'Wilful contravention of the conditions of the licence'. What actually happened was that the touts were giving reduced fares to families, but unfortunately one family contained a Ministry Inspector! This happening in the middle of the then short Summer season could have been disastrous for both companies, but fortunately it did not affect private hire, contract, or Naval leave services. It was after this incident that the two companies were combined.

Originally the Greyhound fleet was based at a small garage situated on North Quay, Weymouth, but this became too small for the larger coaches and a recently rebuilt garage at Charlestown was taken over from A.F. Lewis which had plenty of space! Mr Charles Samson was employed to maintain the fleet, which was originally painted in two shades of brown, later changed to a livery of blue and fawn following the merger. High standards, including the changing of engine oil every 6,000 miles, were maintained. Like most roadside garages of the period there was a petrol pump to sell fuel to the general public.

Following the sale to Southern National the Charlestown premises continued to be used for the garaging of coaches, 13 being kept there. During and after the war and following the bombing of Edward Street, Charlestown became the paint shop and a store until the rebuilding of Edward Street in 1955. The premises were disposed of in 1959, becoming the workshops of the Universal Engineering Company until demolished.

Like many small operators, Austin commenced his operations with a Ford 'T' char-a-banc, and in February 1924 a Fiat char-a-banc was acquired. Like the Ford, this was of small capacity but both having pneumatic tyres they gave a reasonable ride. In May 1924 a Daimler CK of greater capacity was purchased and this also ran on pneumatic tyres.

The char-a-banc concept was to be quickly eclipsed by what was known as the 'all weather coach', which had fixed side windows and a roll-back roof that could be quickly pulled into place - which is more than could be said for the previous arrangements! Austin's first all-weather was a Dennis 30 cwt, PR 8683, powered by a four-cylinder 17.9 litre petrol engine with a four-speed gearbox. The chassis cost £300, the Dennis 14-seat body being extra.

With the commencement of the London service in March 1929 a faster heavier vehicle was required. This came in the form of TK 2299, a 'Star Flyer' with a low framed chassis and excellent suspension, powered by a 3.2 litre 24 hp six-cylinder overhead valve engine driving a spiral bevel gear rear axle via a four-speed gearbox. Vacuum-servo brakes were fitted, and top speeds well in excess of 50 mph were obtainable! The Star Flyer was the only locally owned example, Star having been acquired by Guy Motors in 1928, and production ceasing four years later.

Requiring a back-up for such a service, a Bean coach was also purchased. This was a small lightweight machine powered by a four-cylinder 14 hp engine. The Bean enjoyed a short popularity during the mid-1920s.

In February 1931 the first heavyweight vehicle - a Leyland 'TS3' TK 5933 - entered the fleet, and it also set the pattern whereby all future Greyhound coaches would receive Duple bodies. The TS3 was the single-deck version of the Leyland Titan. A 6.8 litre, six-

The buildings of Frederick Place and Royal Terrace form a backdrop to this line up of Greyhound coaches taken after 1929 showing vehicles about to depart on a British Red Cross Society outing. To the left PR 8683, a Dennis 30 cwt, note the insert single rear wheels, centre is Daimler CK PR 2645, and on the right Star Flyer, TK 2299. The bodywork of the Dennis and Star can be seen as superior to the Daimler although only a few years separates them, within a few more years all will be obsolete. *Author's Collection*

Driver 'Pop' Lee stands alongside Greyhound No. 7 at Corfe Castle. TK 5933 was a 1933 model Leyland TS3 with a Duple C30F body, although the door was not strictly at the front a close view of the coach will show it is the second main pillar back. Within two years this body style was to be completely outdated by Duple's own high standards. Pop Lee was a typical coach driver of the pre- and post-war years, he drove for Greyhound, Southern National, Bere Regis, and Bluebird, it was a seasonal job and the best offer secured the services of the driver. *J. Lee*

cylinder, 55 bhp engine was fitted, and the brakes were vacuum-servo. The chassis had a 16 ft 6 in. wheelbase and cost £1,050. The following year a pair of Dennis Arrow coaches were acquired, TK 7530/1, this model being a completely revised design fitted with an overhead valve six-cylinder 6.13 litre engine, a four-speed gearbox mounted on the rear of the engine giving a top speed of over 50 mph. Braking was by the Dewandre Servo system. The chassis cost £1,100. Only 58 Dennis Arrows were built, within a year the model being superseded by the new Dennis Lancet. Such was the speed of advance in vehicle design.

In 1933 Austin reverted to Leyland with the purchase of a 'TS4' chassis, TK 9099. An improvement on the 'TS3', this model was fitted with a more powerful 7.6 litre engine, and the wheelbase was extended one foot. Triple servo brakes were provided, but the main improvement to the eye was a new style of radiator.

Austin also had several taxis over the years which were licensed as PSVs, these being used to convey the few passengers from outlying areas to the King's Statue and thereby avoiding extra time and mileage on coaches.

Following the amalgamation of the Victory and Greyhound fleets, the older vehicles were quickly disposed of and two Dennis Lancet Is were purchased for the 1935 season, JT 2382/3055. Although not quite such a dashing machine as the Arrow, the Lancet was a steady workhorse. A 5.7 litre four-cylinder petrol engine combined with a four-speed gearbox gave a top speed of just under 50 mph, which at the time was well above the legal limit! From an aesthetic viewpoint, many considered the massive radiator ugly compared with its predecessor, but the chassis cost about £400 less.

The Greyhound fleet at its peak was considered the best in Weymouth, and during its existence not one second-hand vehicle had been purchased, itself a compliment to Austin's abilities as a coach proprietor.

A report in the *Southern Times* on 21st September, 1935, claimed that Greyhound carried 30,000 passengers during that Summer on tours alone, without contract work and the transport of Naval ratings to and from Portland, The final line said, 'The Company are planning even bigger things next year', but there was not to be a 'next year'.

The exact financial circumstances of the company are unknown, except that several of the new vehicles were obtained on hire purchase terms, payments on which still had to be made during the lean Winter months! In November 1935 Southern National, eager to obtain further Naval express services, commenced negotiations with Greyhound, which resulted in the purchase of the entire business on 31st January, 1936. Southern National paid £13,896 5s. for the goodwill of the company, £2,045 for the Charlestown Garage, and £9208 for 13 coaches which were taken into the Southern National fleet.

At a total cost of £25,149 Southern National had acquired a reasonable sized garage, gained more Naval Leave Services, and removed the last tours competitor from the King's Statue. However, the Greyhound reputation stood high, resulting in the tours and excursions continuing to be marketed under the 'Greyhound' name for the 1936 and 1937 seasons, after which the vehicles were completely merged into the Southern National fleet, three of them surviving until 1954.

Following the sale of the business the other Directors of the reformed company, Messrs Dawe, Miller, and Wright, pursued their interests as described on page 151, whilst Austin purchased Ryan's shop and cafe in Royal Terrace. Following alterations to the shop the cafe part became the Weymouth Bay Hotel. Reginald Austin died on 3rd February, 1956 at the age of 56. Although the Hotel has ceased to operate the premises are still owned today by the Austin family. Situated by the main bus stops Austin's is probably one of the best known shops in Weymouth.

No. 10 in the original Austin Greyhound fleet was Leyland TS4, TK 9099 shown posed for the camera outside the Duple factory before delivery in April 1933. The stylish outline of the Duple 32-seat body demonstrated the improvements in the past few years.   *R. Marshall Collection*

Dennis Lancet I, JT 2382, destined for the Greyhound (Weymouth) Ltd fleet, photographed before delivery from Duple the body builders. A quality body on a sturdy chassis, it gave 20 years' service to various owners.   *Author's Collection*

R.G.W. Austin, Greyhound Motor Coaches, Weymouth

No.	Reg No.	Chassis	No.	Body	Type	No.	Built	Acq.	Sold	Notes
		Ford T			CH					
	PR 1988	Fiat			CH		2/24	2/24		
2	PR 2645	Daimler CK			CH		5/24	5/24	12/34	
	PR 8683	Dennis 30 cwt		Dennis	C14F		4/27	4/27		
4	TK 2299	Star Fly/VB4	1041		C		3/29	3/29	12/34	1
	TK 3148	Bean			C		7/29	7/29		
6	TK 4650	Dennis GL	70632	Dennis	C20F		5/30	5/30	12/34	1
7	TK 5933	Leyland TS3	61509	Duple	C30F	2162	2/31	2/31	12/34	1
8	TK 7530	Dennis Arrow	110045	Duple	C32F	2743	3/32	3/32	12/34	1
9	TK 7531	Dennis Arrow	110046	Duple	C32F	2744	3/32	3/32	12/34	1
10	TK 9099	Leyland TS4	2374	Duple	C31F	3218	4/33	4/33	12/34	1

Notes
1. Vehicles transferred into the fleet of Greyhound Coaches (Weymouth) Ltd.

Disposals
Ford T   Not known.
PR 1988   W.J. Barkus (dealer) Caversham Road, Reading. LO.
PR 8683   To Lyne, Tarrant Rushton by 1.34. To Mrs Green, Middle Range Farm, Whitchurch, Canonicorum c. 1935. LO.
TK 3148   Biggs, Winterborne Abbas, then Mrs Green, Middle Range Farm, Whitchurch, Canonicorum. LO.

Other Vehicles
TK 6424   Humber car reg. 22/5/31 licensed as PSV with Austin to Tilleys (dealers), Weymouth.
PR 8377   Humber car reg. 2/27 to Revd Cowley, Stinsford, Dorchester, Dorset. Licensed as PSV with Austin, to Greyhound Coaches (Weymouth) Ltd.

Greyhound Coaches (Weymouth) Ltd

No.	Reg No.	Chassis	No.	Body	Type	No.	Built	Acq.	Sold	Notes
1	OH 2209	Crossley			CH14			12/34		1
3	TK 4979	Dennis GL	70662	Dennis	B20F		8/30	12/34	1/36	1
4	TK 4650	Dennis GL	70632	Dennis	B20F		5/30	12/34	1/36	1
5	TK 2299	Star Fly VB4	1041		C		3/29	12/34	12/34	2
6	TK 4628	Dennis Dart	75704	Duple	B20F	2175	5/30	12/34	1/36	1
7	TK 2584	G/ford 166SD	10613	Wycombe	C26F		5/29	12/34	1/36	1
8	TK 5933	Leyland TS3	61509	Duple	C30F	2162	2/31	12/34	1/36	2
9	TK 7530	Dennis Arrow	110045	Duple	C32F	2743	3/32	12/34	1/36	2
10	TK 7531	Dennis Arrow	11046	Duple	C32F	2744	3/32	12/34	1/36	2
11	JT 990	Commer Cent.	56040	Harrington	B20F		5/34	12/34	1/36	1
12	TK 7892	AEC Regal	6621358	Harrington	C32F		6/32	12/34	1/36	1
13	TK 9301	AEC Regal	6221505	Harrington	C32F		5/33	12/34	1/36	1
14	TK 9099	Leyland TS 4	2374	Duple	C31F	3218	3/33	12/34	1/36	2
15	JT 2382	Dennis L/cet	17087	Duple	C32F	4878	2/35	2/35	1/36	3
16	JT 3055	Dennis L/cet	170980	Duple	C32F	5512	6/35	6/35	1/36	3

Notes
1. Ex-Victory Tours vehicle.
2. Ex-Austin, Greyhound vehicle.
3. New vehicle into combined fleet.

Disposals

OH 2209	Unidentified dealer Brighton 12/34.
TK 4979	SNOC No. 3588. LL 11/37 to W. North (dealer), Leeds, 1937. By 4.38 to Dawson (dealer), Clapham, London for scrap.
TK 4650	SNOC No. 3589. 12/37 to J.A. Watson 'Watsons Coaches', Gunnislake (H), to Ministry of Supply, LL 6/41. LO.
TK 2299	R.W. Toop 'Bere Regis & District Motor Services'. To R.W. Toop, W.J. Ironside and P.W. Davis, trading as 'Bere Regis & District Motor Services', Dorchester. 9/40 to Ministry of Supply.
TK 4628	SNOC No. 3581. To G.C. Cook (dealer), Battersea, London. LL 11/38.
TK 2584	SNOC No. 3591. Sold 1937, by 8/38 G. Castle 'Stotfolder Coaches', Stotfield (F). Withdrawn 12/42. To H.V. Freemantle & H. Dobson 'Progress Coaches', Sanderstead (N). 6/46 to A.H. Hill, Greenwich, London. LL 9/48.
TK 5933	SNOC No. 3587. 1940 fitted with a new Duple body C30F (No. 9870 series 2). 12/52 to Swann (dealer), Weymouth, scrapped 1954.
TK 7530	SNOC No. 3586. 10/40 damaged by enemy action Weymouth. 1947 Beale (dealer), Exeter for scrap. LO.
TK 7531	SNOC No. 3585. 1942 damaged by enemy action at Portland, LL 17/3/42, stored, to J. Miller (scrap dealer), Weymouth, scrapped 10/4/53.
JT 990	SNOC No. 3592. Withdrawn 7/40. 4/4/6 to Beale (dealer), Exeter. By 2/49 with W.E. & L.J. Grundon, Eltham, London. 11/49 to Grundon's Coaches, Eltham, London, withdrawn 11/50.
TK 7892	SNOC No. 3582. 1940 fitted with Duple body C32F, No. 8472. 8/54 to Swann (dealer), Weymouth. 12/54 Scource (scrap dealer), Weymouth; scrapped.
TK 9301	SNOC No. 3583 1953 to Thompson (dealer), Cardiff; scrapped.
TK 9099	SNOC No. 3584. 1941 fitted with new Duple body C32F (No. 9869, series 2). 9/52 to Swann (dealer), Weymouth.
JT 2382	SNOC No. 3593. 1/50 to Dunns Motors, Taunton. LL 9/54. Withdrawn 4/55 LO.
JT 3055	SNOC No. 3590. Withdrawn 10/49. 3/50 to S. Allan 'Beacon Tours', St Austell (H). Withdrawn 3/53. To K. Hartley, Wakefield, scrapped.

Other Vehicles

PR 8377	Humber car. Reg. 2/27 to Revd Cowley, Stinsford, Dorchester. Licensed as PSV with Austin, to Greyhound Coaches (Weymouth) Ltd.
UU 6871	Humber car licensed as PSV by Greyhound by 1934.

J.J. Hodges, Chickerell, Weymouth

W.J. Hodges was in business by the mid-1890s as a blacksmith in Commercial Road, Weymouth. By 1898 James Hodges was engaged as an Engineer, Smith, General Machinist, Cycle Agent & Repairer, and iron fences were made and repaired. Trading from Little George Street (later renamed Westham Road) in later years, the business became a cycle shop. In 1905 he was also trading from the 'Station Cycle Works' Victoria Arcade, opposite Weymouth railway station. In March 1913 the blacksmith's business in Commercial Road was disposed of owing to the ill health of W.J. Hodges.

Hodges resided at Wesley Villa, East Street, Chickerell. In October 1916 he became the owner of FX 634, a Rover 15 hp Landau taxi. During the 1920s he entered into the coach business, a small Fiat vehicle being purchased, and he engaged in various work including conveying children from Langton Herring to Chickerell school. One of his sons, also named James, joined the business, and later grandson Jimmy Hodges succeeded him.

In December 1930 Hodges applied to Weymouth Council for a Hackney carriage licence for one motor coach. This was refused as the Council would not allow more than 30 licensed coaches within the Borough. Hodges took the refusal to appeal with the newly-formed Traffic Commissioners, who granted a tours & excursions licence. The main problem was obtaining space at the King's Statue for his vehicle, the Town Council's argument being that there was no room for more coaches on the site as the steadily increasing size of coaches and the erection of a waiting shelter were causing problems for the existing operators. The matter dragged on for a considerable time, but in late August 1931 Hodges took delivery of a new Bedford coach.

In 1932 Hodges again applied to the Council for permission to use the motor coach stand at the King's Statue for one vehicle, and quickly followed this application by a letter with a change of plan, as he realised that the Council would find many difficulties. He submitted an application to ply for hire from Westham car park, under the same hours and regulations as applied to the King's Statue site, and also sought permission to erect a small sectional hut for use as a booking office.

The use of that site for the commencement of tours was agreed on condition that no obstruction was caused at the car park entrance, a charge of 1s. per day per vehicle being made for use of the site. However, the Council would not grant permission for the erection of a booking office.

Although working away from any competition, at the end of the 1932 Summer season Hodges requested to move from the car park to the King's Statue owing to slackness of trade, the Council replying that they would consider the application. Early in 1933 Hodges applied to the Council for a site opposite the Alexandra Gardens, an application that the Council deferred to a later meeting. James Hodges died suddenly in February 1933 aged 56. Shortly after this his motor coach business was sold to C. Dean & Son of Chickerell garage, who took over the operation of the Westham site.

Despite Hodges operation being small and not well recorded, he had the distinction of owning the first Bedford coach in the area. TK 6827 was a Bedford WLB registered in September 1931. As Bedford coach production had only just commenced the previous month, this vehicle must have been one of the first off the production line. With a wheelbase of 13 ft 1 in. it was powered by a six-cylinder OHV engine with a cylinder bore of 3⁵⁄₁₆ in. and a stroke of 3¾ in., developing 26.33 hp. Brakes were mechanically operated without a servo, the complete chassis costing just over £200.

The cycle business continued to trade from No. 13 Westham Road, until July 1937 when it moved to Frederick Place, in St Thomas Street, when the Westham Road shops were rebuilt. The St Thomas Street business was taken over by Messrs Tilleys as their pram and baby supplies shop in 1949. Jimmy Hodges will be best remembered for his contribution to local football, as he played for both Chickerell United and some Weymouth clubs. He qualified as a referee in 1926, held many appointments within the sport and was still secretary of the Dorset Football Association when he died aged 68, on 25th December, 1968.

J.J. Hodges, Chickerell, Weymouth

No.	Reg No.	Chassis	No.	Body	Type	No.	Built	Acq.	Sold	Notes
	T 8636	Fiat 15/20 hp	F2/172524		CH14		1/20	c./24	3/31	
	TK 6827	Bedford WLB			C20F		9/31	9/31	1933	

Previous Owners
T 8636   New to Western 'Culme Valley', Uffculme.

Disposals
T 8636   No further user.
TK 6827 To Dean 'Monarch Coaches', Chickerell, Weymouth.

C.W. Dean & Sons, 'Monarch Coaches', Chickerell, Weymouth

The Dean family were involved with the Chickerell Brickworks, situated in Putton Lane. Charles Dean was born in 1860 at Lytchett Minster, where he worked in the clay pits and brick kilns with his father. In later years he was involved in similar ventures in other parts of the country, taking out his own patent and building many kilns embodying his own ideas, and he worked for some time in China. In his later years he turned the clay pits in Putton Lane, Chickerell to good account and formed the Weymouth Brick Company. He retired from that business on his 68th birthday in 1928.

However, in 1929 he decided to enter the road haulage business, a garage and filling station being constructed on the main road at Chickerell. In the event only one Ford 'AA' 30 cwt lorry was purchased in March 1929, and the motor coach business was entered into instead, Dean trading as 'Monarch Coaches'. A Chevrolet 20-seat coach was acquired in 1930, and a Ford 'AA' 14-seater the following year.

A stage carriage service between Chickerell and Weymouth, via Westham, on Saturdays only and a service to Dorchester Market via Weymouth on Wednesdays was commenced. With the introduction of the 1930 Act the Chickerell-Weymouth service was refused a licence, but the Chickerell-Dorchester service was allowed. At the same time a licence was granted for a group of seven excursions and tours to operate between May and October, commencing at the Turks Head Inn, Chickerell, with a picking up and setting down point in Weymouth at Westham bridge car park. In 1932 application was made for modification of the tours operated, plus additional picking up points at Wyke Hotel and Weymouth Lido. The tour modifications were granted, but the additional picking up points were withdrawn!

In March 1932 Dean applied to the Traffic Commissioners to have a pick-up point at the corner of St Thomas Street and Westham Road, Weymouth, for excursions and tours operated from Chickerell, but it has to be said that - even with the small amount of traffic of the period - it would have been a dangerous place to stop, and the application was withdrawn. In May 1933 Dean again applied for a pick-up point at the King's Statue in connection with tours, excursions and pre-booked parties, but again this was refused. Within a month Dean had purchased the business of J.J. Hodges, and in July a letter to the Watch Committee requested that he be permitted the same facilities at Westham car park, the application to the Commissioners to take over Hodges' licences having been made on 21st April, 1933 and granted on 26th May. The acquisition of the Hodges' business gave Dean the all-important Westham coach park site, the licences, and the school contract between Langton Herring and Chickerell.

In 1934, under the Western Traffic Commissioners, an application was made to alter and add certain tours, more importantly to pick up and set down at Chickerell Garage in addition to the Turks Head Inn, and an additional pick-up point at the Swan Inn, Wyke Square. Although this application was opposed by Southern National and Hants & Dorset, it was granted! An attempt was made again in October 1936 to change the picking up point to the King's Statue, this being again opposed by Weymouth Corporation and by Southern National and P.J. Jeanes, so once again the move was refused.

In the 10 years Monarch Coaches were in operation five of the six vehicles owned were purchased new. The fleet livery was two shades of blue with various amounts of cream lining, and they reflected the development of motor coaches of the period. The first vehicle purchased, TK 4140 - a Chevrolet LQ - was a quality lightweight

JT 3097 Dennis Lancet I, new to Dean 'Monarch Coaches' in June 1935. Finished in a blue and cream livery complete with the Dean crest on the side, the body style of the period is clearly shown in this manufacturer's photograph.

Reproduced by permission of Surrey History Service

machine of its day, powered by a six-cylinder OHV engine with a cylinder bore of 3⁵⁄₁₆ in. and a stroke of 3¾ in. developing 26.33 hp. The three-bearing crankshaft had splash lubrication for the bottom ends, and the drive was via a four-speed gearbox. It was a lively model capable of 50 mph, and the precursor of the later Bedford models!

The second purchase TK 6310 was a Ford 'AA' this also being a well-proven, lightweight machine of the period. A four-cylinder petrol engine with a bore of 3.87 mm and a stroke of 4.25 mm developed 40 bhp. Fitted with a four-speed gearbox the complete 13 ft 1 in. wheelbase chassis cost £195. The purchase of PO 7597 was a far more expensive proposition, this being a Garner coach with a 20-seat Harrington body. Although well produced it was not widely sold. It had a normal control chassis, and was fitted with an 'Austin Twenty' engine. Sold out of the Monarch fleet, it is believed to have passed to another Dorset operator thought to be Sprackling, of Ivory Coaches, Winterborne Stickland. By 1940 it had passed, via Lee Motors of Bournemouth, to Bodman of Worton, Devizes, and was in regular use on various duties until 1949.

The first Bedford acquired was TK 6827 with the takeover of Hodges as already described. A heavyweight machine was obtained in June 1935 with the purchase of a Dennis Lancet I, complete with Dennis bodywork, and the following year one of the ever-faithful Bedford WTB models was the last vehicle to join the fleet.

The sale of Greyhound to Southern National in 1936 put Dean in the position of being the only private coach operator in the Weymouth district. By 1937 the business was registered with the Traffic Commissioners as W.C.L. & C. Dean, trading as C. Dean & Son, Chickerell Garage, Chickerell, Weymouth, with 32 tours licensed for operation. The Chickerell-Dorchester stage service was still operated plus several taxis, and the garage also sold petrol.

The business carried on until early 1940 when, faced with an uncertain future and the loss of tours income, it was decided to sell. F.C. Hoare of Bluebird Coaches, Portland was in the process of taking over the business, when in July 1940 the Army requisitioned JT 3097, the Dennis and JT 5178, the Bedford WTB, these events ending the first 10 years in the history of Chickerell garage.

Dean, 'Monarch Coaches', Chickerell, Weymouth

No.	Reg No.	Chassis	No.	Body	Type	No.	Built	Acq.	Sold	Notes
	TK 4140	Chevrolet	LQ61454		C20		2/30	2/30	b/34	
	TK 6310	Ford			C14		5/31	5/31	b/34	
	PO 7597	Garner	132500BPC		20F		5/33	5/33		
	TK 6827	Bedford WLB			C20F		9/31	1933	b/36	
	JT 3097	Dennis Lct I	170978		C32F		6/35	6/35	1940	
	JT 5178	Bedford WTB	110751	Duple	C26	7658	6/36	6/36	1940	

Previous Owners
TK 6827   Hodge, Chickerell, Weymouth.

Disposals
TK 4140   To Toop, Bere Regis by 1934, to Bere Regis & District, LL 30/9/40. LO Lancashire Motor Traders.
TK 6310   By 1934 to Clark of Horsham, LO Carter, Plumbers Plain Garage, Horsham.
PO 7597   To Dorset operator thought to be Sprackling 'Ivory Coaches', Winterborne Stickland, Blandford. To Bodman, Worton, Devizes, *circa* 1940. WD by Bodman in 2/49.
TK 6827   To Palmer, Fordham 'Fordham & Dostrict' by 1936. To Ministry of Supply 3/41. LO MOS.
JT 3097   7/40 requisitioned by Army. To F.C. Hoare 'Bluebird Coaches', Chickerell, Weymouth by 1944.
JT 5178   7/40 requisitioned by Army. To F.C. Hoare 'Bluebird Coaches', Chickerell, Weymouth by 2/48.

Walter John Mullins

As described in Chapter One, there were a number of small operators or prospective operators who applied for Hackney licences to operate char-a-bancs. Some never entered the business, whilst others quickly departed with little or nothing recorded of them.

We do however know a little of the business of Walter John Mullins, who became the owner of a 14-seat left-hand-drive Ford model 'T' char-a-banc, FX 8283 which was first registered in October 1921. Mullins was granted a Hackney licence in April 1922, but in May 1925 the Watch Committee were not satisfied with the condition of his vehicle and were not prepared to renew the licence for the following year. However, it would appear that some rectification work was carried out, as in April 1926 the Committee renewed the licence for FX 8283.

No other mention of Mullins appears in remaining Council records, except that in September 1929 the Watch Committee was informed that W.J. Mullins had been plying for hire without a licence. With the forthcoming 1930 Act, operation of the Ford 'T' would have been difficult if not impossible. The Mullins family became haulage contractors and later furniture removers, a business in which they were very successful. In later years CFX 171, their 1947 Bedford pantechnicon with a Lee Motors body in cream livery with red lettering, was a familiar sight on house removals in the Weymouth area.

John Oliver Moore

J.O. Moore resided at 2 Crescent Court, Crescent Street, Weymouth, but of his business little is known. He is recorded as the last owner of a Ford model 'T' char-a-banc, FX 9136. It is reputed that his vehicle was painted red and he traded as 'One Man Band'. Moore survived quite late, as in 1929 the Watch Committee allowed him to stand one coach at the King's Statue, but the forthcoming 1930 Act doubtless caused his demise. It appears that he also undertook taxi driving, a Unic car, PR 2100, being registered to him in March 1924, and he was the last owner of FX 9702. J.O. Moore still held a Hackney licence for taxi work in the late 1940s.

Like many others Moore had used the Ford model 'T'. This indefatigable little machine was the inspiration of many operators, and a brief description of this chassis is a worthy end to this part of the story.

Although almost universally referred to as the Model 'T', later char-a-bancs were constructed on the 'TT' chassis. British production of this modified chassis commenced in 1918. With a 10 ft 4 in. wheelbase, the truck version could carry a 1 ton payload, but like the model 'T', many were over-bodied and in consequence overloaded. The alternative to the 'TT' chassis was one of several conversion kits available to lengthen the 'T' chassis.

The engine and gear box were the same as fitted to the 'T' which, when first introduced in 1908, was ahead of others. The four cylinders were cast in one block which also formed the crankcase, and the cylinder head was detachable - an advance on the former 'fixed head'engine. This new idea forms basic engine design to the present day. The ignition system was supplied by a low tension flywheel magneto. The suspension consisted of large transverse leaf springs at both front and rear.

The most interesting item was the two-speed epicylic gearbox. Driving a Ford 'T' was different to other vehicles, there being no gear lever or clutch pedal. The right pedal operated the brake which acted on the transmission shaft. The centre pedal, when depressed, engaged reverse gear, whilst the left-hand pedal operated the two forward speeds and neutral. Depress the pedal and low gear was engaged, whilst releasing it engaged top gear, neutral being selected by partly depressing the pedal and partly applying the handbrake! The throttle control was on the steering column.

The 'T' and 'TT' models remained in production until 1927. Their spindly features, particularly the fragile-looking, yet strong, vanadium steel front axle, was a trade mark of this remarkable vehicle which formed the basis of many small bus operators' fleets.

AEC 'YC' No. 2221, CC 4240, originally a lorry. The chassis was reconditioned and fitted with a Dodson OT30/26RO body which cost £508 6s. 4d. in 1925, entering service at Weymouth during the Summer of the same year. Photographed at Upwey, Royal Oak. By December 1919, 2221 had passed to the Eastern National fleet. *E. Latcham Collection*

No. 2032, BM 8020, loads passengers in the road outside the King's Statue during the 1920s; to board a bus at that point in later years would be almost suicidal! No. 2032 was a 3 ton Dennis subsidy chassis purchased in 1919 from the Government depot at Slough. Fitted with a Brush B32R body formerly fitted to a Tilling Stevens of Southend-on-Sea Corporation, No. 2032 was sold out of service in April 1932, ending her days on a farm at Osmington. *Author's Collection*

Chapter Seven

The National Omnibus & Transport Company

The history of the National Omnibus & Transport Company, and its successors is long and complex. Originally commencing life as 'The National Steam Car Company' at Chelmsford in June 1909, the initial concept was the manufacture of the Clarkson steam bus. Very quickly it became an omnibus operating company with interests in the London area and Essex, with the steam bus featuring in its operations.

By the end of World War I, operations had spread to Bedfordshire and the surrounding area, and the steam bus had given way to the now improved motor bus. The company was reformed as the 'National Omnibus & Transport Company' on 13th February, 1920.

It was a time of rapid expansion. In October 1919 a depot had been established at Stroud in Gloucestershire, and the tentacles of 'National' were spreading westwards as services commenced at Bridgwater and Yeovil in July 1920. Taunton was added the following year, aided by the closure of the local Electric Tramway system. In the same year a Yeovil-Bridport service had commenced, and by 1922 a depot opened at Bridport, which allowed a service to Weymouth via Winterborne Abbas and Upwey to be commenced on 8th July. On the same date a vehicle was out-stationed at Swanage, and started a Swanage-Weymouth service (36).

The Town Council at Weymouth considered they were already well catered for with existing bus services, clearly not wishing to upset the GWR, Road Motors, or any of the small local operators just starting up by allowing 'National' permission to operate buses within the Borough.

The Bridport and Swanage services ceased at the end of the season, returning the following year when the Bridport-Weymouth service operated via Dorchester, and a service from Yeovil via Sherborne, Cerne Abbas, and Dorchester to Weymouth (35) was added. The lack of co-operation at Weymouth caused the 'National' operations to remain seasonal. Towards the end of 1924 difficulties encountered by the Weymouth Motor Company Ltd allowed 'National' the opportunity it required. The purchase of the company and its operating base at Edward Street gave them the all-important licences.

The acquisition by 'National' of Messrs Road Motors of Luton in April 1925 increased its Weymouth operation with the ownership of Radipole garage and the all-important Upwey-Radipole-Weymouth-Wyke Regis-Portland Victoria Square stage carriage service, this becoming route 33. Thus despite the actions of Weymouth Council, about whom there had been accusations of members having a vested interest in the local operators, the 'National' became well established within the Borough.

In May National approached Portland UDC with a proposal to extend the bus service to Castletown, the Council replying that they did not wish this to take place. However expansion in other directions soon did occur with the takeover of Messrs Jeanes' Chickerell service from 30th July, 1925, certain journeys then being extended to Abbotsbury, where an outstation was established by driver Hurford that October, the fare to Weymouth being 1s. single, 1s. 6d. return. It was the beginning of the end for the Abbotsbury branch railway!

During the July of 1926 two toastrack type vehicles were placed in service between the Pavilion Theatre and Bowleaze Cove, but this service was not operated without difficulty. At the September Watch Committee meeting representatives of 'National' were present, and issues such as recent accidents, overcrowding, and failure to keep to the timetable with the 'Runabouts' ('Toastracks') were discussed. 'National' admitted that the timetable for the service was a mistake, but it applied for licences

One of the four Dennis 'E' types new to Weymouth in May 1927 No. 2380, PR 9052, fitted with a Strachan & Brown B32D body is photographed at Lulworth Cove after working a service from Weymouth. Messrs Leak, Mead and Valance stand alongside. Leak and Mead remained with Southern National until retirement, whereas the Dennis 'E' types were retired for reasons unexplained in 1934 after only seven years' service. *E. Latcham Collection*

AEC Reliance No. 2895, TM 5265, with driver Jack Moore at the King's Statue, before departing for Exeter. Although the photograph states 1928, the vehicle was not built until 1929, and Southern National transfers have been applied to the side, all this adding at least a year to the date. The original Dodson B32R body was replaced by a Bristol B32R body in 1937. *Author's Collection*

Conductor Woodsford, stands alongside toastrack 2858, TK 2830, at Bowleaze Cove. In this pre-1930 photograph note the original small solid-tyred wheels guaranteed to give a rough ride on the roads of the period. 2858 fetched £50 when sold for scrap in 1941.

Author's Collection

for three additional 'Runabouts' for the following year which would enable a seven or eight minute service to be run.

'National' buses commenced to run to the top of Portland following the acquisition of Smith & Hoare in February 1927. On 28th of that month 'National' experienced its first serious incident when a bus was trapped in flood water on the Portland Beach Road. Just after 5pm a Portland-bound bus became trapped on the section of road by the oil tanks, water soon rising to the top of the wheels. A clergyman on board waded through the water to Portland to obtain assistance, but in the meantime a railway wagon was noticed in the siding just over the wall and the passengers were lifted onto the wall and into the wagon. Some men were just starting to push the wagon towards the station when the clergyman returned with a rowing boat, and they were then transferred to it and rowed to Portland. It must be the only time that a passenger between Weymouth and Portland has travelled by bus, rail and boat in a single journey!

The *Southern Times* for 21st May, 1927 referred to members of Portland UDC taking the inaugural trip on the new buses that 'National' had provided for the Tophill route. 'National', now established on the Island with a through route from Weymouth to Easton, Southwell, and Portland Bill, caused despair to the Joint Railway Committee which saw patronage of the Easton section of the Portland branch fall further, as detailed in Chapter Three. Although the shareholding and agreements with the railway companies were still several years away, an agreement was soon reached - at least locally. By late May 1927 a notice appeared on the new buses operating the Tophill route, stating that local passengers would not be carried to Rodwell or Wyke Regis. An official of the 'National' explained to the *Dorset Daily Echo* the reason thus:

AEC Regal No.2905, TK 3024, travels along Dorchester Road, descending the hill from Littlemoor Corner towards the Swan Inn at Broadwey, shortly after arriving in Weymouth during the Summer of 1929. The 'Dome Top' of the Short Bros H24/26RO body is clearly shown. Nos. 2904/5 were the first buses in Weymouth to have the luxury of self-starters! Road widening to the right side has altered the scene from 60 years ago. *Author's Collection*

The garage built in 1928 for 'National', viewed from Edward Street. The house in the distance is the first terrace house of Upwey Street. The entrance in the centre of the photograph was in line with Terminus Street which was off picture to the right. *Author's Collection*

On our new route buses run at almost the same times as the GW&SR buses and cover part of the same route. We have made arrangements with the railway companies not to pick up passengers between the Town Bridge and the top of Boot Hill. After ascending Boot Hill our buses turn to the right and travel through Wyke Road where we can pick up passengers for any point. On the return journey from Portland we do not pick up after reaching Wyke Regis.

The minutes of the July 1927 Watch Committee record the following:

Suggested Runabout Service to Westham: The Town Clerk was directed to communicate with the National, intimating that in the Committee's opinion a service of Runabouts to and from Westham would be very beneficial to the residents of that area, and suggesting that the Company should inaugurate such a service. Note:-The Company has since been communicated with, and they adopted the suggestion immediately.

It is open to question if 'Runabouts' were actually used on the service. If so, it would have been an interesting spectacle!

The takeover of the Weymouth-Preston-Sutton Poyntz-Osmington Mills services of White Star (Jeanes) in May 1928 saw three services a day extended to Wool and Lulworth Cove, and a limited stop service to Exeter and Torquay commenced on 28th July. The closure of the Town bridge for reconstruction later in the year was covered by a shuttle service between the Town bridge and the King's Statue (33B) giving connections to other services. An application to extend the Town bridge service to Westerhall via King Street, Ranelagh Road, Walpole Street, and Avenue Road to Carlton Road South was approved by the Council in January 1929.

With the exchange of vehicles between depots it is impossible to give a full account of all the vehicles allocated to Weymouth, and this process continued throughout Southern National history. However, thanks to Watch Committee records, details of which vehicles were licensed to operate within the Borough during 1924 are recorded as six AEC 'YC' types, Nos. 2168, 2169, 2171, 2173 and 2176, all having 30-seat single-deck bodies.

Following the purchase of both the Weymouth Motor Company and Messrs Road Motors, the details after 1925 became a little less clear as the absorbed vehicles were exchanged for others, particularly when overhauls became due. Three National Dennis vehicles, 2010/27/32, and at least one AEC 'YC' No. 2066, arrived during the 1925 season. Two 14-seat Chevrolet buses and three new Guy coaches 2301, 2304 and 2317 arrived in 1926, the latter being the first Beadle-bodied vehicle purchased by the company. The first two Guy B20T 'toastracks', 2323/4, were purchased to operate the Weymouth seafront service.

During 1927 further new vehicles were added to the fleet, and by May some unspecified single-deck vehicles had arrived to work the Tophill services, followed by four Dennis 'E'-type by the end of the month. Three Guy B25T toastracks 2368/9/70 arrived in July, whilst 1928 saw Leyland PLSC1 single-decks join the fleet. Early in 1929 an AEC Reliance demonstrator underwent trials at Weymouth. Registered as TK 1662 and given fleet No. 2510 it was the first of three chassis, 660001-3, rebuilt from 456 models. Fitted with a Harrington B32F body, 2510 only remained in the 'National' fleet for a few months, going to J. Sharp of Manchester in the May. Records show it was last licensed with that company in December 1946, and was broken up in September 1947.

A further two Guy B32T 'toastracks', 2857/8, were purchased in May 1929, bringing the total up to seven, although at least one was employed during the Summer season between Bridport and West Bay.

July 1929 saw two of the latest buses to go into production enter service at Weymouth - AEC Regent double-decks Nos. 2904/5 (chassis Nos. 661005/7). These were part of the pre-production batch of 12 vehicles constructed. Powered by the '6 type' six-cylinder OHV petrol engine, with a bore of 100 mm and stroke of 130 mm developing 95 bhp driving a four-speed gearbox through a single plate clutch, they were fitted with single servo brakes. The 26/24RO bodies were constructed by Short Bros of Rochester to the designs of AEC, a feature of which was the 'camel roof' raised along the centre line to give headroom in the upper deck, but as with many double-decks of the period the staircase was in the open. Weymouth was honoured to have received the vehicles early in July, as the design was not announced to the public until the August! Known locally as the 'Dome Tops', they gave the company remarkable service.

The two Regents were a contrast to the other AEC double-decks in the fleet, the 'YC' types. Although by 1930 they had been fitted with pneumatic tyres they were no match to the latest design. Likewise the Dennis single-decks, although rebodied, were basically war surplus lorry chassis.

With the expansion of services garage facilities had to be improved, and the Edward Street premises, which consisted of a selection of odd buildings and former stables, were demolished and replaced with a modern garage in 1928. A garage was also constructed on land to the east side of Victoria Square, Portland, and major improvements were made to the former Road Motors' garage at Radipole which, up to September 1930, had cost £1,258 14s. These measures gave the area its own workshop facilities. Previously vehicles had to travel, or at worst be towed, considerable distances to receive major attention.

However, time was running out for 'National', the company having expanded beyond the wildest dreams of its founders. The taking over of major operators in Devon and Cornwall, including the GWR bus services, made it remote from its birthplace, and given the circumstances of the time it had become difficult to control from London and Chelmsford. Thus in 1929 it was split into three separate companies, Western National was registered on 1st January, and on 28th February Eastern National, Southern National, Northern National and Midland National were registered. The last two never traded, but were set up to prevent others adopting the name. Following protracted negotiations with the Southern Railway, the final agreements incorporating Southern National were signed at the end of July 1929.

Principal Services of the National Omnibus & Transport Company

Date	NOTC	SNOC	
8/7/22	36	28	Weymouth, Wool, Wareham, Corfe Castle, Swanage.
8/7/22	37	31	West Bay, Bridport, Winterborne Abbas, Dorchester, Weymouth.
1923	35	26	Yeovil, Sherborne, Cerne Abbas, Dorchester Weymouth. B
16/4/25	33	22	Portland VSQ, Wyke Regis, Statue, Radipole, Upwey. A
7/25	32	20	Statue, Chickerell, via Pye Hill or Westham
7/25	32A	20	Statue, Chickerell, Portesham, Abbotsbury.
3/27	40	22	VSQ, Easton, Southwell, Portland Bill. D
1926	33A	23	Pier-Coastguard Station, Overcombe, Bowleaze Cove.
1928	36B	30	Statue, Warmwell Cross, Wool, Lulworth Cove. C
5/28	41	33	Statue, Preston, Sutton Poyntz, or Osmington Mills. E
1928	41A	33	Statue, Preston, Osmington Mills.
1928	42	42	Weymouth, Dorchester, Bridport, Lyme Regis, Axminster, Exeter, Torquay. F
1928	33B	24	Town Bridge, Rly station, Park Estate, Westerhall.
1929	32B		Statue, Cromwell Road, Adlaide Hotel, Westham Cross Roads.

Notes

A Ex-Road Motors Ltd.
B WD 15/9/40 RS 6/47.
C WD 4/8/40 RS 5/46 WD 9/9/61.
D Ex-Smith & Hoare, Portland.

E Ex-White Star, (Jeanes).
F Limited stop, reduced to Exeter. Joint with Devon General after 1937. After 1/6/56 No.47. 1962 service split at Axminster.

Chapter Eight

Southern National Omnibus Company 1929-1949

The change of company name had little effect on the travelling public, except for a revision of service numbers. In May 1932 a head office was set up in Exeter for both Western and Southern National, staff working for both companies. Their pay was charged proportionately to the revenue each company earned. Management became more localised, and expansion was rapid up to the outbreak of war.

With their considerable shareholdings, the railway companies could, to some extent, influence the actions of the company, and the minute books clearly show where the railway interests vetoed a scheme if it looked like affecting their business. Likewise local Council interests also had to be taken into consideration. With the new Town bridge open in 1930 service 33B to the King's Statue, introduced in 1928, had become superfluous as other services returned to their normal routing. However, at a Board meeting during 1932 it was declared:

Although this service is operated with a 14 seater vehicle, the receipts are so appallingly low that it is suggested that application be made to the Commissioners to withdraw it. This service was, however, put on at the special request of the Weymouth Council, and in view of the fact that this council has treated us remarkably well in the past, the Management Committee may consider it wiser under the circumstances not to withdraw the service. [There was however a pencilled note suggesting the mileage be halved!]

Co-operation with the Council was also on the agenda in April 1930 when it was suggested that a large waiting shelter be erected at the King's Statue, the Southern National being willing to subscribe up to £650 towards the cost, subject to a notice inside reading 'Reserved for the Company's passengers only'. In October the Council estimated the cost of constructing a shelter to accommodate 120 persons at £800, so it was decided to reduce this to accommodate 60 persons and provide an enquiry office, the Borough Surveyor stating that the work would not then exceed £650 and that he would proceed as quickly as possible. The company were not so charitable in 1932 when Portland UDC requested the provision of shelters at Fortuneswell, Easton and Weston, the answer being a direct 'No' as they could be used by persons other than Southern National passengers!

The absorption of the GWR bus service at the end of 1933 and the acquisition of the Portland Express operation in 1936 removed the principal fare stage competition from the area, the few remaining independent Portland operators with their limited licences giving little trouble. It was again time to court favour with the Council, and in 1936 it was decided to contribute £50 towards a shelter at Wyke Hotel, and £30 for a shelter at the Town bridge.

Since taking over the Portland Express service there had been much comment concerning the lack of buses at busy periods on the Portland services, to Tophill in particular, where the service was worked by a mixed fleet of single-decks, mostly of 32-seat capacity. The company decided in 1936 to place an order for six 44-seat single-deck buses, the legendary six-wheelers!

There was also the difficulty of keeping the railway companies happy at the same time, as revealed at a meeting between railway and bus company officials in January

No. 2594, UW 4864, a Chevrolet with a Strachan B15F body. This vehicle new in 1928 was first used in the Essex area. Transferred to Weymouth in March 1929, especially to operate the Radipole Park Drive (60) and other restricted routes such as Sandsfoot Castle, and the Nothe Gardens. Photographed at the Weymouth end of Radipole Park Drive, with Melcombe Regis Gardens in the background. Note the fleet name in the earlier style, as used by 'National'. Like many early lightweight vehicles it had a short life, being sold for scrap in December 1935 valued at £9 2s.   *E. Latcham Collection*

Guy toastrack, No 2323, PR 7177, standing at Weymouth Pier awaiting a journey to Bowleaze Cove. The toastracks were the last vehicles to run on solid tyres, in 1933 it was decided to fit them with pneumatics at a cost of £30 each. The B20T open body clearly demonstrates the joys and dangers of such a machine. This vehicle, along with toastracks 2324, 2369, and 2370, was sold in 1937 for the combined price of £57 10s.   *Author's Collection*

1937 which had been convened to discuss proposed bus operations between Upwey, Weymouth, Portland and Easton during the forthcoming Summer. Mr Roland Buszard, assistant traffic manager for Southern National stated that prior to the acquisition of the Portland Express service, 15 vehicles were necessary to work the services compared with 18 buses after takeover. During the Summer of 1937 it was proposed to use 19 buses and increase the number of journeys, because of the services of Portland Express having been embodied in the Summer timetable.

Another problem was that of timekeeping on certain buses to and from Portland Bill which connected with trains at both Portland and Easton stations, Mr Buszard explaining that the heavy nature of the traffic conveyed over the routes during busy periods often necessitated duplications or triplications, and buses were being acquired with a capacity of 44 seats. The service would also be increased to overcome the problems raised by the railway representives.

The GWR representative was concerned about the loss of rail traffic on the Upwey-Weymouth section of the route, and his company viewed with apprehension the proposal to operate at 20 minute intervals instead of half-hourly during the Summer period - especially as the recent proposals of the former Portland Express operators had been successfully opposed by the Traffic Commissioners. Mr Buszard replied that:

The Southern National Company were the original road operators on the route and suggested that, whilst the joint objection was successful, it does not follow necessarily that the Great Western company alone would have been successful in opposing a similar proposal by this company.

Regarding changed circumstances since 1935, Mr Buszard added that the police objected to buses turning at Grey's Corner (Upwey), and turning at the Royal Oak or Wishing Well were the only alternatives. The whole of the route was built up on one side of the road and partly built up on the other side, and the proposals were designed to meet the needs of the residents all along the route. It was clearly a difficult situation, and to some degree a case of biting the hand that had fed them, but business was business, and the rapidly-developing Dorchester road area was a good investment.

The 44-seat six-wheelers entered service during the first week of July 1937, causing the *Dorset Daily Echo* to comment:

The new 44-seaters which have been placed on the Upwey-Southwell-Portland Bill service have met with general approval. They help to obviate overcrowding and being left behind. They have but one drawback - their length. This only appears in Fortuneswell in the busy hours of the day, when their drivers have to prove themselves expert jugglers at manoeuvring in and out of the frequent traffic jams. It was difficult enough when the 32 and 36 seaters were the biggest on the roads, but now a few feet have been added to the length of the buses hold ups are more frequent.

Only four double-deck vehicles were allocated to Weymouth, all AEC Regents dating from 1929/30, but during July and September six new double-decks arrived thus alleviating problems on the Upwey-Portland route. Although this eliminated the overcrowding and the complaints received from the Dorchester Road residents, it led to complaints from the residents of Church Street, leading to the Wishing Well, where the road is narrow and the majority of the houses low and very close to it, without a footpath. They did not appreciate the large double-decks passing their

The first staff outing of the employees of the Regent Cinema was photographed for posterity with the coach taking centre stage. No. 3405, TK 6402 a 1931 Leyland TS1 with Duple C26D body, clearly shows the green livery carried by coaches at that period. In May 1939 No. 3405 was fitted with a Beadle C31R coach body and transferred to the Royal Blue fleet until withdrawn in 1952.   *Author's Collection*

AEC Regal No. 2993, TK 4883, stands at Portland Bill during 1935 with its original Strachan B32R body. In January 1938 a Duple C32F coach body was fitted, the original body being disposed of for £40. After an eventful life 2993 was withdrawn during 1953.   *E. Latcham Collection*

property. Whilst the main attention had been focused on the Upwey-Portland services, other developments had been taking place. On 1st June, 1931 a 'Summer only' service from the King's Statue to the Nothe Gardens commenced, and the following July a seasonal service to Sandsfoot Castle Gardens came into operation, running from the King's Statue via Westham bridge and Westwey Road. Both services were operated by low capacity vehicles, and sometimes the Guy toastracks. The rapidly expanding council housing estate at Westham received a direct service (20A) to Westham Cross Roads in April 1933, whilst in July 1935 a second service (20B) running through the estate commenced. October 1934 saw a service to Radipole Village (60), primarily intended to serve the isolated housing development at Southill.

In October 1935 a service commenced from Portland station to the Dockyard and HMS *Osprey*. The reason the service started from the station was that the railway members of the Board considered they provided an adequate service from Weymouth. The takeover of the Dorchester town bus service operated by Deacon on 7th January, 1935 created a small sub-depot in the County town. A forerunner of the war clouds gathering was the application in August 1937 to operate excursions from the new aerodrome at Woodsford (RAF Warmwell) to both Dorchester and Weymouth. As part of a tidying up operation of various adjoining routes with Devon General, the Weymouth-Exeter service became a joint operation during that year.

In September 1938 a service to the small hamlet of Nottington situated half a mile off the main Dorchester Road commenced, and in June 1939 the 24 service was revised to run from Grosvenor Road through the Park District to the King's Statue, then on to the new estate at Southlands. Here again was conflict with the Portland branch railway, a halt for Sandsfoot Castle having been opened alongside the estate in August 1932, and a connecting footbridge installed. However as this estate was built on both sides of a valley with steep hills on all roads, and the stations at the Weymouth end were not well suited for the main shopping area, there was little incentive for residents to patronise the railway for local journeys.

At the same time long distance services had also expanded with the introduction of a Weymouth-Bournemouth service on 26th July, 1930 (jointly with Hants & Dorset), certain journeys being extended to Easton on 1st December. Surprisingly the Southern Railway had agreed to the operation of this service. A coastal route from Weymouth to Bridport via Abbotsbury commenced in June 1932, whilst a Salisbury-Weymouth service, operated by Wilts & Dorset, had commenced in June 1929.

The tours and excursions side of the business at Weymouth had also been developed, the small operators which had not gone before or shortly after the 1930 Road Traffic Act virtually out-paced by the new coaches that Southern National could afford. The takeover of the Greyhound fleet in 1936 cleared most of the remaining opposition from the King's Statue, the non-appearance of any coaches belonging to the Jeanes family and the acquisition of their licences the following year completing the process. Dean (Monarch Coaches), operating from Westham coach park, was the only independent remaining!

The acquisition of the Greyhound express services added to the long distance services provided. In January 1935 the express services of Royal Blue were taken over by the Southern & Western National companies, and shortly after Southern National express services were transferred to the Royal Blue side of the business.

The booking office moved from Edward Street to No. 5 Royal Terrace, at the King's Statue, during 1937. At that time Weymouth had 77 vehicles allocated to the

Photographed at Portland Bill during 1937 is Tilling Stevens No 63, FJ 8983, with its original 1933 Brush B35R body, rebodied by ECW in 1945, and withdrawn from service during 1954. It continued in use as a demonstration van for F. Mitchell of Chapelthorpe, Wakefield.

R.C. Sambourne

Bristol GO5G No. 239 stands at Radipole before departing for Portland, Victoria Square On the side of the Beadle H30/26R body the letters 'GW & SR' can be seen under the Southern National fleetname, this short-lived device was applied to vehicles 237-240 but had been removed by 1939. No. 239 with the remainder of the batch was rebodied with ECW L27/28R bodies in 1949, all being withdrawn in 1958 after 21 years' service.

Author's Collection

depot, Edward Street could accommodate 41, the others being kept at Radipole and Portland, whilst 13 coaches were garaged in the former Greyhound premises at Chickerell. Expansion of the Edward Street premises was the answer, and in March 1937 the whole of Terrace Street and Nos. 12 and 13 Commercial Road were purchased at a cost of £7,964 5s. 2d. In October 1938 a 'stopping up' order was placed on Terrace Street, but little else was done until the air raid of October 1940 decided the matter!

The Portland garage fuel tank was converted to store diesel oil during 1938, indicating that diesel-engined vehicles were allocated there. At least one six-wheeler (probably two) was kept at Portland, the 8.40 am from Victoria Square to Weymouth being worked by one of these vehicles with a Portland crew, and a duplicate using a Bristol L5G, also with a Portland crew, then worked the 10 am Weymouth-Swanage (28). Portland-based vehicles often worked other routes not connected with the island at various times of day, and likewise Portland crews often worked Weymouth-based buses and routes before joining a Portland vehicle for their return to the island. As well as being a working garage, Portland was useful to store delicensed vehicles, the toastracks often taking refuge on the island during the winter months.

During the 10 years just reviewed great advances had been made in the types of vehicle available. The first two vehicles to arrive under the new management were AEC Regents with bodies by Short Bros, L24/24R double decks Nos. 3031/2, which arrived in Weymouth in March and May 1930, followed by a batch of AEC Regals with Strachan & Brown B32R single-deck bodies. During 1932 the delivery of three Tilling Stevens saloons with Beadle B32R bodies, Nos. 3346/7/8, allowed the withdrawal of three former 'National' Dennis saloons which were, by then, completely outdated.

The original 'National' fleet numbering system had been continued, and by the end of 1932 it had reached No. 3397. From 1933 Western and Southern National used a new combined numbering system based on vehicle classes for new stock, the old system from No. 3398 upwards being retained for acquired vehicles. The registration procedure was also revised. Previously vehicles had been registered in the county in which they first operated, but after the registration of vehicles Nos. 50-65 with Exeter City Council, all subsequent vehicles were registered with Devon County Council.

The first vehicles to enter the fleet under the new numbering system were Tilling Stevens Brush-bodied B32R single-decks Nos. 50-65, several being allocated to Weymouth for various duties. By this time the remaining AEC 'YC' double-decks and the Dennis saloons of the former Road Motors' fleet had been withdrawn. An interesting purchase in January 1935 was former Southdown No. 153, a Leyland G7 of 1923 rebodied with a Short Bros B27/24RO body in 1929. The intention was to run a seasonal open-top service between Bridport and West Bay, but the Traffic Commissioners refused to license the service, and at least during the Summer of 1937 it worked local services at Weymouth as fleet No. 3506.

Also during 1935 the decision was made to fit two of Weymouth's AEC Regents with diesel engines, No. 3031 receiving a Gardner 6LW in April and 3032 in June.

The first Bristol chassis were purchased by the company in 1935 when 27 'JJW' type joined the Royal Blue fleet. In 1936 a batch of J05G with B32R bus bodies were acquired, Nos. 192-193 had Eastern Counties' bodies whilst No. 232 had a Beadle body.

The arrival of the six-wheelers put a new dimension into the bus operations on the island, and they quickly proved to be the most successful and reliable vehicles on the route, becoming a legend in their own time!

Weymouth's first Bristol double-deck No. 237, ETA 984, stands at the King's Statue before departing for Portland, Victoria Square. In this photograph taken just before the war the 'GW & SR' device had been removed from under the fleetname. The original Beadle H30/26R body shown in the photograph ended its days on a farm at Catsburg Cross, Bideford, when 237 was rebodied in 1949. To the left is the shelter of 1932, one of the six-wheelers is parked in the background. *Omnibus Society*

The pre-war Edward Street garage looking out into Terrace Street. To the right is No. 3105, a Leyland TS1 with a Duple 26-seat body. To the left a Leyland and an AEC parked under the low beam that was to cause problems after the bombing. Compare this view with that on page 217 taken in October 1954. *E. Latcham Collection*

The Leyland Tiger (or 'TS7' model) was introduced in 1935, improvements on the previous 'TS6' including replacement of the triple-servo brake system by a Lockheed vacuum-hydraulic system, a larger clutch and a fully floating rear axle. The electrical system was of the standard 12-volt CAV Bosch type.

The chassis of the 'TS7D' (driven rear axle) was an extended version of the TS7 model. The wheelbase was 18 ft 10 in., this measurement being taken between the centre of the front axle and the centre point between the rear axles. The overall length was 30 ft, the legal limit, it was only 27 ft 6 in. for two-axle buses! The rear wheels were mounted on a bogie constructed with inverted springs, an axle being fitted at the fore and aft end of the springs. The unit was fixed to the chassis by large bearings mounted on the centre of the springs, these being fitted with needle roller bearings which allowed the bogie to swing in the vertical direction. By removing the bearing caps, the entire bogie could be wheeled out from under the rear of the jacked-up chassis.

Southern National was at that time under the control of the legendary B.V. Smith, who was both General Manager and Engineer and had a policy of fitting Gardner oil engines into most vehicles. The Leyland engine was not acceptable, and an outside contractor fitted the 5LW units into the chassis. The B44C bodies were constructed by J.C. Beadle of Dartford, Kent, the first two chassis arrived from Leyland on 4th and 6th April, 1937, the other three following on 7th May. They were numbered 1000-1005 in the fleet, ETA 233-238, chassis Nos. 13900-5 and body Nos. 614-9. Each chassis cost £751 15s. 3d. and each body £552 15s.

The local populace having been awe struck by the appearance of the six-wheelers, were in for a further treat on 23rd July when three Bristol GO5G double-decks, Nos. 237/8/9, arrived from Messrs J.C. Beadle, and were put straight into service. No. 240 followed on 29th July and entered service on 1st August. The 'G' was the second double-deck chassis produced by Bristol, the previous 'A' type being obsolete by the early 1930s. However the 'G' had a short production run, only 248 chassis being produced, the Southern National chassis being numbered 197-200. They were powered by Gardner 5LW diesel engines.

The 'G' chassis was quickly superseded by the 'K' type during 1937, the first two purchased by Southern National, Nos. 243/4, arriving in Weymouth from Messrs J.C. Beadle on 25th September, 1937 and entering service from the 1st October. These were early production models with chassis Nos. 42.10 and 42.11, and as with the previous 'G' type chassis, the bodies fitted were Beadle H30/26Rs.

The 'K' type was without doubt the finest double-deck chassis produced by Bristol, ranking alongside the Leyland Titan and the AEC Regent - and many say it was superior. It was known as 'The Engineer's Bus' because of its ease of maintenance. In 18 years of production 4,146 'K' chassis and variants were produced.

By August 1937 the six-wheelers and new double-decks were responsible for the main Upwey-Portland services, allowing the original AEC Regents 2904/5 to operate the Westham service, which at that time was the only other route operated by double-decks. The Tilling Stevens and AEC Regals were working occasional trips to Portland Bill, Chickerell, Sutton Poyntz, and Osmington, and recently rebodied Leyland PLSC3s 3531/5/71/2/3 were also operating various services, whilst Bristol JO5G No. 232 was the principal bus on the Exeter service.

The arrival of new Bristol L5G single-decks during 1938 allowed 2988-2995, the 1930 AEC Regals with Strachan & Brown B32R bodies, to be rebodied by Duple as C32F coaches, whilst 3091 had its original Beadle B32R body replaced by a Duple C32F during 1939.

In 10 years between 1929 and 1939 Southern National had become well established, and during the Summer of 1939, as war clouds gathered, King George VI came to Portland twice to review the fleet. This event brought massive crowds to the resort, but it all came to an abrupt end with the declaration of war.

In the early days of hostilities Southern National vehicles collected evacuee children from Weymouth railway station for dispersal around the area, and there was an immediate reduction of services, with many Sunday morning and evening journeys being taken off. This included the Summer-only services to Bowleaze Cove (23), Weymouth-Wool-Lulworth Cove (30), Sandsfoot Castle (34), Nothe Gardens (35), Radipole Park Drive to Radipole (60), Bridport via Abbotsbury (21A), and the Taunton-Weymouth (219), also the Saturdays-only service to Nottington Village (22F). The 22F, 34, 35 and 60 were never reinstated. The Thursday, Saturday & Sunday Weymouth-Sherborne-Yeovil (26) service was also withdrawn, as was one Weymouth town service, Wyke Square-Grosvenor Road (24), much of the route being covered by other services. The local town service in Dorchester was also withdrawn for the duration from 14th October.

Fuel rationing was introduced on the 16th September, 1939. Vehicles were fitted with masked headlights, and white paint appeared on front mudguards and rear corners to assist in the blackout, during which a speed restriction of 20 mph was imposed, whilst the interiors were illuminated with only a few blue-coloured bulbs, making fare collection very difficult. With many staff joining the forces conductresses soon became a common sight on the town's buses. The formalities of the Traffic Commissioners were laid aside for the duration, the Southern Regional Traffic Commissioner making direct decisions and giving orders. The normal PSV test was abandoned, drivers holding 'Defence Permits', and competition between bus and railway ceased as they both struggled against mounting odds.

On 28th December Portland garage closed, the 16 drivers and conductors being transferred to Weymouth. The garage became a store and was used for other war purposes. The service from Portland railway station to the Anti-Submarine School within Portland Dockyard (88) still operated, although now starting from Weymouth. During January 1940 freezing conditions for several days caused the cancellation of services after 8 pm, and as private motoring ceased more passengers used the few buses. At a Council meeting early in the month Councillors complained of the 'Unsatisfactory Bus Service', and in true Council tradition appointed a sub-committee to interview Mr J.C. Cousins the local manager. In February the Council discussed 'the undignified scramble for buses at the King's Statue'. Queue rails were suggested to ease the situation, one Councillor stating that 'there were instances of people getting there in plenty of time for their buses, only to be trampled on and pushed aside by others who came running up at the last moment'.

Weymouth & District Trades Council favoured a Municipal bus service. At a Portland Urban District Council meeting on 21st February it was reported that the Trades Council had passed a resolution to the effect that the attentions of Weymouth Corporation and Portland Council be called to the ever-growing dissatisfaction of the general public with the present service of buses, with a view to joint action being taken to establish a municipal bus service for the district. Many complaints had appeared lately, the outstanding one appearing to be the struggle of Portland people to board a bus at the King's Statue at certain times. Conditions had not improved in April, one of the main causes of complaint being that short distance passengers took up seats, leaving the bus only partially loaded after covering the first section of its route, there being no fuel available to run duplicate vehicles for short distances.

The fall of France and the Channel Islands saw the arrival of many ships loaded with refugees at Weymouth Harbour, the buses and coaches of Southern National being quickly assembled to move them from the immediate area. The threat of invasion was now a real prospect, and in July the Weymouth and Portland area officially became a 'War Zone' with restrictions on visitors, the seafront and sands being defended with barbed wire and scaffolding. There were also tank traps to dodge, part of the town becoming an 'Anti-Tank Island'.

Further reductions in services took place, when the Southlands Estate route (273) was withdrawn. The war then took a grim turn. From occupied airfields in Cherbourg a Junkers 88A could reach Weymouth in just over 15 minutes, its deadly load of bombs causing much damage in the Weymouth and Portland area. Following several heavy raids in the district, Edward Street garage was almost destroyed at lunch time on 21st October, 1940. The destruction of the garage and surrounding property caused the deaths of two bus company employees, tyre fitter Cyril Stevens and painter Ronald Balch. Also killed was eight-year-old Margaret Serle and her friend Patrica Thompson who were playing outside their houses in Edward Street. Mrs Serle was buried under the rubble of her home, where husband Clifford, the depot cashier, would normally have been having his dinner, but this being a Monday he had gone to the Post Office to collect insurance stamps for staff. Garage foreman Jack Boon, trapped under concrete in his office, received serious injuries from which he never fully recovered. £50,000 was claimed for the loss of the garage and four adjoining houses owned by the company, £476 for plant and furniture, £247 for stores, and £22 for stationery.

With Edward Street out of use all maintenance and fuelling was carried out at Radipole garage which had been used as a heavy dock facility. The former Greyhound garage at Charlestown was brought back into service as the paint and body shop, and for a short time some vehicles were garaged at Rocky Knap. Weymouth Town Council also allowed the parking of vehicles on various sites as part of the dispersal plan to avoid mass destruction in the event of an air raid. The Edward Street site was cleared and brought back into use for parking, although with large sections of the building missing and parts of the steel framework exposed by missing walls. There were several low beams that double-deckers had to avoid!

The transportation of workers to Portland Dockyard was giving rise to problems. Early in 1942, early morning and evening peak journeys between Weymouth and Victoria Square were extended to the Dockyard, an extra 1d. being added to the cheap day return fare. There was also the problem of the closure of the Portland-Easton section of railway to passenger traffic during the winter months between 1940-1945, causing the issue of combined rail-bus season tickets - particularly to scholars and apprentices - and the proportions to be charged by both railway and bus companies. Although the Easton train service had not been well patronised, its loss added to the already overcrowded buses. From 1st June, 1942 the issue of workmen's cheap day return tickets was suspended, being replaced by weekly tickets obtainable from the company's booking offices, although for many workers tickets were obtainable on the Friday from conductors who visited works' canteens.

Royal Blue coach services were finally withdrawn from 13th November, special fare stage services operating over certain parts of routes not covered by other forms of transport. One such service was the 402 Bournemouth-Dorchester-Bridport-Exeter which was operated by Weymouth depot.

During the same month to save fuel 23 bus stops were abolished in the Weymouth area, and from 20th December all services ceased after the departure of buses from

A view taken shortly after the bombing of Edward Street garage on Monday 21st October, 1940. In the foreground is an unidentified AEC Regal coach, behind can just be seen the rear blind box of Leyland TS7D No. 1004. In the centre is Leyland TS2 No. 2974, and on the left Leyland SKP3 No. 3647 with a Thurgood B26 body. This ex-Sully's of Chard vehicle was the only one not returned to service following the raid. *Author's Collection*

Despite the complete destruction of the front of the garage, coaches parked in the back only received superficial damage. To the left is AEC Regal No. 2732, a former Elliott Royal Blue coach fitted with a Duple C31F body in 1938. In front in bus livery is Leyland TS1 No. 3111, whilst just protruding is the rear end of 1930 AEC Regal No. 2988, the original bus body having been replaced by a Duple C31F coach body in 1938. *Author's Collection*

the King's Statue at 9 pm, and no buses ran on Sundays before 1 pm except the Bournemouth and Exeter services. This action brought letters of protest in the local press from the Clergy: 'In allowing buses to run after 1 pm it seems as if the Government wish to give preference to the pleasure seeker rather than the Christian worshipper'. A letter of reply from a bus driver pointed out that 'most people live within half a mile of a place of worship, and that many churches conduct afternoon services'. He also noted 'that no ministers of the church have laid their cars up to save fuel and tyres!' If the service reductions were not bad enough, on Sunday 13th December severe storms and floods struck Portland, cutting off both the road and railway, the latter being closed for several days.

To assist with the saving of fuel some buses were converted to operate on producer gas, one such vehicle being Leyland TD1 2985. The exact date of its arrival is not recorded, but the first advert extolling the benefits of the gas bus appeared in the local press during September 1942. In March 1943 it was involved in a fatal accident on the Westham route, when a pensioner leaving the platform of the moving bus was struck by the following trailer. It was not only passengers who could forget there was a trailer behind, a conductress also being injured when she jumped off before the vehicle stopped! Although it saved valuable fuel, it was difficult to handle as turning at the end of routes was a problem. The producer unit was temperamental in operation, and often when climbing the hill past St Paul's church a minor miracle took place to ensure it reached Westham estate!

Staff shortages were a problem; at one stage there were only two conductors, the remainder being female, although bus driving had been a reserved occupation since the end of 1940. By 1943 two conductresses had become drivers, the first being Miss Lucy Bartlett, followed by Ivy Humphreys. They drove all vehicles except the Leyland six-wheelers on which the steering was considered too heavy!

During that March (1943) there was a threatened strike of conducting staff, reported as being 'over the actions of a woman supervisor' who the conductors wanted dismissed, but following prolonged discussions between the company and union the matter was resolved and no strike took place. Shortly after this conductress Hilda Wearne was promoted to inspector, and was highly respected by all staff. The pressures that bus crews were working under at that time must be remembered, a typical example being that on several nights drivers and conductresses had to sleep on their vehicles in the Portland garage, the Beach road being closed because of air raids. Buses were fully loaded, and there was the blackout - plus working an average 70 hour week. On top of this there was fire watching duty. Staff also formed a Home Guard unit, but despite all this they managed to find time for their concert party to provide entertainment in aid of many causes.

In September Portland Council, still complaining about the lack of bus shelters and bus services in general, decided to explore the question of applying for the necessary powers to run a transport service of their own. Complaints concerning services, queues, and the lack of shelters were common in Council meetings and in the local press, the truth being there was very little the hard-pressed bus company could do about the situation. Vehicle 2985 came in for special mention at a Council meeting in April 1944, regarding the complaints by Westham people of the frequent breaking down of the bus, humorously described by a member of the Council as the 'gas works'. Mr Cousins reminded the deputation that, by order of the Ministry of War Transport, certain buses had to be gas-driven. He added that Weymouth was lucky not to have had more of them, but they might have to make do with more in the near future.

Bristol L5G No. 340, DOD 529, parked at Exeter Central railway station during the war, awaiting to return to Weymouth with the No. 42 service. Note the white patches on the front wings and rear corner to assist visibility during the blackout. This 1940 vehicle had its Bristol B35R body replaced by a Beadle B36R body in May 1950. Sold out of service during 1961, three years were spent with Lockwoods Foods, of Long Sutton, before being scrapped in 1964.
Bristol Vintage Bus Group

The remains of Edward Street garage after the clean up following the bomb damage. The area in the foreground had been the approach road to the garage (Terminus Street), and the site of terraced houses, this had been put to use as a starting point for long distance services. Most buses are out on service whilst a few coaches are parked under the 'low girder'. In the background a double-deck stands on what had been the site of Terrace Street.   *B. Thompson*

Just before D-Day bus services were in chaos owing to the mass movement of military traffic, it being reported that on one occasion it took a bus two hours to travel the four miles from Upwey to the King's Statue. A total of 518,000 troops embarked from Weymouth and Portland, and 144.000 vehicles were loaded at Portland. Throughout all this activity bus services ran as best they could.

The vehicle shortage was relieved by the loan of two AEC Regent OT27/28RO open-toppers from Brighton Hove & District, and as D-Day approached there was the bizarre sight of Nos. 6009 & 6229 in faded cream livery operating services to Upwey and Westham.

With the war entering its final chapter, the travel ban was lifted and visitors again arrived at Weymouth by both bus and train for the August Bank Holiday. In September the blackout restrictions were eased, and at the end of the month - to the relief of crews and passengers alike - the 'Gas Works' reverted to petrol propulsion!

On 1st January, 1945 a limited town service was restarted in Dorchester, and with the war now entering its final months the future was considered. The Weymouth Borough Surveyor produced plans to remove the central shelter at the King's Statue and cover the area with lawns and a fountain, and to place the bus shelters on the Esplanade side and at Royal Terrace. It was to be 10 years before this plan became a reality. For many years it had been the Council's wish to remove the buses from the centre of the Statue site, but the war had made the situation worse, as spare buses were often parked there to save fuel or through the lack of other facilities. In February Portland Council complained that the long-awaited bus shelters, recently erected, were not large enough!

Throughout the war there were only three serious bus accidents that could be attributed to the blackout. One where a bus struck a traffic island, and another involving a motor cyclist running into a bus (which proved fatal), and a pensioner falling whilst leaving a bus. However, the conduct of some passengers left much to be desired. Whilst people would queue without question for food supplies and other items, a bus queue brought out their worst behaviour, and there were several court cases following fights at bus stops!

Despite making a break of journey on single-deck services between Upwey to Portland at the King's Statue from early 1944, to deter short distance passengers who could use other services, the matter was not fully resolved until July 1946 when, following the intervention of Sir Arnold Musto, Chairman of the Traffic Commissioners, it was decided to charge 7d. minimum from the King's Statue to Fortuneswell on Tophill buses. On 8th May, 1945 the war ended, V.E. day was celebrated, and no fares were charged that day. However, two days later it was back to 'business as usual' when Weymouth Town Council complained of damage caused to kerbs in the narrow roads of Westham housing estate, particularly in Kitchener Road which was little wider than a bus.

The reinstatement of all services was going to take time. The Weymouth-Abbotsbury-Bridport (21A) restarted in June, as did the Weymouth town service to Wyke Square (24). At the August meeting of Weymouth Council the bus situation was described as 'desperate'. At the May meeting they had complained of overcrowding, the situation being that many people were now taking their first holiday for years, and although visitors were plentiful there were no extra buses or fuel available.

During 1945 there was a wage increase for road staff, drivers' pay being increased to 1s. 4d. from 1s. 2d. per hour and conductors' to 1s. 2d. from 1s. 1d. Despite all the problems of the war years, the buses had carried the maximum number of passengers on the minimum number of vehicles and generally profits were high, an indication being the proportion of profit paid to the railway companies on the Wyke Regis-Radipole service, which amounted to £5,175 1s. 7d. for the year ending 30th September, 1945, compared with the £2,373 in 1939.

In April 1946 a few Royal Blue Express services restarted, some Associated Motorways operations following in June, and the summer service between the Pavilion and Bowleaze Cove restarted in July, a Dennis Ace often being used. The Southlands Estate service (273) also recommenced during the year, and on 22nd December a new service serving the newer part of Westham estate, via Norfolk Road and Hereford Road, commenced and was numbered 20C.

On 2nd November, 1946 a double-deck was taken to the top of Portland, aboard which were members of Portland UDC to observe if it would be possible to operate double-decks on the Island routes. The Council Surveyor, Mr R. Davison, followed in a car making his own observations! However, it was to be another 22 years before double-decks were introduced to Tophill services.

A perusal of the Council minutes for the years following World War II, gives the impression of a 'wish list', and the saying 'What you want and what you get are different things' was to prove true as Councillors asked for the impossible. For although the war was over shortages of vehicles, finance, and materials remained for years to come. However, to be even-handed the Council were also giving the railways the same persistent questioning over their shortcomings, both on the Portland branch and the main line!

The vehicle situation during 1947 improved a little with new double-decks joining the fleet, but coaches were still being used on fare stage work.

A new service, Weymouth-Dorchester via Osmington, Warmwell Cross, and Broadmayne (73) commenced on 24th February, 1947. The following year a Dorchester-Broadmayne-Warmwell Cross-Wool-Wareham service (76) was applied for, and although largely parallel to the railway there were no objection from the railway company, as there was the risk of another operator applying for a licence!

Gradually services were being restored, and the industry was again moving forward, although in different circumstances. The Nationalisation of the railways under the 1947 Transport Act also involved the Tilling Group of bus companies, of which Western/Southern National were part. The 50 per cent of shares previously held by the railway companies meant that the industry was already half nationalised, and a deal concluded with the British Transport Commission in September 1948 finalised the matter.

Thankfully, to a great extent the business of running the companies was left to busmen and there was not the direct political interference which the railways suffered. There was no change of name or outward signs that anything had altered. Locally it also removed the financial payments covering the former Great Western bus route, as now all the finances went into the BTC coffers!

Early in 1948 it was agreed to lay concrete floors for the new Edward Street garage, although there was little hope of rebuilding the garage in the immediate future. At the same time Nos. 11 and 15 Commercial Road and five properties in Terminus Street were purchased and demolished in readiness for the eventual rebuilding. With these improvements carried out, all long distance bus and coach services and tours started from Edward Street after 6th June, 1948. From 1st August the Salisbury service become jointly operated between Wilts & Dorset and Southern National, and an improved timetable was introduced.

From the outbreak of war the Weymouth fleet had been put to its greatest test, but fortunately, vehicle losses were few.

Former Victory Tours AEC Regal 3582 received a Duple C32F body in September 1940, whilst former Greyhound Leylands TS3 3584/87 received Duple C32F bodies in August and December 1940, and, together with the rebodied Regals, they performed sterling service - mostly on stage carriage work. Following air raid damage to Whitehead's Works at Wyke Regis the main office section moved to Upwey Manor, a daily coach picking up at Whitehead's and Wyke Hotel. Most commonly used was AEC Regal 3583 painted in a grey wartime livery and known as 'The old Grey Mare'. Having an outward opening door, she was unsuitable for stage carriage work if it could be avoided.

During June four new Bristol L5G single-decks with Bristol B31R bodies arrived at Weymouth. Numbered 337/8/9/40, they often operated the Bournemouth (36) and Exeter (42) services

Of the 14 vehicles in the garage at the time of the October 1940 raid only one was not returned to service - 3647, a 1935 Leyland SKP3 with a Thurgood B26F body, acquired in 1936 with the fleet of Sully of Chard. The chassis was used for spares and many parts in the construction of No. 2000 after the war, the body being sold to a farmer at Chickerell. The other vehicles suffered from only minor body damage and broken windows, these being Bristol L5G 277, Leyland TS7D 1004, Leyland PLSC 2800, Leyland LT2 2974, AEC Regals 2988/90/2/4 3091 and 3732, Leyland TS1 3111, and Dennis Arrows, 3585/6. A war damage claim of £215 was made for these vehicles. No. 2800 had been converted for use as an ambulance to collect the injured from ships and ambulance trains or evacuate hospitals in the event of air attack.

The following year, 1941, saw the arrival of the first ECW-bodied vehicles to be based at Weymouth, three Bristol K5G models with L30/26R bodies, Nos. 357/8/9, which were quickly put to work on the main routes. The previous year Bristol K5G ECW-bodied vehicles had entered the Wilts & Dorset fleet and several were allocated to their Salisbury-Weymouth service (20). During the year Weymouth received a new depot lorry in the form of No. 664 - a former Dennis Mace bus - the body of which had been destroyed by fire at Yeovil. A lorry body, costing £124, was fitted by Tiverton Coach Works.

Pre-war bodies with mainly timber framework suffered from the stress and strain of movement, and this was not helped by the then rigid mounting of the diesel engine. In 1942 Nos. 237/9/43/4 had to have major rebuilding work carried out, No.238 had been rebuilt the previous year and 240 was rebuilt in both 1941 and 1943! Nos. 2904/5 - the two 1929 AEC Regents - were the worse for wear by 1943, the original Short Bros L26/24R bodies being life-expired. Following rebodying by J.C.Beadle, both vehicles went to North Devon for the remainder of their lives.

The six-wheelers also suffered from body fatigue. Nos. 1001/3/4/5 had body rebuilds during 1941, 1002 was dealt with during 1942, and 1000 during 1943. The remaining Royal Blue coaches were put to other uses. No. 1062, a 1937 AEC Regal, operated on fare stage services in the Weymouth area - still in Royal Blue livery - as did Bristol JJW C32R coaches 164/6.

The gas bus, Leyland TD1 No.2985, was originally a Western National vehicle which had been converted to diesel. The petrol engine from 2955 was fitted, and 2985 entered service at Bideford on 12th May, 1940. In the original installation the burner unit was placed under the stairs, but this arrangement only lasted 12 days, it being pure luck that the entire vehicle did not become part of the burning arrangements!

Later, when the standard trailer gas producers were introduced, 2985 was again converted and later sent to Weymouth where, fortunately for crews, she was the only bus to operate on producer gas, usually working the Westham route. In

Bristol K5G No. 244, ETA 989, stands alongside the shelter at the King's Statue in the years following the war, the original Beadle H30/26R body appears to have been freshly painted. Adverts appearing on the vehicles are in themselves a reflection on social history.

Author's Collection

Bedford WTB No. 481, DDV 47, stands at the King's Statue whilst operating a Goldcroft Estate service (38). This 1939 model with a Duple C25F body spent much of its life on fare stage work owing to vehicle shortages. Withdrawn in 1955 it was broken up locally by Scource.

R.H.G.Simpson

contrast, during 1943 Wilts & Dorset were supplied with four Daimler CW 5G vehicles fitted with Brush L27/28R utility bodies. Numbered 260-263, they were allocated to Blandford and operated the Salisbury-Weymouth service.

It is impossible to list fully all vehicles employed during the war, as variations took place over a period of time. The two Dennis Lancet coaches 3590/3 were put in store at Yeovil during 1942, following air raid damage at Portland the same year. Dennis Arrow coach 3585 was placed in store at Rocky Knap garage, never to re-enter service.

During 1941 Bristol L5Gs, 310/1/36 were operating on the 22 route, and in 1944 two Tilling Stevens - 54 and 60 - appeared at Weymouth, both in grey livery. Dennis Mace 776 saw service during 1943, being joined the following year by 762, 777 and 779. Four more appeared in 1945, 760/4/70/2, plus two 'Aces' (666/7). Bedford Duple coaches were also used, mostly on fare stage work, No. 476 between 1943-45 and Nos. 477/8/84 and No. 3518 between 1944 and 1945, the latter vehicle formerly being in the fleet of 'Baker' of Lyme Regis.

Also running at the end of the war were a selection of Leyland Lions that had been rebodied with Mumford B32R bodies during 1936-7. Having served with the Army as an ambulance, No. 2407 was returned during 1943 and was repainted in green during June 1945. No. 2517 spent a short while at Weymouth in grey livery during 1943 before going to Yeovil the following year. After spending the earlier years of the war at Bideford, No. 2518 ended up at Weymouth, later being sold to Mr R. Pover for whom she served as a mobile barber's shop visiting surrounding villages. In the end she went to a permanent site at Sams' yard, Radipole, until the final journey to Scource's scrap yard in 1950.

No. 2531 returned from the Army in May 1944 and continued working in grey livery, and No. 2572 was also at Weymouth during the latter days of the war, as was 2608 which later become a caravan at Chickerell. Having survived the Edward Street raid, 2800 continued in service, eventually ending her days as a caravan at Charmouth. Little was wasted, the chassis of the producer gas trailer being used to construct a rubbish trailer towed by the depot lorry for trips to the Council tip.

The first signs of some return to normality was the reconstruction of the Tilling Stevens' saloons in 1945. They were rebodied with ECW and Beadle B32R bodies, fitted with Gardner 4LW diesel engines, and Bristol front axles and radiators, giving them an entirely different appearance and a further nine years' service to the company.

During 1946 the following vehicles still had perimeter seating: Bristol J 192/3/4 232, Bristol L5G 275/8/9/80, Leyland TS2 2874, Leyland LT2 2979 and Leyland TS1 3546. However, the bright spot was the arrival in July of Weymouth's first two post-war buses, Bristol K5Gs Nos. 821/2. Each cost £2,781 8s. 6d. They were put to work between Upwey and Portland Victoria Square.

The year 1947 saw little provision of extra services as vehicle shortage continued, and No. 531 - a new Bedford OB Duple C29F - spent much of its first two years on fare stage work, as did many other coaches. Leyland Titan No. 2985 had its original Leyland L27/24R body replaced in February 1947 by a Beadle L26/26R, and the following year a Gardner 5LW engine replaced the petrol unit. The situation eased in 1948 with the delivery of more Bristol 'K' types, including No. 903, fitted with an AEC 6-cylinder engine. At the end of the year 237/8/9/40, the Bristol G05G double-deckers, were sent to ECW for re-bodying. Upon their return they spent a considerable time working from Dorchester depot.

A wolf in sheep's clothing, GF 7254! The chassis commenced life in 1930 as London General double-deck No. 1000, whilst the 34-seat Duple coach body was displayed at the 1937 Commercial Motor show. United at some stage during the war years, this unusual historic marriage is shown parked at Portsmouth whilst operating a Naval leave service.

Omnibus Society

The smart Duple C41F bodywork belies the fact that underneath is one of the few Sentinel SLC chassis. GTK 992 of the Bluebird fleet is seen in London operating Royal Blue relief services. Following is Bluebird Leyland Royal Tiger EPR 265, still in the older blue and cream livery.

R. Marshall

Chapter Nine

Weymouth and Portland Post-War Independents

Bluebird, Chickerell, Weymouth

F.C. Hoare transferred his Bluebird coach business from Portland to Chickerell garage in July 1940, when he acquired the business of Monarch Coaches from C.W. Dean & Son. There is little doubt that the purchase of the business and the move from Portland was a gamble in those uncertain times. At the time of takeover the Army requisitioned the Bedford WTB and the Dennis Lancet from the Monarch fleet, and the Dennis Lancet from the Bluebird fleet.

However, the business survived, and it would appear that limited private hire work was still allowed. In June 1941 one of the rear entrance Bedfords was involved in a accident at Weymouth whilst returning a skittle team from Dorchester. But Government contracts to transport workmen formed the backbone of work during the war years. The former Dean Bedford JT 5178 was returned by 1944, and in January that year a 32-seat Bedford OWB utility bus, BFX 264, was added to the fleet,

With the end of hostilities business was slow to return to normal, as there was still fuel rationing and a restriction on the length of tours and private hire operated. There was however a great demand for Naval leave services.

In April 1946 Hoare requested that Weymouth Council grant him the facilities formerly allowed to Dean at Westham coach park, offering to pay £30 per annum for a maximum of two coaches at any one time in connection with excursions and tours. The Council agreed to accept £15 per annum in respect of each specified vehicle using the park. A second-hand Dodge SBF had been obtained in March and a limited number of tours were operated that Summer.

The following March Hoare applied to continue using the previous facilities, but plying for hire with three unspecified vehicles and paying £45 for the season, and in the event of more than three vehicles standing in the car park he would pay the normal parking fee for the excess vehicles. Also for £10 he was allowed to place a small hut as a booking office on the site, all these terms being agreed by the Council. The hut became a fixture, not being removed at the end of each season, the Council then deciding to charge £15 per annum for the site!

Gradually the business developed as times improved. The Westham site was well suited for holiday makers and residents in the Westham area, and it was less than a five minute walk from the sea front. Later a booking office situated in the south end of the information centre on the esplanade was acquired, giving equal opportunity with Southern National to obtain passengers from the sea front area. Over the years the fleet has been maintained in excellent condition, either new or high quality second-hand vehicles being purchased to keep the fleet in the top league of coach operations.

In March 1947 the first new post-war vehicle was purchased, a 29-seat Bedford OB, BTK 624. June 1947 saw the purchase of what must historically be the most interesting vehicle to enter the fleet, and it is worthy of a full description. On the surface it appeared to be just a second-hand six-wheel coach, GF 7254. The chassis had been constructed at the Chiswick works of the London General Omnibus Company in July 1930 and fitted with a double-deck body. It was numbered LT 1000, retaining that number with the formation of London Transport in July 1933. Withdrawn in May 1939, it passed to Mitchell (dealer) of London SW 12 in the August. At a point unknown the chassis was fitted with the 34-seat Duple body carried by the Tilling Stevens six-wheel 'Successor' chassis displayed at the 1937 Commercial Motor Show, but the chassis, not being a success was dismantled!

The chassis of LT 1000 fitted with this luxury body then appeared with Susen's Coaches of Twickenham before sale to Bluebird, with whom it still ran in its white and green livery. It was purely a stop-gap and not a very well liked vehicle in the Bluebird fleet. It passed to White Heather of Southsea in June 1949, and two years later became a caravan ending its days at Bosham - a sad end for two components that had been at the forefront of PSV history!

In February 1948 JT 3097, the requisitioned Dennis Lancet I from the Monarch Coaches fleet, was returned to Bluebird, but unfortunately JT 5828, the former Bluebird Dennis Lancet II, was never returned, going into the fleet of Mid Wales Motorways before ending its days cut down as a low loader for the Aberystwyth Tractor Company.

By that time the opportunities to purchase new vehicles were improving, three Dennis Lancets and a Crossley chassis being purchased in the next three years, and the last Bedford OB, EFX 173, was purchased in 1950. May 1951 saw the purchase of EPR 265 - a Leyland Royal Tiger with a Plaxton C41C body, one of the first of the type to be owned by a Dorset independent. It was very impressive at the time, as the most modern coach in the Southern National fleet was a Bristol LWL!

Later in the year a Commer Avenger was acquired, and by this time all the pre-war vehicles had been sold out of the fleet. The purchase of the Royal Tiger also marked a point where any half-cab or bonneted vehicle appeared dated overnight from a passenger's point of view. This was partly overcome by the purchase of conventional chassis with 'fully fronted bodies' such as FJT 114, a Dennis Falcon, in July 1952. However this did not come up to expectations, and was disposed of that December. A little more successful was GNV 978, a second-hand Dennis Lancet II. The 'fully fronted' coach was the vehicle of the future. During 1953 FJT 950, a Commer Avenger II with a Plaxton C33F body was acquired, joining KLJ 30 of the same type acquired three years previously from Excelsior, of Bournemouth.

A second Royal Tiger, HMR 444, also with a Plaxton 41-seat body, was acquired from Hillman of Westbury. A popular vehicle in the Bluebird fleet, she was lengthened to 36 ft with 49 seats during 1963. Following eventual sale to Munden's of Bristol in 1972 the chassis was reduced to 30 ft, and a Plaxton C33F body fitted, the vehicle then being re-registered as EHY 111K. A surprise purchase by Bluebird in the November of 1954 was GTK 992, a new Sentinel SLC6 with a Duple C41C body, the only Sentinel coach known to have operated in Dorset.

Within the next few years the remaining half-cabs would depart from the fleet as Bedford and Ford vehicles were acquired. In February 1963 EFX 173, the remaining Bedford OB, departed, thus bringing to a close a chapter in Bluebird history. The following year saw the purchase of VJT 907, the first Bedford VAL six-wheeler, to be followed by 11 other various chassis, bringing us up to the cut-off point for this history. It is interesting to note that the Bedford OB had cost approximately £1,750 whilst the replacement Bedford VAL just in excess of £5,500!

Over the years the fleet livery changed to suit the tastes of the period, the original pre-war blue with orange livery remaining into the early 1950s when cream relief was also added. By 1956 several vehicles had appeared in a predominantly white livery with orange and blue relief, although the well known 'Bluebird' motif remained on the vehicle sides, and this livery with slight variations remained until recent years.

Having always purchased good quality vehicles, Bluebird have kept abreast of the latest trends in the coaching business, changing to suit the requirements of the travelling public. Today the day trip to Cheddar Caves or the evening mystery tour do not hold the attraction they did 50 years ago, and extended tours and Continental travel now form part of the company's operations. Although Westham coach park is now buried under the Weymouth by-pass, the business is still very much alive, run by the third generation of the Hoare family. More than 120 vehicles have passed through the fleet in the past 76 years.

Bluebird, Chickerell, Weymouth

No.	Reg No.	Chassis	No.	Body	Type	No.	Built	Acq.	Sold	Notes
	JT 4425	Bedford WTB	110365	Duple	C26R	6661	3/3/6	3/36	2/49	1
	JT 5828	Dennis Lct 2	175100	Duple	C32F	7648	10/36	10/36	1940	1
	JT 7273	Bedford WTB	111388	Duple	C26R	8989	5/37	5/37	6/52	1
	JT 5178	Bedford WTB	110751	Duple	C26	7658	6/36	b/44	2/51	
	BFX 264	Bedford OWB	17072	Duple	B32F	34045	1/44	1/44	1/54	2
	LMF 230	Dodge SBF		Duple	C30			3/46	10/51	
	BTK 624	Bedford OB	44045	Duple	C29F	43485	3/47	3/47	8/54	
	GF 7254	LGOC		Duple	FC34F		7/30	6/47	6/49	2
	JT 3097	Dennis Lct 1	170978	Dennis	C32F		6/35	2/48	2/51	
	CPR 699	Dennis Lct 3	408J3	Duple	C33F	42919	5/48	5/48	12/56	
	DFX 475	Crossley	97883	Burlingham	C33F	3691	3/49	3/49	1/54	
	DJT 424	Dennis Lct 3	643J3	Whitson	C33F		7/49	7/49	9/56	
	EFX 173	Bedford OB	142539	Duple	C29F	49201	9/50	9/50	2/63	
	HRU 755	Dennis Lct 3	515J3	Plaxton	C33F	442	1/49	1/51	3/61	
	EPR 265	Leyland	510078	Plaxton	C41C	1311	5/51	5/51	11/59	
	KLJ 30	Comm. Av 1	23A0420	Plaxton	C33F	1249	8/50	10/51	1/58	
	FJT 114	Dennis Fal.	158L6	Plaxton	C33F	1725	7/52	-7/52	12/52	
	FJT 950	Comm. Av 2	44A0002	Plaxton	C33F	2003	12/52	12/52	3/61	
	GNV 978	Dennis Lct 3	122J10A	Yeates	FC37F	243	1/51	3/53	7/57	
	HMR 444	Leyland PSU	511000	Plaxton	C41C	1482	10/51	12/53	11/66	3
	GJT 893	Bedford SB	18677	Burlingham	C35F	5531	4/54	4/54	10/62	4
	GTK 992	Sentinel SLC	6/30/21	Duple	C41C	215/2	11/54	11/54	12/63	
	JJT 128	Comm. TS3	T85AO264	Plaxton	C41F			3/56	3/56	12/63	
	KFX 507	Bedford SBG	50498	Duple	C41F	1074/105	1/57	1/57	10/64	
	KFX 506	Bedford SBG	50537	Duple	C41F	1074/106	1/57	1/57	10/64	
	KTK 262	Bedford SB8	54679	Duple	C41F	1074/333	7/57	7/57	12/64	
	LJT 945	Bedford SB8	58475	Duple	C41F	1090/132	3/58	3/58	10/64	
	LWK 353	Karrier Q25	32A0687	Reading	C14C		1952	3/59	2/60	
	OPR 262	Ford 570E	510E39042	Duple	C41F	1126/89	3/60	3/60	5/61	
	OPR 543	Austin J2VA	58424	Kenex	C12R		3/60	3/60	9/65	
	RJT 91	Ford 570E	510E62906	Duple	C41F	1139/218	3/61	3/61	11/66	
	PRJ 678	Ford 570E	510E38267	Duple	C41F	1126/129	1960	5/61	7/61	
	RPR 742	Bedford SB1	87752	Duple	C41F	1133/499	6/61	6/61	1/71	
	RPR 950	Ford 570E	510E61054	Duple	C41F	1139/335	6/61	6/61	11/66	
	YRV 302	Bedford SB5	89547	Duple	C41F	1145/239	1962	10/62	11/67	
	YRV 303	Bedford SB5	89546	Duple	C41F	1145/240	1962	10/62	10/69	
	YLK 599	Bedford C4Z2	4217	Duple	C19F	1127/11	1960	2/63	8/67	
	VJT 907	Bedford VAL	1229	Plaxton	C52F	632855	1/64	1/64	2/73	
	645 GBU	Bedford SB13	93981	Plaxton	C41F	642922	2/64	10/64	6/74	
	648 GBU	Bedford SB13	94472	Plaxton	C41F	642207	4/64	10/64	4/74	
	BPR 70B	Bedford VAL	1588	Plaxton	C52F	652721	12/64	12/64	1/73	
	AMK 192A	Bedford J25Z	2162491	Plaxton	C14F	632452	4/63	9/65	10/68	
	BMT 100A	Bedford SB5	92167	Duple	C41F	1159/361	5/63	12/65	1/70	
	DXE 533C	Bedford VA14	1651	Duple	C52F	1185/57		11/66	1/71	
	DXE 534C	Bedford VA14	1641	Duple	C52F	1185/58		11/66	1/71	
	477 PYB	Bedford CALV	203321	M. Walter	B11R	UB72327		12/66	9/69	
	LRO 887C	Bedford VAS1	2190	Duple	C29F	1201/2		10/67	4/73	
	HJT 424F	Bedford VM14	6870411	Duple (N)	C45F	172155	11/67	11/67	12/77	
	GBK 992E	Bedford VAS5	7836632	Duple	C29F	1211/17		10/68	b/85	
	OOW 612G	Ford Transit	55150	South Hants	B12F		11/68	11/68	6/79	

Notes

1. To Chickerell with the purchase of Dean 'Monarch Coaches' 1940.
2. Later reseated to B29F.
3. 6/62 lengthened by Sparshatts of Southampton from 30 ft to 33 ft 5 in., to 49 seats. 1972 chassis reduced to 30 ft, Plaxton C43F body (79025) fitted, re-registered as EHY 111K (with Munden, Bristol).
4. Delivered in black and silver livery, which was retained for some years.

Bluebird, Leyland Royal Tiger, HMR 444, shown in its lengthened form, 3 ft 5 in. having been added in June 1962, allowing another 8 seats. Painted in the later all cream livery, the Bluebird motif is clearly displayed.   *Author's Collection*

Having come a long way from the Crossley and Chevrolet models of the 1920s, VJT 907, a Bedford VAL with a Plaxton C52F body, represents the latest in the Bluebird fleet of 1964. Photograped at Portland, Victoria Square in November 1968. To the left the original Portland station of 1865, to the right the bay window of the offices of the former gas works, and the Southern National garage.   *C.L. Caddy*

Previous Owners

JT 3097	Dean 'Monarch Coaches', Chickerell, Weymouth - via War Department.
JT 5178	Dean 'Monarch Coaches', Chickerell, Weymouth - via War Department.
LMF 230	Valiant, Ealing, London.
GF 7254	New to London General as LT1000. To London Transport. WD 5/39. 8/39 to Mitchell (dealer), London SW12.
HRU 755	New to Excelsior, European Motorways Ltd, Bournemouth.
KLJ 30	New to Excelsior, European Motorways Ltd, Bournemouth.
GNV 978	New to Seamarks, Rushden.
HMR 444	New to Hillman, Westbury, Wilts.
LWK 353	Ex-Stanbridge Motor Services, Stanbridge.
PRJ 678	Ex-Croker, Salford, Manchester.
YRV 302	Ex-Byng, Portsmouth.
YRV 303	Ex-Byng, Portsmouth.
YLK 599	Ex- Conway Hunt, Ottershaw.
645 GBU	Ex-Southsea Royal Blue.
648 GBU	Ex-Southsea Royal Blue.
AMK 192A	Ex-Tecfax, London W2 new to 'World Wide' SE5.
BMT 100A	Ex-Tex Tours Ltd, Bournemouth.
DXE 533C	Ex-Seamarks, Westoning.
DXE 534C	Ex-Seamarks, Westoning.
477 PYB	Ex-A.E. Salmon, Coxley.
LRO 887C	Ex-Knightswood, Watford.
GBK 992E	Ex-Byng, Portsmouth.

Disposals

JT 4425	To L. Saunders, Portland. LL 3/54. Scrapped c. 1957.
JT 5828	Requisitioned by Army 6/40. By 5/46 with Mid Wales Motorways. LO Aberystwyth Tractor Co.
JT 7273	To Smiths, Portland. LL 6/57. Scrapped by Smith.
JT 3097	To Kents Coaches, East End, Baughurst, Hants, 11/53 to H.A. Black, Shaw, Newbury (showman) LL 9/56.
JT 5178	To Fountain Coaches, Twickenham, LO Cowdell, 121 Malpas Road, Newport, Mon. scrapped.
LMF 230	To Springvale, Winchester.
GF 7254	Via Sparshatt (dealer), Southampton to 'White Heather' Southsea as No. 12. Later as caravan at Bosham, 4/61 to Sullivan, Bosham for scrap.
BTK 624	To C. Shepheard 'Bluebird Coaches', Aberford, Yorks. WD 10/57 to Coastal & Country, Whitby. 1/58 to Ernest Ledgar, Sunderland, used as mobile shop. LL5/64.
EFX 173	To Miller 'Rambling Rose', Bristol. 3/64 to Miller, Farnborough, Bath, WD 3/66. To Spiller 'Arleen', Peasdown St John, WD 4/67, scrapped.
BFX 264	To Tidey, Public Works Contractor, Brighton.
CPR 699	To Pond, Nazing, LL 9/60. LO Hepworth, Norton, Doncaster.
DFX 475	To Morton, Lymington LL 6/59. LO Heavy Motor Services, Kirkstall, Leeds.
DJT 424	To Elmhurst, Loughton, LL 9/58. LO Barnard & Barnard (dealers).
HRU 755	To Chiltern Queens, Woodcote. Withdrawn 4/67. 5/68 to Passeys scrapyard, Benson, remained in yard a number of years then broken up.
EPR 265	To Bolton, Coventry, to Bernard Kavanagh & Sons, Urlingford, Kilkenny LO.
KLJ 30	To J.H. Smith, Syston. 1960 to N.A. Reed 'The Ferrers Coaches', South Woodham not licensed, 1961 to Yeates (dealer), Loughborough.
FJT 114	To Matthews 'Greyfriars', Winchester. 1/61 to S.G. Sherman, Totton, Southampton, LL 7/62.
FJT 950	To Wolstenholme 'North Dorset Coaches', Wincanton LO in Northumberland.
GNV 978	To Whitchurch Service Station, Winterborne Whitchurch, Blandford.
HMR 444	To Creed, London. 4/72 to Munden, Bristol. 4/86 to Perry, Bromyard.
GJT 893	To Smith, Portland. To Mosley (dealer).
GTK 992	To Brewer, Cobham LL 11/65, LO Dorran Construction Co., Perth, scrapped by 3/70.
JJT 128	To Soul, London SW19.
KFX 506	To Elgar, Inkpen.
KFX 507	To Elgar, Inkpen.
KTK 262	To Howarth, Middlestown.
LJT 945	To Kent, Baughurst, Hants. 2/71 to Phillips, Brookfield, Shiptonthorpe, Yorks.
LWK 353	To Dennett, Yeovil.
OPR 262	Withdrawn after accident, then to Foster, Ellesmere Port.

They say, 'Imitation is the sincerest form of flattery'. The Austin CXB was not known as the 'Birmingham Bedford' without good reason. HAH 786, a 1947 CXB with a Mann Egerton C29F body in the ownership of Smith's 'Royal Manor' coaches of Portland, clearly shows the point.
G.R. Mills Collection

The real thing, Bedford OB, HAA 558, new to the fleet of Hants & Sussex in March 1949. It had passed to Leonard Saunders of Portland in March 1954, with whom it remained until January 1962, when sold to Smith of Portland. Photographed at Easton in September 1966, it had been repainted from Saunders' red livery into Smith's cream. Withdrawn in October 1968 it was the last of the once ubiquitous small Bedfords that had worked in the area. *C.L. Caddy*

Disposals (continued)

OPR 543	To Potter, Skewen.
RJT 91	To Gold Line, London E7.
PRJ 678	To Heard, Hartland.
RPR 742	To Smith, Portland.
RPR 950	To Croxley Coaches, Croxley Green.
YRV 302	To Foster, Glastonbury.
YRV 303	To K. Shaw & Son Ltd, Dobcross, B. 1/72 to Judd, Byfield.
YLK 599	To Butler & Henley, London SE26.
VJT 907	To Hudson, Rowlands Castle.
645 GBU	To King, Whitehill.
648 GBU	To Smith, Portland.
BPR 70B	To Monk, Staplecross.
AMK 192A	To King, Kirkcowan.
BMT 100A	To Morgan, Great Bedwyn.
DXE 533C	To Ring Road, Bradford.
DXE 534C	To Cruse, Warminster.
477 PYB	To D. Smith, Portland.
LRO 887C	To Browing, Box.
HJT 424F	To Baker, Yeovil.
GBK 992E	Mobile home, Bristol by 5/81.
OOW 612G	Not known.

D. Smith, Easton, Portland

Following the sale of the Portland Bus Service to 'National' in 1927 (*see Chapter Five*), the Smith family business continued with road haulage and taxi work, the haulage side later falling into decline. In 1934 part of the Easton Garage was converted into a fish shop, the family business then becoming a combination of fishmongers and taxi proprietors!

Following World War II Richard Smith's son Douglas purchased a second-hand Bedford WTL from a Government sale near Bristol. Operations commenced in 1947, the coach carrying the title *The Royal Manor*. At first just private hire work was undertaken, until June 1950 when licences were granted for a selection of tours and excursions starting from Easton Square.

No doubt in anticipation of the pending closure of the Portland branch railway, in November 1951 Smith applied to operate a fare stage service from Castletown Pier to Weymouth, as required by Naval personnel, and a daily fare stage service between Portland Victoria Square and Portland Bill, according to traffic requirements. There was a sudden awakening like that of the 1930s, as Southern National objected to both applications and Weymouth Council objected to the former, mainly because of proposed dropping off point at the 'Electric House' in Westham Road, or in nearby Park Street.

On Portland it was considered there was a requirement for extra buses during the Summer, when local people had difficulty in boarding a service to Portland Bill as these buses were always loaded, and likewise there was always a long queue at the Bill when it was time to return. The application was supported by Portland UDC, and there was no objection from Saunders who also operated a bus on the route. Following a public inquiry by the Traffic Commissioners at Yeovil in January 1952 both applications were refused, at which point the matter rested for the next 10 years!

Like many small operators the purchase of second-hand vehicles was a practical means of updating the fleet. The original Bedford, dating back to 1935, was nearing the end of its life in 1952 and was replaced by Bedford WTB JT 7273 obtained from Bluebird of Chickerell. It was a case of 'The Return Of The Native', as JT 7273 had been new to Bluebird of Portland in 1937! By June 1957 this vehicle, again having served both owners well, was replaced. However its final job saw it travelling to places far beyond its normal activity. Fitted out as a caravan complete with a double bed it was used for a touring holiday by Mr & Mrs Douglas Smith before it was finally broken up for spare parts.

The replacement vehicle, HAH 786, was unusual in being an Austin CXB, a type often known as 'The Birmingham Bedford', with a bonnet and body style, that could at a distance be mistaken for the real thing! First introduced in mid-1939 it was powered by a six-cylinder OHV engine with a cylinder bore of 88 mm and a stroke of 101.6 mm developing 50 bhp. Chassis modifications following the war saw a four-speed constant mesh gearbox and Clayton Dewandre brakes fitted. New in 1947, HAH 786 had served Norfolk Coachways of Attleborough for seven years before moving to Gourd's Coaches of Teignmouth, Devon. Purchased by Smith's in February 1957 for £250, following an engine rebuild it served its new owner for another seven years.

Smith's bought its first new vehicle, a 12 seater mini-bus, at Easter 1960. Ideal for small private hire jobs, the Karrier-bodied BMC gave good service. With the acquisition of Saunders' business in February 1962, Bedford OB HAA 558 joined the fleet, and following a refit gave another six years service. Also in 1962, a Bedford SB from the Bluebird fleet was purchased bringing the fleet strength up to two coaches, a mini bus and several taxis. The success of the SB and the mini-bus resulted in two more SBs and another mini-bus later being purchased. The business had grown with the increase of private hire work and various contracts, including the transportation of inmates from both the Island's prisons. In 1954 the fish shop in Easton Square closed, and the garage roof was altered to allow entry to larger vehicles. The opportunity to purchase the business and licences held by Saunders gave Smith all he had been refused 10 years previously by the Traffic Commissioners. Since 1969 - the point where this history ends - Smith's expanded to operate 15 vehicles and a fare stage service between Weymouth and Portland Bill, taking over the former Southern National garage in Victoria Square in January 1977.

Later the business was sold out of the family to Milverton, who then sold it to the Cawlett Group, by then owners of Southern National, Early in 1999 Southern National became part of the FirstGroup. On 4th September, 1999 Smith's ceased trading as a separate company, the Portland garage being closed and the services absorbed into the main company. A repeat of 1927!

D. Smith, Portland

No.	Reg No.	Chassis	No.	Body	Type	No.	Built	Acq.	Sold	Notes
	VN 7272	Bedford WTL	875102		C26		6/35	5/47	5/52	
	JT 7273	Bedford WTB	111388	Duple	C26R	8989	2/37	6/52	6/57	
	HAH 786	Austin CXB	106968	Mann/Egg.	C29F		8/47	2/57	11/62	1
	OPR 260	Austin J2/VB	57967	Kennex	M12R		3/60	3/60	11/67	
	HAA 558	Bedford OB	93639	Duple	C29F	46614	3/49	2/62	10/68	
	GJT 893	Bedford SB	18677	Burlingham	C35F	5531	4/54	10/62	11/67	
	MDP 449	Bedford SB3	43691	Duple	C41F		1956	6/65	1/71	
	VCE 521	Bedford SB1	73593	Duple	C41F	1120/100	10/59	8/67	4/74	
	PLF 355	Karrier AF	AF 2523	KW	C14F			4/68	4/69	
	5710 SM	Bedford SB1	88439	Duple	C41F	1133/517	1961	3/69	2/75	
	477 PYB	Bedford CALV	203321	MW	B11R	UB72327		9/69	7/72	

Notes
1. Seats fitted into HAA 558.

Previous Owners

VN 7272	New to G. Barker & Sons, Scarborough. Purchased by Smith from War Department sale at Bristol.
JT 7273	New to Bluebird, Portland. To Bluebird, Weymouth, to Smith, Portland.
HAH 789	New to J.C. Brown 'Norfolk Coachways', to Gourd's Coaches, Teignmouth.
HAA 558	New to Hants & Sussex. to Saunders, Portland, 1962 to Smith.
GJT 893	Bluebird, Chickerell, Weymouth.
MDP 449	New to Smiths of Reading.
VCE 521	New to Harris 'Progressive', Cambridge carried 'Harveys' fleetname. To Bryan, Didcot 11/61.
PLF 355	Ex-Newsam, Weymouth, ex-Weare, Kirkham 4/67. Original owner not traced.
5710 SM	Ex-Jolly, South Hylton.
477 PYD	Ex-Bluebird, Weymouth.
RPR 742	Bluebird, Chickerell, Weymouth.

Disposals

VN 7272	Broken up in Powell's yard, Easton, Portland.
JT 7273	Broken up for spares at Portland.
HAH 789	To Powell, Easton, Portland as store, then broken up.
GJT 893	To Moseley (dealer).
RPR 742	To South Central, Dorchester via Moseley (dealer).

Bere Regis & District Motor Services, Weymouth Depot

In its heyday Bere Regis & District was one of the largest independent coach operators in the Country. With a colour scheme of two shades of brown, its vehicles were a familiar sight throughout the County of Dorset. Like many country operators it started with humble beginnings in 1929 when Mr R. W. Toop commenced operations from Bere Regis with a 14-seat Model 'T' Ford. The following year W.J. Ironside, a carrier-cum-bus-operator who provided services from the village of Winfrith to Dorchester, Weymouth and Wareham, sold out to Toop, the combined service operating under the fleet name of 'Pioneer'. A local operator from Bloxworth, Mr P.W. Davis, joined Toop in 1936, and Ironside - after being out of the industry for six years - acquired a financial interest, and the fleet name Bere Regis & District was adopted, having been used originally by another local operator. By the outbreak of war in 1939 two other small operators had been acquired. The war years provided much extra traffic with the military camps and other establishments in the area, and during that time 111 other small operators in the Dorset area were added to the business, the most important being F. Whitty of Dorchester, who provided valuable premises and a filling station, which later became the company's head office.

Expansion continued to take place with the acquisition of companies around the county, and by 1965 no fewer than 27 various operators had become part of Bere Regis & District. Expansion then slowed down, although Messrs Elliot & Potter of Wimborne was acquired in 1982 and the last takeover was Mid Dorset Coaches during 1987.

At its peak the company operated over 100 vehicles, many different types having been employed over the years which represented most of the chassis and body manufacturers of the time. In the 10 years following the end of the war 37 new vehicles were purchased and almost 90 second-hand vehicles, including ex-Chester Corporation and Hants & Sussex Leyland double-deckers, used mainly on the Piddlehinton Camp and Poole-Dorchester services.

At that period services were operated to all four corners of the county daily, together with market day-only fare stage services, works journeys, school contracts, excursions & tours and private hire, whilst express services for both Navy and Army personnel from the various establishments in the area took Bere Regis coaches as far north as Yorkshire, Liverpool, and many other parts of the Country, as did relief work for both Royal Blue and Associated Motorways.

Garages were maintained at Bere Regis, Wimborne, Longham, Marnhull, Winterborne Stickland, Sherborne, Blandford, Hazlebury Bryan, Weymouth, and Dorchester, and many coaches were parked on land near the driver's home in the more remote parts of the county.

Weymouth had never featured greatly in their operations apart from a pre-war Winfrith-Osmington-Weymouth service on Saturdays, which terminated in Gloucester Mews. This service was resumed post-war, but the Town Council were displeased with the parking arrangements - as they had been on 19th March, 1948 when 11 of the company's coaches took 20 minutes to pick up passengers in Westwey Road! Many private hires visited both Weymouth and Portland and private hires also commenced in both towns.

During 1951 applications were made to operate a fare stage service between the Riviera Holiday Camp at Bowleze Cove and Weymouth, but following various difficulties the application was withdrawn.

In May 1953 Bere Regis acquired the premises of Ellis & Betts, Motor Engineers, situated at Radipole, on the Dorchester Road. The newly appointed manager, John Woodsford, and his family lived in a caravan placed in a lock-up garage on site, but later a 'Woolaway' concrete bungalow was built as his residence. The retail sale of 'Cleveland' petrol was continued, and later a small shop at the site entrance used as a dry cleaner's was taken over for a booking office.

Unfortunately for the company, the conditions applied to their tours and excursion licences allowed passengers to be picked up only at the garage and points northwards, and with the garage being situated a mile from the centre of Weymouth this created a distinct disadvantage. However, at its peak over 20 vehicles were based at Weymouth, many employed on contract and private hire work. Three vehicles were employed in taking workers to the net factories in Bridport, whilst others conveyed workers to Bovington Camp. Staff transport was provided to holiday camps at Bowleaze Cove and Osmington, and Naval leave services operated from Portland.

During March 1961 part of the garage site was let to Pat McCausland for the sale of Renault cars, and in 1967 the Weymouth depot closed. The site became a car dealer's showroom, owned by various companies until cleared and replaced by a supermarket.

Owing to the complexities of the fleet and the constant changing of vehicles at depots it would be impossible to give a list in this publication of Weymouth-based vehicles. However, it is hoped one day somebody will write the full story of Dorset's most interesting operator!

Staff outing early 1950s style, 9 coaches from the Bere Regis fleet line up on Weymouth Esplanade. L to R. Leyland PS1/1 HTB 187, NRF 174; AEC Regal MMH 18; Maudslay Marathon 111 CJT 535/6/9/4/3; and Leyland PS1/1 ORE 580. The Leylands all had Santus C33F bodies. The Maudslays Whitson bodies, and the AEC a Duple C33F. The Maudslays were new to Bere Regis for the 1948 season, whilst the remainder were second-hand purchases.   *J. Woodsford Collection*

Chapter Ten

Southern National
1949-1969

The new era started badly with the death on 10th May, 1949 of Mr John Cousins, the area traffic superintendent. Cousins had moved from Luton in 1921 to become manager of the Weymouth branch of Messrs Road Motors, and following the acquisition of that company by the National Omnibus & Transport Company became their local manager.

Fuel rationing, which lasted until January 1951, had kept private motoring to a minimum, and there was much talk of a unified public transport system - a subject still under discussion 50 years later! In truth, bus services had reached their peak, and were to plunge into decline. A fare increase took place during 1950, this coming as a shock to passengers as it was the first increase since before the war. Unfortunately it was the first of many to come.

By early 1951 there was serious talk of closing both the Abbotsbury and Portland branch railways to passenger traffic. Arguments for keeping the Abbotsbury branch were few, as the bus had already made its mark. The Portland branch was different, although the bus already provided the door-to-door or at least street-to-street service, the railway suited servicemen with through bookings beyond Weymouth, and of course their kit bags, which were a little difficult on a bus! Also in the age before the small folding 'baby buggy', mothers with prams and pushchairs were forced to use the train. However as fully described in Volume Two, the cases for and against closure were argued by both British Railways and local Councils, and (needless to say) the Portland branch closed as from 3rd March, and Abbotsbury from 1st December, 1952.

Southern National found no difficulty in providing the additional services in both cases, the problems of the kit bags being resolved by a dockyard lorry taking them to Weymouth station for either forwarding or collection, but the problem of mothers with pushchairs was ongoing. The boot of a saloon would hold a few, but space under the stairs of a double-deck was severely restricted!

The Abbotsbury branch closure created two new services, one from Abbotsbury and Portesham via Buckland Ripers to Upwey Junction (20D), principally to convey pupils for Dorchester grammar schools, which was later replaced by county school transport. The other service was longer lasting, a 'Friday only' trip from Coryates Halt (20E). Just as the branch auto-train had chugged through the countryside searching for passengers, the bus crew now surveyed the remains of the halt, and looked over the hedgerows for signs of life in the hope that their journey had not been in vain!

On 10th June, 1953 the traditional bell punch type ticket system was replaced by 'Speed Setright' machines issuing a ticket from an unprinted reel. The burden of carrying racks of tickets was done away with. As these tickets had been priced and numbered, they had a value even before issue, and if they fell into the hands of some unscrupulous person, left the conductor with a debt. Basically, a conductor paid in cash to the difference in the serial numbers of tickets issued by the cash office and those returned at the end of duty. With the setright system a ticket had no value until issued, and with machine counters for half pence and shillings, the waybill system was greatly simplified. The departure of buses from the centre of the road at the King's Statue was becoming a problem even in those days, for the prospective passenger to get into the centre of the road was a hazardous process! During June 1954 the central area was fenced off, the displaced services being moved to stops on

Resting at Edward Street is Tilling Stevens No. 65, FJ 8984 in its rebuilt form, the original Brush B35R body being replaced by an ECW B35R body in 1945. The KV type Bristol radiator and front axle complete the disguise of this 1933 vehicle, withdrawn in 1954 it was later used by Ashtons (contractors) Leeds. *Author's Collection*

Once pride of the Weymouth fleet and principal bus on the Exeter service Bristol JO5G No. 232, ADV 84, had been reduced to local duties when photographed at Edward Street during the early 1950s, fitted with a 1948 Beadle B36R body fitted with, by then, dated drop windows. The original Beadle B32R body resided on a farm at Bere Ferrers, Devon. When withdrawn in 1958, No. 232 passed to a local showman appearing at local fairs painted in shocking pink and blue liveries. *E. Latcham Collection*

AEC Regal No. 3093, TK 6518, new in 1931 as a bus with a Beadle B32R body and allocated to Bridport. Rebodied in May 1939 with a Duple C32F coach body, it stands at Edward Street near the end of its life, withdrawn in 1953 and ending its days in a Cardiff breaker's yard. Alongside stands Bedford OB No. 352, HUO 685, a 1947 model with Duple C27F bodywork, withdrawn in 1955 being exported to E. Kyriakou of Limassol, Cyprus.   *E. Latcham Collection*

The last petrol-engined bus in service at Weymouth, although a few Bedford OB coaches still remained. No. 3822, a 1947 Bedford OB with Mulliner B28F body, had been purchased with the business of Wintle, Martock, in 1953. Used in the Weymouth area during 1954/5 it mainly operated on the Grosvenor Road-Goldcroft Estate service (38) withdrawn during 1955 it passed through Comberhill Motors (dealer) the following year to Associated Motorways, Colombo, Ceylon.   *Author's Collection*

Bristol L5G No. 337, DOD 526, stands at the King's Statue, Weymouth in the years following the war showing the original Bristol B35R body, replaced by a Beadle B36R type during 1950 giving the vehicle another 15 years' life. Arriving at Weymouth in June 1940, 337 and her sisters transported refugees from Weymouth Harbour following the fall of France.

Bristol Vintage Bus Group

Bristol L5G No. 278, ETT 944, loads passengers for Bridport at Edward Street during the early 1950s, in the days when fitting both passengers and luggage into the bus was a struggle. The Beadle B36R body of 1949 replaced the original Mumford B1R which had been rebuilt during the war. No. 278 was withdrawn in 1959 and sold via a London dealer to a showman.   *B. Thompson*

Conductor Bing Richmond and driver Jim Wild stand alongside Leyland TS1 No. 3111, DR 8639, at the King's Statue, the Beadle DP32R body of 1939 having replaced the original 1931 Mumford C26R. 3111 spent many years on stage carriage work, withdrawn in 1953 and sold to Thompson (dealer) Cardiff. *Author's Collection*

the sea-front side of the road and into Frederick Place at the top of St Thomas Street. To add further confusion, at the same time the Portland group of services serving the Island were re-lettered, becoming Portland Bill (22A / B), Southwell via Courtlands (22D), Southwell via Wakeham (22E), The Grove (22F), During the Winter timetable there were 10 buses per hour on that route as far as Dumbarton Road, Wyke Regis. Seven continued to Portland Victoria Square and three of these went to Tophill. During the Winter months only eight services operated to Portland Bill per day, much of the route being common to all services. A new hourly service from Haywards Estate (Radipole) to Portland Victoria Square (22C) also started during the year.

On 18th October work at last commenced on the rebuilding of Edward Street garage, the cost of which was to be £42,629. During rebuilding the buses were parked at Westham coach park, where a 1929 Leyland LT1 No. 3439, VE 2144 - until 1945 Eastern Counties No. 83 - acted as an office and mess room. Buses were still refuelled, sometimes with difficulty, amongst the building work at Edward Street, and it was an operational nightmare with staff spread over four operational bases!

The shelter in the centre of the King's Statue site was demolished in October 1955, the experimental new system having been successful, a large flower bed and zebra crossing becoming a feature of the site thereafter.

Portland Beach Road again had a victim on 30th November when Bristol K5G No. 244, proceeding through flood water, lost the road and tilted at an angle in the roadside ditch. The passengers, mainly girls travelling to work in Weymouth, were carried clear of the water by the crew pick-a-back fashion!

In December the low railway bridge over the main Dorchester Road at Ridgeway was replaced, ironically by which date Highbridge double-decks had ceased to exist in the local fleet. Until this was done these vehicles had to proceed via Gould's Hill when entering or leaving Weymouth. The new bridge did however allow Devon General to use Highbridge-bodied AEC Regent IIIs on the Exeter service.

Devon General AEC Regal III No. SR597, LUO 597, waits to depart from Edward Street with joint service No. 47 to Exeter. No. 597 was delivered in March 1950 and had a Weymann B35F body. and was in the last batch of five vertical-engined single-deck vehicles purchased by Devon General.
Author's Collection

During the early 1950s when Exeter City Transport showed a deficit in returns on the joint working arrangements in Exeter with Devon General, Exeter City adjusted the matter by entirely working joint Devon General, Western/Southern National services from Exeter to Plymouth and Weymouth, using tickets over printed in red 'Devon National'. Exeter City Daimler CVD6 No. 73, JFJ 873 with Weymann B35F body, stands at Edward Street before returning to Exeter. New in 1949 this interesting vehicle was withdrawn in October 1966 and survives in preservation.
R.K. Blencowe Collection

Bristol K5G Nos. 358, FTA 641, and 359, FTA 642, stand parked in the centre of the road at the King's Statue during August 1952, giving a detailed rear and front view of their original 1941 ECW L30/26R bodies. No. 359 on the right has been repainted in the revised Tilling livery, eliminating much of the cream relief. In the background to the right can be seen the Southern National office on Royal Terrace.   *A.B. Cross*

Bristol K5G No. 243 of 1937 stands at Edward Street alongside 1947 K6A No. 860 which is fitted with the standard TT type L27/28R body. The 1950 Beadle L27/28R body on 243 differs in many respects particularly with internal detail, whilst the retention of the pre-war KV type radiator and bonnet caused a slight design problem around the windscreen. No. 243 was withdrawn and scrapped in 1959, 860 was withdrawn in 1965 then worked for a North London independent for a further three years.   *R.H.G. Simpson*

Bristol K5G, No. 871, JUO 975, awaits to depart from the King's Statue with a Westham service during 1965. Built in 1948, 871 was an archetypal Bristol 'K' with ECW L27/28R body, showing the two aperture destination blinds of the period, the side blind box above the platform, a feature discontinued on later models, blanked off. Withdrawn in May 1965, No. 871 had spent many years operating the Westham services. *C.L. Caddy*

Bristol KSW6B No. 1833, LTA 943, heads down Dorchester Road past Lodmoor Hill. Nos. 1832 and 1833 were the first two 8 ft wide buses in Weymouth, collected from ECW on 15th December, 1950. Strict instructions were issued that they be confined to the Upwey-Portland, Victoria Square route owing to their width! *Bristol Vintage Bus Group*

Reconstruction of the garage was delayed by a strike of the men erecting the steel framework, but with the commencement of the Summer season Westham coach park had to be vacated. This resulted in some buses being parked in the uncompleted garage, and the majority in the approach road to the disused Melcombe Regis station. The coaches were however kept overnight at Westham coach park.

A new seasonal service between Edward Street and Littlesea Camp (61B) commenced and the Bowleaze Cove service (23) was amended to run to and from Edward Street, whilst work on the new garage dragged on. However, more pressing problems were to arise with the Suez Crisis in the late Summer. Fuel rationing brought a drastic cut in services, many of which were never replaced, and this was quickly followed by several sharp fare increases as fuel prices soared. It was a turning point for the bus industry.

Never recovering from the crisis of 1956, the decline in bus patronage has continued. The National Bus Strike between 20th-28th July, 1957, was over a claim for a pay increase of £1 a week. The employers offered 3s., the eventual settlement being 11s. a week. It appears a small amount, but one has to take into account what could be purchased for that money over 40 years ago! It is interesting to note that the staff of Western and Southern National were members of the National Union of Railwaymen - a strange arrangement but one common to companies that had previous railway involvement. The GWR had recognised the NUR for its omnibus staff since 1916, but a Board meeting of Southern National in 1931 decided that recognition of a union would not be accorded until it became necessary. However, at a meeting in December 1936 the Chairman reported that 'satisfactory arrangements have been made with the NUR, and the agreement is nearing completion'. It was an unusual marriage, the busmen becoming members of the Weymouth No. 2 branch, neither branch assisting the other or taking advantage during industrial disputes!

The dispute was followed by a 7 per cent fare increase, and cuts began to appear in services as the family car started to make an impact on people's travel habits - although most still took the traditional seaside holiday, which boosted Summer trade. Works and school journeys were still an important source of revenue. Pupils for Weymouth grammar school were transported from Portland, well over a dozen buses served the Dockyard from various points, others serving the AUWE at Southwell, whilst Whitehead's factory was served by a small fleet, including several dinner-time buses over short distances. This was all to change shortly, the first major reduction of staff in the Dockyard taking place during 1957 allowing some buses to be cut out. Those workers with a car often carried several of their workmates, depriving the bus of still more custom.

Reconstruction work at Edward Street was completed by late 1956, the new dockshop facility allowing Radipole to become a garage for the coach fleet whilst the former Greyhound garage at Charlestown was sold in October 1959 to become an engineering works.

Open top buses returned to Weymouth on 18th June, 1958, with one vehicle operating between Upwey (Royal Oak) and Portland (Victoria Square). In October 1959 the Salisbury service became one-man operated with single-decks. Weymouth-Swanage was shortly to follow, and Dorchester depot went over to one-man operation during 1962. The commencement of the 1962 Summer service also saw the end of joint working of the Weymouth-Exeter service with Devon General; henceforth it was operated as two separate services, meeting at Axminster.

In April 1964 an 'assisted travel' scheme was introduced for workers at the Atomic Energy Establishment, Winfrith. Buses from various part of Weymouth, Portland and

Leyland TS7D No. 1000 turns into Edward Street from Kings Street during August 1952. Note the centre entrance and destination blindboxes, there were four, one at front and back, and one in the centre each side.

A.B. Cross

Not long before their withdrawal from service the six-wheelers were photographed lined up under the remains of Edward Street garage early one Sunday morning. From the left, 1004, 1002, 1000, 1001, 1003, 1005. Used exclusvely on the Portland Tophill routes, each vehicle had covered over a million miles between 1937 and 1954, not only proof of a good vehicle, but the quality of the maintenance staff at Weymouth, particularly the body builders. Not forgetting the difficult conditions everybody had worked under since 1940.

B. Thompson

Dorchester travelled to this remote site a mile west of Wool. Although the site was alongside the Weymouth-Bournemouth railway, a station or halt was never constructed, doubtless because any scheme that involved first getting to either Weymouth or Dorchester stations would not have been so attractive as a direct bus service!

At the same time Weymouth grammar school moved to a new site at Charlestown, on the Chickerell side of Weymouth. This involved more services as new routes were set up to convey pupils to and from Upwey, Preston, and other areas.

Exactly 30 years after the arrival of the six-wheelers, the Tophill routes were again to sample the newest and largest single-decks available, when seven Bristol RELL ECW B53F buses took over the services in June 1967, and as with their illustrious predecessors, they were an instant success.

The advancements in the design of buses between 1929 and 1939 were again to be repeated between 1949 and 1969. Although there was a shortage of new vehicles and other equipment throughout 1949, in that December the 75 vehicles allocated to Weymouth covered a recorded 200,834 miles. The influx of new and rebodied vehicles during 1950 allowed the sale and delicensing of some pre-war vehicles. In January 1950 Bristol L5Gs 272, 280 and 337 returned from J.C. Beadle with new B35R bodies, whilst Dennis Ace No. 776, which had worked Bowleaze Cove and Dorchester town services, was delicensed and later sold, becoming a mobile shop in Kent. A further batch of Bedford OB Duple C29F coaches relieved older vehicles for the Summer trade.

Weymouth's two original Bristol K5G double-decks Nos. 243/4, returned from J.C. Beadle on 16th June with new L27/28R bodies, thus eliminating the last Highbridge double-decks from the depot. The delivery of new double-decks continued with Bristol KS5G ECW L27/28R vehicles 1829/35/37/39 during October, November and December. The first two Bristol KSW6B ECW L27/28R for Western/Southern National were delivered to Weymouth on 15th December, 1950, these being the first 8 ft-wide vehicles in the fleet. By contrast the pre-war BSA motor cycle used by inspectors was taken out of service!

A further intake of new vehicles during 1951 included Bristol K5G Nos. 1840-43, these having chassis for 7 ft 6 in.- wide bodies, but were fitted with the new 8ft-wide bodies - easily recognised as the wheels were inset from the mudguards and, from the driver's point of view, the seat was a little offset from the steering wheel! The coach fleet was enhanced by the introduction of Bristol LWL6B ECW FL37F coaches, No. 1336 being the first to arrive. Compared with previous vehicles they appeared massive, and with a very high quality interior finish, they were known locally as 'Brabs', after the giant airliner of the time - the Brabazon.

December 1951 saw the new Bristol LS5G B45F saloon buses enter service. The first two allocated to Weymouth, Nos. 1680/1, commenced working Tophill services from the beginning of the month, and soon others arrived. When a chassis cross-member failed on No. 1681 the following Summer sceptics thought the vehicles not suitable for Portland, but this proved to be an isolated incident, the LS being a thoroughly reliable vehicle. The reign of the six-wheelers was over!

The coach version of the LS, the LS6G ECW C39F, arrived for the Summer of 1953, the first job for No. 1342 being a Coronation trip to London. Instantly these coaches, where the driver was with the passengers, reduced the 'Brabs' to second class, and the Bedford OB lost favour with drivers (small coach, small tips).

The rebodying programme virtually came to an end when, early in 1954, Bristol K5G Nos. 357/8/9 had their ECW L30/26R bodies replaced, and following rebuilding these three sisters did not return to Weymouth but ended their days in North Devon.

Weymouth's warime gas bus No. 2985, DR 6957, with a Beadle L26/26R body fitted in 1947 and a Cov-Rad radiator. Photographed before departure to the breaker's yard in April 1956, now like the Groves Beer she advertised, just a memory. *B. Thompson*

Bristol LS5G No. 1698, OTT 53, new in 1953, stands in Victoria Square before proceeding to Tophill. Behind is the Southern National garage and the bay window of the Portland Gas Works office. No. 1698 passed via dealers to Cream Line, of Tonmawr in November 1971.

E. Latcham Collection

The new Bristol LS vehicles having proved themselves capable of handling the Tophill services, the six-wheelers were relegated to duplicates and school duties. Each vehicle had travelled over a million miles! Nos. 1001 and 1003 were delicensed on 1st February, 1954, and on 24th, 1004 was taken out of service following collision with a milk float. At the end of the month 1000 and 1002 were also withdrawn, all being placed in store at Portland garage. No. 1005 - the last in service - ran during the Summer of 1954, but left Weymouth on 27th September to join her sisters at Dartmouth, to where they had recently been moved. They remained in the garage yard until August 1955, when they went to Kingsbridge garage for the Gardner engines to be removed before the vehicles were sold to Noyce, a local scrap dealer. By 20th August work had commenced on the breaking up of 1001, the remainder being sold to local farms. By mid-September 1000 and 1005 were on the farm of Buckingham Bros at Washbourne, Harburtonford, who had paid £14 for the chassis and £20 for the body of each vehicle. Mr Croft paid £30 for 1003 which was put to use as a fowl house. No. 1002 ended its days at East Allington Farm, and 1004 at Well Farm, Chillington. Within 10 years all had disappeared, 1000 and 1005 being broken up in 1964, whilst 1004 is reputed to be buried in a disused quarry.

The first two Bristol 'Lodekkas' commenced service in October 1954 (Nos. 1873/4) and were placed on the Upwey route, both of these vehicles had open platforms. No. 1873 had a single window on the rear platform, but others had the rear window split into two, and subsequent deliveries had manually-operated platform doors, and when new were placed on the Salisbury and Bournemouth routes.

Early 1955 saw the last petrol-engined bus in service, although a few Bedford OB coaches still remained. No. 3822, a 1947 Bedford OB with a Mulliner B28F body, mainly operated on the Grovernor Road - Goldcroft Estate service (38). Also withdrawn during the year was Bedford OB, Duple C27F coach No. 531. New in 1947 she had spent much of that year and 1948 operating on stage carriage work. Except for a touch-up in 1951 she still retained her original 1947 paintwork when sold to work with other former Southern National Bedford's in Limassol, Cyprus.

April 1956 saw Leyland Titan No. 2985, the former Weymouth gas bus, stripped of its valuable Gardner engine and towed to a field at Winterborne Abbas where it was broken up by a local scrap merchant.

Three Bristol MW5G ECW B45F saloons arrived during 1958, shortly after converted to B41F with a luggage rack at the front nearside and equipped for one-man operation. Nos. 1789/90/1 were put to work on the Salisbury service where they spent most of their lives, with one vehicle covering three round trips each day, a distance of 300 miles. In 1959 the first 'K' (No. 243) was transferred to Western National and was almost at once broken up by Rundle & Owen of Plymouth. 244 became a Western National tree lopper in 1961, later suffering the indignity of being painted white to act as a bus washing machine guide at Plymouth!

The first Bristol FLF6B ECW H38/32F double-decks were allocated to Weymouth in September 1961, Nos. 1979/80/1 were put to work on the Upwey-Downclose Estate service, and the following year the first pair of lower deck offside seats were removed to form an extended luggage rack. These vehicles, with driver controlled power operated doors, stairs at the front end, and a higher passenger capacity, were one of the major advances in the local fleet for some years.

A further batch of Bristol MW5G ECW B45F single-decks arrived in 1963 and were put to work on Tophill routes. They were of a revised body design and fitted with fluorescent interior lighting. At the same time two MW6GG ECW C39F coaches arrived, Nos. 1410/1, the first to be painted in the Royal Blue livery of blue and cream but with 'Southern National' fleetnames on plastic panels at waist level. All

1956 Bristol LS5G No. 1781, TUO 497, climbs Meissner's Knap, Fortuneswell, Portland. The incline behind and the blind bend were the scene of the Bus Race of January 1927 described on page 99. After 20 years' service 1781 passed via dealers to J. & P. Wood of Craven Arms.

E. Latcham Collection

Weymouth's first Lodekka No. 1873, OTT 46, stands in Victoria Square, Portland soon after entering service in 1954, and fitted with the original design of full apron radiator grill. The shop window to the rear of the vehicle, was pre-1936, the office of Portland Express. After 17 years' service at Weymouth 1873 was withdrawn in 1971, going to the Wakefield Shirt Company as staff transport until scrapped in 1976.   *Author's Collection*

Edward Street cleared for rebuilding in October 1954, the concrete floors and pits having been
in place since 1948. Looking through the remains of the garage Melcombe Regis station can be
seen in the distance. The exposed low girder on the left had succeeded in reshaping a few
double-decks!   *E. Latcham Collection*

'K' type double-decks parked at Westham coach park during the winter of 1954/5 whilst
Edward Street was under reconstruction. In the background beyond Radipole Lake and
Melcombe Regis Gardens, the timber sheds of Messrs Betts & Co. and the twin spires of
Gloucester Street Congregational church have, with the passage of time, disappeared. Where the
buses stand is now part of the Weymouth relief road.   *B. Thompson*

Following the floods of July 1955, Southern National coaches parked overnight at Westham coach park were left half full of water. MOD 971, No. 1344; OTT 78, No. 1369; and OTT 84, No. 1375, await rescue. To the left the Miniature Railway, to the right the Bluebird Coaches' booking hut. Behind the inner harbour is Weymouth town centre, drastically changed since this photograph was taken. *Author's Collection*

The return of an open top double-deck in 1958 for a Summer-only service between Upwey Wishing Well and Portland, Victoria Square. No. 3821 stands at the Island terminus. New to Bristol Tramways in 1938 as City Service vehicle No. C3133, it was purchased by Southern National in 1958 and converted to OT30/26R and painted in cream livery. Not successful on the main road route, the service was switched to Littlesea Holiday Camp until the vehicle was withdrawn in 1964. *Author's Collection*

future coach deliveries were to be in this livery, it being considered there was less confusion amongst passengers when these vehicles worked Royal Blue reliefs at weekends! The revised bodystyle had what could be described as a 'piano front', and was mounted on air suspension.

The final delivery of Bristol FLF double-decks arrived in 1965, powered by a mixture of Bristol BVW and Gardner six-cylinder engines with interiors illuminated with fluorescent lighting, and as with their predecessors, the seating was reduced to provide extra luggage space. The Bristol LWL6B 'Brab' coaches were disposed of with the arrival of more Bristol MW6G ECW C39F coaches for the 1966 season, the earlier 'piano front' having given way to a new style of body.

The Bristol RELL6G ECW B53F vehicles, Nos. 2700-2707, were the first in the Southern National fleet to have semi-automatic gearboxes. They were also 36 ft long! The only problem was the lack of luggage space, no rear locker being provided and the side lockers being far from ideal for short-distance stage work. Within a year the front four nearside side-on bench seats had been converted so as their backs tipped forward to form a luggage pen when required. The REs were the pride of the fleet, but after the 'Lord Mayor's Show came the muck cart', this being in the form of second-hand Bristol Omnibus Bristol FSF6G ECW L2426F vehicles. Numbered 1014-1019 in the Southern National fleet, they had previously been 6018/9 in the Cheltenham & District fleet, 6004/7 in the Bristol fleet, and 6020/1 in the Bath Services fleet. They were never as popular at Weymouth as the Bristol FLF, as they tended to give a rough ride on uneven roads.

Their arrival allowed several older vehicles to be withdrawn including No. 987, a 1949 Bristol K5G and one of two diverted from the Caledonian Omnibus Company upon completion. She was readily identified by the different shade of interior trim. For a number of years 987 regularly worked the Park Mead Road service (24), and was also the depot driver training bus.

Over the period from 1967 the fleet of Bristol LWL single-decks was reduced, and by the Summer of 1968 only one remained at the Weymouth depot, No. 1613. Fortunately in that November this excellent example of a Bristol single-deck was purchased for preservation by the Dorset Transport Circle, and is now part of the National collection with the Science Museum.

The Summer of 1968 also saw the first three Bristol RELH6G ECW C45F coaches arrive at Weymouth. With older coaches moving down the fleet, the final Bristol LS6G coaches departed following the 1969 season. Although 16 years old, right to the end they had operated tours, and carried out Associated Motorways services to Derby and Mansfield and Royal Blue duplicates to London. Like all vehicles in the past 20 years, they had served well.

During the late 1960s minor alterations to services took place to keep pace with traffic requirements, and on 29th December, 1968 the last Sunday services ran on the Westham (20A/B/C), Park Mead Road (24), and Southlands Estate (273) routes. Towards the end of 1968 a double-deck bus was again tested on the Tophill routes, and this time it was successful. This was followed on 22nd December 1968 with Bristol KSW No. 1844 touring the island routes with members of the Dorset Transport Circle, regular public services commencing on 5th January, 1969, when during the day all Tophill services were extended to Radipole. Forty years after the first National bus reached Tophill the double-deck had at last arrived. It is also the point where our story ends.

In January 1969 Southern National became part of the National Bus Company, and a year later, in January 1970, Southern National ceased as an operating entity, it being integrated into Western National. It was the end of an era!

With Chesil Beach and Chiswell forming a backdrop, Bristol RELL No. 2704, HDV 630E, climbs around the hairpin bend on the climb to Tophill, Portland, shortly after entering service during the Summer of 1967. The REs, 36 ft long and with a capacity of 53 arrived exactly 30 years after the 'six-wheelers', the previous high capacity vehicles used on Tophill services. Like their predecessors the REs are now history, and the hairpin bend replaced by a new road.

C.L. Caddy

The first official passenger-carrying double-deck to reach Portland Bill, Bristol KSW6B No. 1844, LTA 954, is posed by the lighthouse on 22nd December, 1968, after bringing a party of Dorset Transport Circle members to tour the Island's bus routes. In January 1969 double-decks commenced regular services to Tophill, the Island had been conquered!   *C.L. Caddy*

Weymouth Area Principal Services of the Southern National Omnibus Co.

Date	No.	
1930	23	Pier-Bowleaze Cove. E D
1930	24	Statue, Wyke Road, Wyke Regis. F
1930	22A	Easton Rly Stn, Portland Bill/Grove. C
1/6/30	30A	Bovington Camp, Wool, Lulworth.
26/7/30	11	Weymouth, Dorchester, Bere Regis, Poole, Bournemouth. I
1/7/31	35	Statue-Nothe Gardens. A D
1/6/32	21A	Weymouth, Abbotsbury, Bridport. M
4/7/32	34	Statue Sandsfoot Castle. A D
1/4/33	20A	Statue-Westham Cross Roads.
8/4/33	33A	Statue, Preston, Sutton Poyntz.
8/4/33	22A	Upwey RO, Radipole, Statue, Rodwell, VSQ, Easton, Portland Bill.
8/4/33	22B	Grove, Easton, Portland Bill.
1/7/33	29A	Weymouth, Dorchester, Wool. G
1/7/33	60	Statue, Radipole Park Drive, Icen Road. A D
9/7/34	22C	Upwey WW, Statue, Easton, Portland Bill.
9/7/34	22D	Upwey RO, Statue, Rodwell Easton, Portland Bill.
1/10/34	61	Statue, Pye Hill, Radipole Turn, Radipole Village.
7/7/35	20B	Statue-Corporation Road. L
25/10/35	88	Portland Rly Stn. Dockyard, HMS Osprey.
1936	98	Weymouth Railway Station-Weymouth Quay.
28/9/36	22E	Statue, Wyke Road, Easton, Portland Bill.
12/9/38	22F	Statue, Radipole, Nottington Village. D
17/6/39	273	Grosvenor Road, Statue, Southlands Estate. J
1946	88	Statue, Rodwell, Dockyard, HMS Osprey.
1946	273	Statue-Southlands Estate.
22/12/46	20C	Statue, Links Road, Hereford Road.
3/47	73	Weymouth, Preston, Warmwell Cross, Broadmayne, Dorchester.
5/6/48	61A	Statue, Pye Hill, Lanehouse, Camp Road.
1/49	33B	Statue, Chalbury Corner, Littlemoor New Inn.
1/1/49	34	Weymouth, Dorchester, Blandford, Salisbury. H
26/9/49	38	Statue-Haywards Avenue.
12/52	20D	Abbotsbury, Portesham, Upwey & Broadwey Station. B
12/52	20E	Weymouth, Chickerell, Coryates.
1952	22C	Statue-Haywards Estate.
14/6/53	38	Goldcroft Avenue, Statue, Park Estate, Grosvenor Road.
13/9/54	22A	Edward St King's Statue, Wyke Road, VSQ. Easton, Wakeham, Southwell, Portland Bill.
13/9/54	22B	Edward St King's Statue, Wyke Road, VSQ, Easton, Weston St, Southwell, Portland Bill.
13/9/54	22D	Statue, Rodwell, Easton, Reforne, Weston, Southwell, Portland Bill.
13/9/54	22E	Statue, Rodwell, Easton, Wakeham, Weston Corner, Southwell, Portland Bill.
13/9/54	22F	Statue, Rodwell, Easton, Grove.
20/1/55	35	Weymouth-Salisbury, via Blandford Camp.
14/5/56	61B	Edward Street, Littlesea Holiday Camp. A

Notes

A Summer season services.
B WD 12/1/57.
C WD 9/30.
D WD 11/9/39.
E RS 1946.
F WD 20/9/49. RS 1945 extended to Ferrybridge. 21/12/47 Via Wyke Square to Park Mead Road.
G WD 29/5/33.

H Ex-Wilts & Dorset No.20. To joint service.
I 8/4/33 joint with Hants & Dorset. 11/11/33 extended to Southwell, extension WD 6/6/40. 4/6/58 to No. 36.
J WD 1/6/40.
L extended to Westham Cross Roads 1950.
M WD 20/9/39 RS 6/45.

Index

References to Volume One are shown in **Bold**, Volume Two in Roman and Volume Three in *Italic* type.

Southern National No. 1613, LTA 772, a 1951 Bristol LWL5G with ECW B39R body. Originally in the Western National fleet, in March 1960 transferred to Southern National, and later to Weymouth depot, from where it was withdrawn in October 1968. Purchased by the Dorset Transport Circle for preservation, it attended many events before being handed over to the Science Museum in March 1981, being a considered a perfect example of a post-World War II single-deck service bus.
C.L. Caddy